FOUCAULT
AND
THE CRITIQUE
OF INSTITUTIONS

STUDIES OF THE GREATER
PHILADELPHIA PHILOSOPHY CONSORTIUM

Already published:

Joseph Margolis, Michael Krausz, and Richard Burian, eds.,
Rationality, Relativism and the Human Sciences
(Martinus Nijhoff Publishers, 1986)

FOUCAULT AND THE CRITIQUE OF INSTITUTIONS

Edited by
John Caputo and Mark Yount

The Pennsylvania State University Press
University Park, Pennsylvania

Library of Congress Cataloging-in-Publication Data

Foucault and the critique of institutions / edited by John Caputo and
  Mark Yount.
      p.   cm.
    Includes bibliographical references and index.
    ISBN 0-271-00881-4 (alk. paper)—ISBN 0-271-00938-1
  (pbk.)
    1. Foucault, Michel. 2. Associations, institutions, etc.
  I. Caputo, John D. II. Yount, Mark, 1954–
  B2430.F724F684   1993
    194—dc20   92-33881
                                                                    CIP

Copyright © 1993 The Pennsylvania State University
All rights reserved

Printed in the United States of America

Published by The Pennsylvania State University Press,
Barbara Building, Suite C, University Park, PA 16802-1003

It is the policy of The Pennsylvania State University Press to use acid-free paper for the first printing of all clothbound books. Publications on uncoated stock satisfy the minimum requirements of American National Standard for Information Sciences—Permanence of Paper for Printed Library Materials, ANSI Z39.48–1984.

To Michael Krausz and Joseph Margolis,
The Spirit of the Consortium

CONTENTS

I. INTRODUCTION
JOHN CAPUTO AND MARK YOUNT
   Institutions, Normalization, and Power   3

II. FOUCAULT AND CRITIQUE
JITENDRA MOHANTY
   Foucault as a Philosopher   27
JOSEPH MARGOLIS
   Redeeming Foucault   41

III. THE SELF AND ITS SEX
MARK POSTER
   Foucault and the Problem of Self-Constitution   63
JUDITH BUTLER
   Sexual Inversions   81

IV. THE UNIVERSITY AND ITS DISCIPLINES
CHUCK DYKE
   Extralogical Excavation: Philosophy in the Age of Shovelry   101
MARY SCHMELZER
   Panopticism and Postmodern Pedagogy   127
JOSEPH ROUSE
   Foucault and the Natural Sciences   137

V. THE WORKPLACE
ROBERT MOORE
   Law, Normativity, and the Level Playing Field:
   The Production of Rights in American Labor Law   165
MARK YOUNT
   The Normalizing Powers of Affirmative Action   191

VI. HEALING INSTITUTIONS
JOHN CAPUTO
    On Not Knowing Who We Are: Madness, Hermeneutics,
    and the Night of Truth in Foucault   233

Notes on Contributors   263

Index of Names   265

Index of Subjects   269

Part I

INTRODUCTION

INSTITUTIONS, NORMALIZATION, AND POWER

John Caputo and Mark Yount

INSTITUTIONS

This volume is the collaborative work of the Greater Philadelphia Philosophy Consortium. It grew out of a series of conferences organized around the work of Michel Foucault that was conducted by the Consortium in 1985–86 under the title "Institutions, Normalization, and Power." Yet, while this volume had its beginnings there, almost none of the papers included here are taken from that series. Rather than issue a conference volume, we decided to cast a broader net in consortial waters, to invite a broader range of participants into a more integrated, longer-term project. The resulting volume still draws its character and range of contributions entirely from the Consortium, as we solicited those faculty of member institutions and guests of Consortium programs who work closely with Foucault and with issues raised by Foucault. The objective of the volume—realized here, we believe—is to collect studies that not only read but *apply* Foucault. The focus of that application in the present volume is the question of the institution, including specific questions put to specific institutions such as the university and the workplace.

Our Introduction to this collection will do some normalizing of its own, we hope for the reader's benefit. We begin by normalizing the real author-ity here—Foucault—by briefly highlighting some of the most important theoretical strategies his works offer, especially those on which our other authors have drawn. We will focus, as the essays do, on Foucault's genealogical terms (normalization, power/knowledge) and then on resources his work suggests for critical practice, intervention, or resistance. Our Acknowledgments are ushered in by our Admonitions. Treat the Introduction as you would the book, reading by your own lights and to your own order. We have arranged the volume in a way that suits us; its pages can clearly be read in any order that pleases you.

NORMALIZATION AND POWER

The connection between Foucault and institutions seems an obvious one, but not because he wanted to make the institution the basic unit of analysis. On the contrary, Foucault situated institutions within the thin but all-entangling web of power relations. He did so explicitly in *Discipline and Punish*, and he subsequently read his later analysis between the lines of his earlier works. In this genealogy, institutions are the more readily definable macro-objects, grosser instruments for the finer, more elemental workings of power. Power is the thin, inescapable film that covers all human interactions, whether inside institutions or out. Institutional structures are saturated with sexual relations, economic relations, social relations, etc., and are always established *of* these power relations: relations between men and women, old and young, senior and junior, well-born and starved, colorless and colored, Occident and Orient. Institutions are the means that power uses, and not the other way around, not sources or origins of power. The analysis of power is thus always more fine-grained than any analysis of classes, of states, or of institutions in their own terms would be. That is why for Foucault—and for all of the studies that follow here—the workings of power cannot be described from the standpoint of a master discipline, especially a perspective that would seek an *origin* for power, or take political power to be its initial or privileged form. It is always a question of analyzing institutions from the standpoint of power, and not of analyzing power from the standpoint of institutions.[1]

But we ought not to speak of power in the substantive, for there is no such thing. Instead, sets of "power relations" bathe the structures and edifices of human life, without power ever amounting to a thing or substance. It is not the very substance-and-subject of the historical process, like the Hegelian spirit; not the driving movement of contradictory social relations, as in Marx; not the unifying-gathering power that holds sway over all in Heidegger's history of Being. (The similarities might not be entirely accidental, though: see Mohanty's paper herein, "Foucault as Philosopher.") Power is not one thing, but multiple and multiplied, scattered and disseminated.

This means that power is not concentrated at a central point of organization and domination. Power is not first of all the power of the sovereign. There *is* power over freedom, and action on the action of others, but this is a domination that traverses the fields of power, that operates variably in various relationships. "In so far as power relations are an unequal and relatively stable relation of forces, it's clear that this implies an above and a below, a difference of potentials."[2] These potentials of power cannot be understood as brute force, though brutality is among their possible outcomes—as is seduction. Power relations are embedded in the very heart of human relationships, springing into being as soon as there *are* human beings. Power need not be harsh and abrasive or constrain narrowly and painfully; without overt violence it seeks its objectives in the more subtle, thus all the more effective, mode of "suasion," of "conduction." Power relations clear the ways for human behavior (*conduire*) to be subtly conducted (*conduit*), so that human actions are led as surely and as effortlessly through their channels as water through a "duct" (*ducere*).

Power has not always been conducive to such gentle persuasions; Foucault locates a shift in the workings of power between the seventeenth and eighteenth centuries. The mode in which power was previously exercised could essentially be defined in terms of the sovereign-subject

---

[1] See Michel Foucault, "The Subject and Power," in Hubert Dreyfus and Paul Rabinow, *Michel Foucault: Beyond Structuralism and Hermeneutics*, 2d edn. (Chicago: University of Chicago Press, 1983), p. 222.
[2] Michel Foucault, *Power/Knowledge: Selected Interviews and Other Writings, 1972–1977*, ed. Colin Gordon, tr. Colin Gordon et al. (New York: Pantheon, 1980), pp. 200–201.

relation. But as power relations evolved new techniques and instruments incompatible with relations of sovereignty, power passed from the physical existence of the sovereign to a tightly knit grid of material coercions, to continuous and permanent systems of surveillance: disciplinary power. Where sovereignty had held lord over the land and its bounty, disciplines now directed the eyes of power to bodies, allowing meticulous control over their operations by a strategy distinct from repression. Disciplines introduced the power of norm, and from that point forth power has demanded the productions of truth that its new techniques make possible. Power is no longer repressive but productive; does not say no but yes; does not prevent but invent; does not prohibit but promote; does not negate but affirm; does not annihilate but create.

Where power takes the form of normalization it does not bend our virtues to a narrow Aristotelian mark, a pinpoint standard to be hit dead center. Normalization *does* impose homogeneity, but at the same time makes it possible to individualize, to measure gaps, to differentiate according to the norm whose function is to make differences intelligible *as such*. The norm has tolerances for a vast range of individuals, a duction ample enough to promote diversity even as it constrains all deviations by its standard measure. Normalization keeps watch over the excessive and the exceptional, delimiting the outcasts who threaten the order of normalcy. There are institutions to contain these outcasts and—if possible, this is at least the idea—to redirect their course to the latitudes of the normal. Institutions will form and well-adjust the young into supple, happy subjects of normalization. Institutions will reform the abnormal who stray beyond the limits.

But normalization proceeds by way of confession rather than repression. Far from abolishing the individual, power's strategy is to produce legions of adapted, ambient individuals to move easily through the manifold channels of modern social relations. Patients are brought out of the dark chamber of the prison and endowed with the power to speak a language that experts understand. By wanting to know everything, all about the childhood, the personal history, the fantasies of the patient/inmate/believer, the "subject" is produced. And power produces its subjects in an unlimited, interminable subjectification, by exceedingly detailed personal dossiers, elaborate records of the individual life and personal history.

Thus, for Foucault, power is "power/knowledge." Beyond the Baconian theme that power is applied knowledge, Foucault contends that knowledge is applied power. Knowledge is what power relations produce in order to spread and disseminate all the more effectively. Against the liberal notion that truth is something that will "out" (emerge *as* truth) if all distortive power is removed, Foucault holds that without power no "truth" could be brought forth at all. It is not as if, were power removed, the truth of an undistorted subject would be liberated. Quite the opposite: it is power that produces the science of subjectivity in order to produce subjects.

Consider Foucault's analysis of "madness" (*folie*). When in the nineteenth century enlightened reformers declared the mad "mentally ill" and placed them in the hands of the physicians, medical professionals found it necessary to produce the science of mental illness. It was incumbent upon them to invent a knowledge parallel to the science of bodily illness, one that cures and normalizes behavior the same way that medical science cures and straightens broken limbs. Foucault's first study of sexuality shows the same pattern. Freud did not liberate sexuality from Victorian repression but rather, being himself a "new Victorian," produced "sexuality" as the most intimate secret of behavior, as the hidden key to conduct, as the code that the physician reads in order to unlock the secrets of subjectivity for the patient. *Scientia sexualis* produces the patient as one who is to be liberated from sexual repression. Psychiatrists and psychologists, criminal justice professionals and social workers, confessors and spiritual directors: all produce the knowledge they apply. They create the knowledge they require in order to fashion functioning, well-formed individuals. They do not discover but invent; they do not "liberate from" but "produce for."

THE CRITIQUE OF INSTITUTIONS

But, for Foucault, the same agents of normalizing might also be instigators of critique. There is no formula for critique in Foucault's varied texts, but from the genealogical perspective (on which most of these essays draw), critique must begin from an analytic of relations of power. It is those most immediately caught up in these fields of power who can best expose them for what they are. To expose the intelligible structure of a local power regime, to show how the differentials in power relations work from their microstructures to their larger effects, is to expose a regime to criticism, to assist resistances not yet imagined. So, if a narrow claim to "expertise" allows one to operate machineries of domination, that person is also positioned to leak the secrets of the machine, even to calibrate its parts toward opposite functions. This is why Foucault was particularly interested in the historical emergence and recent ascendency of the "specific intellectual." Unlike the "universal intellectual" who would speak as a master of truth and justice, the specific intellectual operates her intelligence where she is already situated, at the precise points of her own conditions of life or work. (Foucault's examples are an interesting mix, including Darwin, Oppenheimer, and himself. They are less marked by the feminine pronoun.)

One dimension of criticism for the specific intellectual is the critique of universality per se:

> I dream of the intellectual destroyer of evidence and universalities, the one who, in the inertias and constraints of the present, locates and marks the weak points, the openings, the lines of power, who incessantly displaces himself, doesn't know exactly where he is heading nor what he'll think tomorrow because he is too attentive to the present. . . .[3]

But what does this poststructural effusiveness have to do with the struggles of real people, of people who are displaced in more material ways, whose death will not be that of the author? The eternally recurring complaint is that criticism by intellectuals of *any* kind comes to naught. But Foucault was able to address that charge by providing a new conception of what the work of criticism *is*. Problems are not always already there—not *as* problems, anyway. It has taken the work of hundreds and thousands of people for problems like the prison, medical power, and the like to come onto the agenda. The specific work of the specific intellectual begins with this problematization: "[t]his development of a given into a question, this transformation of a group of obstacles and difficulties into problems to which the diverse solutions will attempt

---

[3]Michel Foucault, "The End of the Monarchy of Sex," from *Foucault Live: Interviews, 1966–1984*, tr. John Johnston, ed. Sylvere Lotringer (New York: Semiotext(e), 1989), p. 155.

to produce a response. . . ."⁴ The *problem* is to the mature Foucault what the *question* is to Heidegger: not something to be taken for granted as an occasion to produce a solution, but something that must be wrested forth by the highest activity of thought.

But this is also how the poststructural liberations of a specific intellectual can be turned to explicitly political ends. Foucault's specific intellectual can say to the people: "I would like to produce some effects of truth which might be used for a possible battle, to be waged by those who wish to wage it, in forms yet to be found and in organizations yet to be defined."⁵ In the all-extensive fields of power, the battle is always already under way. Where there is power, there is resistance or, better, *points* of resistance throughout the power network, each one a special case. The specific intellectual will not suppose a sovereign point from which power exercises dominion or domination. Foucault believed that the very idea of power-as-right serves to conceal the fact of domination and all that domination effects. Thus to give due weight to domination, to show its ruthlessness, requires this new analytics of power to expose the domination within *lateral* relations of power: "the multiple forms of subjugation that have a place and function within the social organism."⁶

That is where criticism of institutions comes in. Institutions are where power "becomes embodied in techniques, and equips itself with instruments and eventually even violent means of material intervention."⁷ Criticism attempts to flush out the thought that animates even the most stupid institutions in order to try to change both thought and institution, to show as much that it *can* be changed as that it *must* be:

> to show that things are not as self-evident as one believed, to see that what is accepted as self-evident will no longer be accepted as such. Practicing criticism is a matter of making facile gestures difficult.⁸

---

⁴Michel Foucault, "Polemics, Politics, and Problemizations," in *The Foucault Reader*, ed. Paul Rabinow (New York: Pantheon, 1984), p. 389.
⁵Foucault, "The Question of Power," in *Foucault Live*, p. 191.
⁶Foucault, *Power/Knowledge*, p. 96.
⁷Ibid.
⁸Michel Foucault, "Practicing Criticism," in *Politics, Philosophy, Culture: Interviews and Other Writings, 1977–1984*, ed. Lawrence D. Kritzman, tr. Alan Sheridan et al. (New York: Routledge, 1988), p. 155.

But how is criticism to do any of this? For these specific resistances, a global theory of revolution proves not only unhelpful but actually disabling. The logic of Marxism terrorizes every local action with this dilemma: "either you attack on a local level, but you must be sure that it's the weakest link, the one whose breakage will demolish the whole structure; or else, since the whole structure fails to collapse, the link wasn't the weakest one, the adversary needed only to re-organize his front, and a reform has reabsorbed your attack."[9] The alternative strategy Foucault calls genealogy would combine erudite knowledge and a popular knowledge (*le savoir des gens*), so that "a painstaking rediscovery of struggles together with the rude memory of their conflicts" could be used tactically today.[10] Criticism can only perform its work by recovering this popular knowledge: this "differential knowledge incapable of unanimity and which owes its force to the harshness of everything surrounding it. . . ."[11]

For Foucault, then, critique is always a strategic exercise within networks of power (/knowledge). If power is everywhere as Foucault says it is, and if wherever there is power there are differentials of power, and if we have any care for those on the wrong end of inequalities, then critique calls us to a continuous vigilance. "If everything is dangerous, then we always have something to do."[12]

Most of the essays in this volume are engaged in "doing something" in the above sense: addressing the dangers, exposing pretensions, affiliating to struggles. They *use* Foucault. But Foucault has himself been subject to critique, and a recurring objection from the modernist left is that his account of power leaves no way for truth to find a clearing and no privileged ground for political (or ethical) intervention. We have placed two essays at the beginning of the volume for those readers unsure of whether one *can* begin from Foucault. Whether or not Foucault is "redeemed," as Margolis ambitiously attempts here, the critical attentions of these first two essays offer a horizon that would *allow* for the uses made more explicit in the sections that follow.

---

[9]Foucault, *Power/Knowledge*, p. 144.
[10]Ibid., p. 83.
[11]Ibid., p. 82.
[12]Michel Foucault, "On the Genealogy of Ethics: An Overview of Work in Progress," in *The Foucault Reader*, p. 343.

I. Foucault and Critique

The first two essays are critical estimations of Foucault's status as a philosopher, and each is authored by a philosopher whose own stature makes his reading of Foucault especially important. Jitendra Mohanty's "Foucault as a Philosopher" begins from this paradox: Foucault denied that his work belonged to the discipline of philosophy, yet that work has been widely acclaimed and attacked for its considerable importance *for* philosophy. Mohanty surveys a variety of ways we might figure the bearing of Foucault's work on philosophy, and he focuses on the implications of Foucault's displacement of three concepts that had prevailed until Foucault's emergence in the 1960s: subjectivity, constitution, temporality and history. Like Hegel's *Geist*, which it resembles, Foucault's 'power' proves to be a philosophical (even speculative) concept, as no science of fact could arrive at this *sort* of thesis. Mohanty argues convincingly that "one does not understand Foucault unless one understands the nature of his continuing concern with transcendental philosophy."

Mohanty focuses on three philosophical theses advanced by Foucault: that domains of objects are constituted by discourse; that subjectivity is itself constituted; that the concepts of one history and one time need to be rejected. For Mohanty, these positions challenge only half of the transcendental tradition, the priority accorded subjectivity. (Even there, to say that subjectivity is constructed is not to say that it is false or imaginary.) What is often overlooked, writes Mohanty, is that Foucault retains the general theory of constitution. On this account, what Foucault has shown is how subjectivity is *objectified*, in which case Mohanty suspects Foucault of confusing subjectivity with "its distorted forms." Mohanty's critical engagement with Foucault on the issue of subjectivity is itself an important contribution to the tradition of transcendental philosophy, which all of Mohanty's work so ably articulates and defends.

Joseph Margolis offers the promising title "Redeeming Foucault." Like Mohanty, Margolis takes up the philosophical status of the main claims of Foucault's genealogy. But Margolis's intent is to free Foucault from a slightly different paradox: if truth is an artifact of large historical movements (according to genealogy), does this genealogy not claim to be the truth about truth? No one could bring a better appreciation of the logics of reflexivity and relativism than Margolis, having developed these themes at length in his recent works. In order to redeem Foucault, he takes on Habermas, offering the latter's reading as "the best introduction to what we should avoid in theorizing about Foucault." Foucault does not throw reason into chaos; rather, what so disturbs Habermas is "the bewildering proliferation of serially competing forms of order." (Even the casual reader will want to know that Foucault is neither a modernist nor a postmodernist, but a poststructuralist.)

While an extensive critique of Habermas confirms the initial plausibility of Foucault's thesis about truth, the last part of Margolis's paper attempts to resolve the paradox of that thesis. He does so by analyzing the interplay of its two levels. Ultimately, Foucault is not attempting a transcendental or second-order invariant truth. Margolis argues that where Foucault makes a seemingly universal claim, such claims should be understood as "perceived invariances": contingent, empirical, *produced* invariances. These first-order truths proclaimed by Foucault are precisely at odds with the status claimed by "legitimative invariances," whose second-order claims function as exclusionary rules, always operating at the expense of "the other." Genealogy is the conceptual instrument designed to block such exclusionary moves, even though this resistance is itself contingent, "a risked sense of doubt."

II. The Self and Its Sex

The two essays in this section shade from the theoretical concerns of the first two papers to the analyses of specific institutions in the sections that follow. It is by virtue of Foucault's work from the 1960s and 1970s that we can think of "the self" *as* an institution, a social-historical construction. But Mark Poster's essay, "Foucault and the Problem of Self-Constitution," focuses on the shifted concerns of Foucault's last period. Poster periodizes Foucault's work in this way: the "archeology" of the 1960s pursued critique of the self by a motif of reversal (madness versus reason); the "genealogy" of the 1970s utilized critique by displacement (from subject to structure); the "ethics" of the 1980s sought a hermeneutics of the self by using a strategy of historicism. (Compare Caputo's essay on the hermeneutic reading of Foucault.) Poster finds the key to this last period in Foucault's reexamination of the Enlightenment, and much of his comparison and contrast of Foucault with Sartre (and with Habermas) turns on that point. The central issue here recalls both essays in the first section: "How can the activity of self-constitution through rational critique of the present avoid giving universal status to the subject?"

Poster believes that Foucault avoids a totalizing stance by only claiming for his concerns (insanity, labor, prisons) the exigency "that they have continued to recur up to our time." But Poster argues that this reliance on the past deprives Foucault's position of its grounding in the present and thus of its potential for political intervention. Poster sees Foucault's genius in raising the issue of self-constitution at a time when it is undergoing radical changes, but he would describe those changes in very different terms. Instead of linking changes in self-constitution with bio-power or the constitution of sex, Poster would focus on discursive practices, especially the drastic changes in the structure of language in late twentieth-century culture. The change *he* sees as crucial is posed in terms as close to Lyotard or Baudrillard as to Foucault: "Data banks designate the truth of the individual as a credit risk, as political subversive, as criminal, as customer, client, agent, friend, parent, and lover." Self-constitution has entered the "Mode of Information."

Foucault, of course, saw the constitution of the self as inseparable from its sex, with sex being a social-historical construction (institution?) as well. Judith Butler's "Sexual Inversions: Rereading the End of *The History of Sexuality, Volume I*" complicates one chapter of the history Foucault tells. (Her analysis would also conflict with some of Poster's claims, as she takes more seriously the Foucaultian connection between sex and self-constitution, bringing a different sort of critique to this connection.) Foucault argues that, with the disappearance of famines and epidemics in eighteenth-century Europe, power turned from a defensive formation protecting against death to the production, maintenance, and control of life (bio-power). Death is expelled from Western modernity into our past or a nonwestern exteriority; life takes the form of productive power; and sex takes on the power to characterize and constitute identity.

Butler upsets this account by arguing that to defend against death is already to promote a certain version of life. The distinction between these periods of power will not hold. The AIDS epidemic is a more graphic and disturbing demonstration of this point. Sex serves not only life; it is also made to serve in the regulation and apportionment of death, as technology is differentially deployed to save some lives and to condemn others. Thus, instead of seeing a historical shift from power as constraining to power as productive, Butler sees a "constraining production" that works by linking the categories of sex and identity. Butler asks whether "sex" can be understood as a historical category apart from the *sexes*, and she offers both an Irigarayan critique of Foucault and a Foucaultian caution not to treat femaleness as an identity to be liberated. Foucault's inversion of sex and sexuality has inverted the logic of identity that makes "inversion" possible; now Butler subjects Foucault's history to inversions that "he taught us how to perform." Foucault warned us not to think that by saying yes to sex we say no to power; warns Butler, we must not think that by saying yes to power we say no to death.

III. The University and Its Disciplines

With this section we are thick in the midst of institutions in a more ordinary sense of that term, beginning with that institution to which we "belong" (along, we suspect, with most of our readers)—the university. We "professors" ply our profession where the life of thought is institutionalized (like the criminal or the insane) and normalized (as well reflected in the French label *école normale*, a school for training teachers).

In "Extralogical Excavation: Philosophy in the Age of Shovelry" Dyke uses Foucault to make a stinging and insouciant rebuke to the institution of analytic philosophy. Analytic philosophy, he thinks, is a relentless—if futile—search for discursive power: the power of a scientific-technical discourse, the juridical power to adjudicate the logic and epistemics of other discourses, situated at the center of the most powerful institutions as the voice of reason and morality. It wants to forge an autonomous, foundational discourse that gives clarity to our thoughts, conceptual foundations to empirical matters of fact, and liberal compassion to our ethico-political lives. Dyke (a Brown-trained analytic philosopher of science who has evidently gotten to be "postanalytic") is out to desacralize the sacred object of analytic philosophy and to demythologize its sacred prehistory from Descartes through Locke, Berkeley, Hume, and Kant. Of an early twentieth-century academic "artifact"—the "founding father" of ordinary language philosophy, G. E. Moore, who can prove to us that here is a hand—Dyke says, "if he could prove both his hand and his ass to exist, then he could commodiously scratch his ass." The search for disciplinary autonomy and scientific respectability—ahistorical, cognitive minimalism, Dyke calls it—leaves analytic philosophy flipping vainly like a fish on a hook between the old theological agenda and the physical sciences, never succeeding in acquiring the authority of the former or the disciplinary respectability of the latter: a discipline (as Rorty said) in search of a subject matter (and an assured place in the core curriculum).

Analytic philosophy tries to breathe in an impossible element, to occupy an impossible space—a "phase space," in Dyke's very complicated image of synchronic Poincaré sections with four axes. Such a space, Dyke argues, is constantly being deconstructed as conceptual issues keep getting contaminated by empirical information (even as the very distinction itself wavers) and as intuitions keep getting historicized. Dyke blows the whistle on the sociology of analytic philosophy: the only space it succeeds in occupying at all stably is in elite universities where elite students are well insulated from common knowledge and common people (people who use, rather than prove the existence of, their hands). It prospers in a space where academic philosophers are free to pursue their race for maximum credentialization, mutual reenforcement, and self-congratulation. The end result is that elite students are credentialized by elite universities in order to be hired by other elite institutions, thereby reproducing their own in an insular, institutional self-perpetuation, debating issues of no concern to anyone but themselves, leaving the world not only unchanged but also not very well understood.

This reproduction of knowledge and its knowers, this regurgitation of graduates, does not happen without us. We—though perhaps not you, reader—are the specific intellectuals of a more general pedagogy. That is the vantage from which Mary Schmelzer writes "Panopticism and Postmodern Pedagogy," a first-hand account of forces that contour, coerce, and normalize our activities as teachers. To be in the classroom is to occupy a surveillant role even as you are yourself subjected to surveillance. But the mechanism distributing these gazes mystifies their relations by the same operation, establishing not a hierarchy but diffuse and lateral oppositions. Surveillance does not issue from a center or pinnacle, as if the architecture of power conformed to the organizational charts so reassuring to trustees. Schmelzer offers some very different examples to show how the surveillant gaze is disseminated throughout lateral relations. As the institution trains every "I" to its requisite viewpoint, these gazes are set upon each other—each set to a different watch, labors divided, each assigned a site where her gaze is privileged, even imperative.

The postmodern pedagogue, she who would resist the role of professor in order to teach, has to create the space in which to question the knowledge system these power relations figure forth. Consider these operational imperatives of the norm: that teaching is a category distinct from research; that a lesson, and a course entire, must have a "plan," a defined objective; that certain texts are canonical and that the text is the canon of the course; that all questions have answers; that pupils look to the teacher, and that they not be made too uncomfortable by the process;

ultimately, that these roles are measurable against their assignments. Evaluative mechanisms traverse every intersection of gazes, from before the syllabus to after the exam. In deviating from its appointed norms, performative pedagogy is always at risk of being marked as a standard deviation. The teaching stance Schmelzer shares tries to uncover the enabling assumptions of the institution, even as the teacher continues to work in it—an instance of Derrida's "double gesture." The surveillant gaze will not be occluded, but acts of resistance might redirect that gaze. And the redirected gaze interrupts, or at least shifts, that network of power relations that supports the university's claim to truth, its regulation of what can count as true and of who can do the reckoning.

One might hope to find a more "objective" view of truth in another corner of the university, in the "harder" disciplines of natural science. But Joseph Rouse shows in "Foucault and the Natural Sciences" that such knowledge is also produced in dynamic relations of power. Laboratories have joined prisons and asylums as "complete and austere institutions," producing standardized and normalized objects and forcing *things* to "speak" according to these new dividing practices. Rouse proposes a "how" of knowledge comparable to Foucault's analytics of power, one that will "cut off the head of the king" in epistemology. Epistemological sovereignty reproduces the central features of political sovereignty: a unitary regime, legitimated through law, standing impartially over particular conflicts, and enforced by suppression of illegitimate claims.

Rouse shows how the actual practices of natural scientific knowledge transgress this model of epistemic sovereignty. Application is not consequent upon discovery; the lines assumed to separate what is "internal" to knowledge from external factors do not hold; the circulation of knowledge is directed by conflicts as much political as epistemic. Knowledge can be resisted where there are gaps in the data, but also where its development would be unprofitable, or environmentally unsound, or of too much or too little interest to the military.

Those alarmed by the "relativism" of this analysis suppose that since there is *no* epistemic sovereignty, *all* knowledge claims must have equal claim to validity. But Rouse argues that such relativism actually *depends* on an epistemic sovereignty whose "rights" can be extended to all knowledge and all knowers. By displacing the pretension to sovereign knowledge, we thereby displace the supposed dangers of this relativism. Questions about legitimation are on the same level as any other conflicts over truth, which means that they always emerge in a real setting, with something at stake, interested parties, and a burden of proof enforced by strategic alignments. That arrangement is subject to challenge, of course, and Rouse concludes by comparing the very different challenges creationists and feminists bring to the natural sciences.

IV. The Workplace

Robert Moore and Mark Yount both apply power/knowledge analyses to employment practices, showing in both cases how disciplinary and legal frameworks converge. Moore, who directs the Comey Institute for Labor Relations at St. Joseph's University, disrupts traditional categories of labor law analysis in "Law, Normativity, and the Level Playing Field: The Production of Rights in American Labor Law." Drawing on the resources of Foucault, he exposes contemporary American labor law and collective bargaining as a complicitous system of discipline and social control. Moore traces the legal evolution of this regime to show both its normalizing effects and its constitution of a new form of disciplinary truth. Like the systems underlying psychiatry and criminology, labor-management conflict is constituted as an object of scientific knowledge by the "sciences" of society, whose dominant paradigms proclaim harmony, stability equilibrium, gradualism, and reformism as "normal" and conflict (class or otherwise) as "pathological." It is within this larger discourse that collective bargaining law ensures the status of the arbitrator as "expert," authorized to intervene wherever necessary in order to restore harmony and a "level playing field."

Moore shows convincingly, though, that this legal-disciplinary system has had an opposite effect, making labor inequalities even more extreme by the very mechanisms supposed to "level the field." The "rights" employees can claim are all produced and constrained by these normalizing procedures, and workers are precluded from imagining forms of resistance that would transcend these acknowledged constraints (including measures such as sit-down strikes, which had been effective in the past). The relative decline in authorized strikes and near disappearance of wildcat strikes show how difficult it has been for workers to develop effective forms of resistance. At the same time, the courts have increased the powers of management to lock out striking workers and hire permanent replacements. Thus procedural rights like the right to strike serve less to restore a balance of power and more to legitimate the "truth" of claims brought within the system, to channel all conflict within that system, and ultimately to legitimate the system itself. The end result is a process that rationalizes, rather than challenges, the inequalities of power in labor relations.

Mark Yount's essay, "The Normalizing Powers of Affirmative Action," offers a genealogical critique of both sides of the familiar liberal versus conservative debate on that subject. Affirmative action reproblematized equal opportunity by grafting measures of substantive justice onto procedural standards, and that was a real gain in the provision and enforcement of civil rights and women's rights. But that shift has given rise to a network of legal, administrative, and employment practices so governed by statistical norms that the law requires social scientific expertise for its application, with wide variation in both interpretation and enforcement as a result. While massive inequalities by race and gender certainly justify some *kind* of affirmative action, Yount argues that these inequalities are so great that the affirmative action programs now in effect cannot seriously address the problem, even if properly enforced. Once opportunities have been this massively blocked, Yount contends "the blockages belong to the system"; they are coextensive with the whole social-economic network and cannot be removed with such partial adjustments. Having criticized liberal support for affirmative action as we know it, Yount exposes the power logic of conservative arguments against affirmative action to show that they are misanthropic, only serving to excuse gross inequalities by feeding the "new racism" of whites.

Foucault's genealogy helps explains this network of power/knowledge, and it allows a more nuanced analysis of the logic of the so-called new racism, which uses the existence of affirmative action to deny its own status as racism. But Yount finds genealogy better suited to criticism than to constructing alternatives. Drawing on Foucault's remarks on social security, Yount suggests that genealogy requires a complementary "care perspective," possibly following feminist researches in the wake of Carol Gilligan's work—a line of critical research Yount finds exemplary of genealogy. (Compare the attention to care in Caputo's essay.)

V. Healing Institutions

In the final section, John Caputo claims to find a hermeneutics—what Caputo would call a "radical hermeneutics"—in Foucault. To be sure, Foucault leaves behind the "tragic hermeneutics" of the earlier writings, which seek out a pulsating madness as a kind of originary truth concealed by psychology. But in Foucault's later writings Caputo sees what he calls a "hermeneutics of refusal," of the irrepressible capacity of human beings for being-different, for being otherwise than we are presently constituted. Foucault's more "radical" hermeneutics is thus a "negative" hermeneutics, of the sort described in Bernauer's treatment of Foucault's "negative theology," which rejects the idea of a hidden master name or concealed truth.[13] Such a hermeneutics turns on the idea of what Foucault called in the early writings "the night of truth": the truth that there is no capitalized "Truth," no truth *of* truth. In Caputo's hermeneutics of Foucault, Foucault's is a hermeneutics that confesses that we do not know who we are.

Caputo rejects the complaint that Foucault treats human beings as a kind of pure *hyle* who simply undergo successive historical constitutions—a complaint that would undermine his own idea of resistance. On the contrary, Foucault defines human beings in terms of their freedom and resistance, their capacity to be otherwise. Moreover, by insisting on a certain "hermeneutic depth" in Foucault's work, an ineradicable capacity for being otherwise, the notion of difference or being-different acquires a certain "depth of otherness." On such an approach, the Other comes to us from "on high" (Levinas), from out of the abyss of Otherness. Far from being the object of a medical gaze, we are put into question by the Other.

Caputo's final pages clearly move beyond the scope of Foucault's own reflections, as he turns to implications for therapeutics and the Christian confessional. Caputo gropes for a new way to conceive therapy and the confessional that retains a Foucaultian point of departure and that does not reduce to normalizing power. He suggests a therapeutics that proceeds, not from science and *episteme*, but from nonknowing: a caring that proceeds from the cold truth that we are not alone in the "dark night of truth," that we are all of us—mad and not so mad, sinners and not so sinful—siblings of the same dark night.

---

[13] See James Bernauer, *Michel Foucault's Force of Flight: Toward an Ethics for Thought* (Atlantic Highlands: Humanities Press International, 1990).

ADMONITIONS

> A nightmare has pursued me since childhood: I have under my eyes a text that I can't read, or of which only a tiny part can be deciphered; I pretend to read it, but I know that I'm inventing; then the text suddenly blurs completely, I can no longer read anything or even invent, my throat constricts and I wake up.[14]

If the term 'institution' applies to "all the field of the nondiscursive social,"[15] "the book" may be the dominant institution of discourse. This volume, too, is of that institution. It, too, is traversed with the markings of micropowers, produced and disseminated in networks of power/knowledge, subject throughout to more specific and worldly institutions. That these essays are collected here in this way, that the volume has this shape, or claims a shape at all, especially a unified one: all this belongs to the institution of the book.

Foucault, of course, was suspicious of this institution, and especially critical of the dominance of "the author function" as a "principle of thrift in the proliferation of meaning." Foucault once thought that as the author function disappears, all discourses will then develop "in the anonymity of a murmur."[16] The book you have before you does not suppose that effacement or contribute its volume to that murmur. Yet the author function is at least triply split here: by its character as anthology, grouping many authors; by its doubling of editors; but also by its unifying authority deriving not from any editor or contributor but from the name "Foucault." If Foucault, too, is an institution of sorts now, this anthology repeatedly *uses* Foucault in the contrasting senses this little word allows. So beware of the normalizing powers of books, and of prefaces, and of summaries such as you find herein. Beware of the critic of institutions made an institution for criticism.

But to be an institution in that sense, to be thus *used* will not be the simple betrayal it might appear, precisely because of logics we have learned from Foucault. We might say of him what he remarked of Freud and Marx as "founders of discursivity": that he has created the possibility

---

[14]Michel Foucault, "The Discourse of History," in *Foucault Live*, p. 25.
[15]Foucault, *Power/Knowledge*, pp. 197–198.
[16]Michel Foucault, "What Is an Author?" in *The Foucault Reader*, pp. 118 and 119.

for something other than his discourse, yet something belonging to what he founded.[17] We might claim of him what he claimed of Nietzsche:

> [His] contemporary presence is increasingly important. But I am tired of people studying him only to produce the same kind of commentaries that are written on Hegel or Mallarmé. For myself, I prefer to utilise the writers I like. The only valid tribute to thought such as [Foucault's] is precisely to use it, to deform it, to make it groan and protest.[18]

Foucault's thought is made to groan more loudly in some of these essays than others. It is for you to register those protests, to transfer, resist, or further deform the forces that interrupt or impel your reading.

If the book is an institution, if this book is of the "Foucault" institution, the institution that has most literally and directly shaped this work is the Greater Philadelphia Philosophy Consortium (GPPC). Much of that background has already been explained, but some reflexivity seems appropriate here, where even the greatest acknowledgment allows for admonition. If Foucault is correct, knowledge is only produced in circuits of power. Only in such a power/knowledge regime is it possible to establish or operate institutions devoted to truth. The GPPC has emerged and grown through the overlapping and competing powers of its member universities, and especially their departments of philosophy or humanities. We hope this volume is a worthy testament to the consortium that has given the book its character.

But this volume reflects its institutional nexus in what it lacks as well as what it offers. University philosophy departments are dominated by white males, and the present volume grudgingly succumbs to those statistics. Programs are planned mostly by white males and anthologies are edited by white males. This is but one example of the confluence of powers in the reproductive and circulatory systems of knowledge, and it is one of the more visible and more objectionable. Foucault believed the university hierarchy to be "only the most visible, the most sclerotic and least dangerous form" of power/knowledge.[19] Battered, untenured, and disqualified colleagues might argue the point. The articles by Dyke and

---

[17]Ibid., p. 114.
[18]Foucault, *Power/Knowledge*, pp. 53–54.
[19]Ibid., p. 52.

Schmelzer show how complicated it is to inhabit a university: to be "in" a discipline, or even "in" the classroom. Rouse offers another measure of this problem in the domains of the natural sciences, and it may be the common structures of these disciplinary powers that envelop "the university" with the unified shape its catalog requires.

One could conclude that a consortium forged of such raw material is a morally or politically doomed venture, or that books like this one only serve a system that ought to be escaped or opposed. But if Foucault is right, we may not be able to conceive an institution that leaves our hands clean—certainly none with a connection to knowledge. Would it be unfair to say that the Consortium shows the same confluence of limitation and possibility that Foucault attributed to philosophy as a discipline? On the one hand he spoke of escaping from philosophy and of how the remnants of traditional philosophical discourse hampered his earlier work. But he found in the texts that most interested him "something that began with philosophy, put it into play and into question, then left it and came back. . . ."[20] So it is better *not* to escape philosophy, if such a thing is even possible. "The Masked Philosopher" (guess who?) explains:

> From philosophy comes the displacement and transformation of the limits of thought, the modification of received values and all the work done to think otherwise, to do something else, to become other than what one is. . . . It's a way of asking oneself: if such is the relation that we have with truth, then how should we conduct ourselves?[21]

ACKNOWLEDGMENTS

Perhaps the more suspicious we are of the mechanisms of power, the more appreciative we should be when philosophy is able to work its way through those mechanisms, the more grateful we should be for institutions like this Consortium. We thank the GPPC, its directors and constituent members, for their support in making both the original 1985–86 series possible and also the present volume. We owe a special debt of thanks to

---

[20]Michel Foucault, "On Literature," in *Foucault Live*, p. 119.
[21]Michel Foucault, "The Masked Philosopher," ibid., p. 201.

the Pennsylvania Humanities Council and its Executive Director, Craig Eisendrath, for a generous grant that made the 1985–86 series possible. We thank as well the Office of Research and Sponsored Projects at Villanova University, which administered this grant; Allene Murphey, Conference Coordinator, who managed the nuts and bolts of running four conferences at four different institutions; and Andrew Gallinger, who helped prepare the index. And we especially thank Joseph Margolis, Michael Krausz, and John Caputo, who planned that series.

We would also like to thank all of our authors: the original participants, for their great patience over the years this project has developed; and our subsequent contributors, for their willingness to join such a project on shorter notice. We are especially grateful to Mary Schmelzer under these circumstances.

Part II

FOUCAULT AND CRITIQUE

FOUCAULT AS A PHILOSOPHER

Jitendra Mohanty

Although Foucault has often said that his work is not in the discipline called "philosophy" ("of the universities," he would add), it has been generally claimed that some of his theses, if true, must be of considerable importance for philosophy. This is indeed as it should be, for being the sort of discipline that philosophy is, it cannot but be stirred by new ideas in any other science, natural, social, or human. But, in the case of Foucault, there are special difficulties in claiming large philosophical significance for his work, and it is to some of these that I shall begin by drawing attention in the first part of this essay. In the second and the third parts, I shall focus on a couple of Foucault's theses that are as such philosophical and of great importance, no matter whether they are in the long run acceptable or not.

FOUCAULT'S WORK AND PHILOSOPHY

> *I have never had the intention of doing a general history of the human sciences, or a critique of the possibility of the sciences in general.*[1]

Foucault celebrates the rise of specific revolutionary movements as contrasted with the global ones, and also of specific intellectuals.[2] His own scientific work focuses on certain specific conflicts—notably, those in medicine, psychiatry, and penal systems. The idea of grand universal histories and of universal revolutions is, in his mind, connected with the conception of philosophy as a universal discipline, a discipline that allegedly provides all human knowledge and action with a foundation, purpose, and meaning. The question that I want to ask, first, is: if we take Foucault at his own word—if we take him as a specific intellectual abjuring philosophy as a discipline—what philosophical significance can his work nevertheless have? I shall not even attempt to call into question the validity of his historical studies in medicine, psychiatry, and penal systems. Assuming their validity (or truth in the only sense admissible by Foucault, that is, in the sense in which 'truth' is not separable from 'power'), one still would want to be clear about their bearings on philosophy. Clearly, there are several possibilities to choose from: One may hold that studies such as Foucault's in such areas need have no bearing on philosophy; or, one may concede that the bearings they may have on philosophy need be of no greater significance than the vast changes in the natural sciences in this half of the century; or, one may contend that, despite Foucault's denial that he is doing philosophy, his work cannot but have profound influence on philosophy. Let us consider these three possible views.

The first view is that Foucault's work in such specific areas as history of medicine, psychiatry, and penal systems, like any work in the empirical sciences, can at best only underdetermine philosophy. Work in these areas can be of momentous importance for the social sciences, but philosophy is not a social science, although it may have the social sciences, or at least

---

[1] Michel Foucault, *Power/Knowledge: Selected Interviews and Other Writings, 1972–1977* (henceforth cited as *P/K*), ed. Colin Gordon, tr. Colin Gordon et al. (New York: Pantheon, 1980), p. 165.
[2] *P/K*, p., 65.

some aspects of them, as its subject matter. By augmenting or modifying what philosophy has to think about, work in the social sciences and in history may indirectly influence philosophy, but it cannot by itself determine what shape philosophy will take. It cannot do so anymore than developments in quantum mechanics or discoveries of the structure of DNA can by themselves force a change in the course of philosophy, excepting by way of providing philosophy with interesting results to focus upon. If observational data underdetermine the sciences, the scientific theories for their part underdetermine philosophy. The point can be made in the following way: The methods of writing history have been changing, with new methodologies being advanced and new looks taken at the past. These changes in what historians do have affected the nature of history as a science, but not the nature of philosophy in general. They may at best provide grounds for a new philosophy of history, in the same way as quantum mechanics provides the basis for a new philosophy of physics that radically departs from the philosophies based on classical physics. But such change is conceived within philosophy in a certain manner; it does not entail a radical departure in the very nature, conception, and role of philosophy.

This brings us to the second view, which concedes that Foucault's fascinating historical studies should provide new problems for philosophical thinking and necessitate revisions of some marginal concepts, especially in philosophy of the social sciences or perhaps in philosophy of history—but none of these changes need be more radical than those occasioned or necessitated by many sea changes taking place in the sciences today. So why specifically focus on Foucault? The only reason his pioneering and in some respects revolutionary work may seem to be of greater philosophical import than many other pioneering and revolutionary achievements in biology, genetics, and the information sciences is that philosophy may be regarded as in a certain sense *closer* to the concerns of the social or human sciences than to the natural sciences. But this last is a questionable assumption. If we reject this assumption and hold that philosophy is neither a social or human science nor a natural science, but is a mode of thinking that derives some of its subject matter from all those sciences equally, then there is no reason why Foucault's specific historical studies should have any more importance for philosophy than work in those other fields. Such a position is perfectly consistent with his disclaimer that he is doing philosophy, although it would leave most philosophers dissatisfied. They would prefer the third alternative and insist that his researches do profoundly affect philosophy in a manner in which researches in physics and the life sciences do not. Let us see how a case can be made for such a view.

To appreciate Foucault's importance for philosophy, one needs to bear in mind the state of philosophy that prevailed in France up until the sixties. That state of philosophy may best be described as a confluence of the ideas of the three H's—Hegel, Husserl, and Heidegger—culminating in the existential phenomenologies of Sartre and Merleau-Ponty. To Husserl, it owed the idea of transcendental subjectivity as constitutive of all mundane objectivities. To Heidegger, it owed the centrality of *Dasein* as being-in-the-world, being characterized by a hermeneutic preunderstanding of itself and its world and by historicity and temporality that make the Husserlian transcendental-constitutive role unattainable. To Hegel, it owed a conception of subjectivity as developing through history towards a comprehensive self-knowledge or, rather, of history as a process through which spirit progressively comes to know itself. The key concepts and concerns of this era were: subjectivity, constitution, temporality, and history. Foucault's researches may then be seen as contributing to the destruction of the centrality of the nexus of these concepts. This is achieved (a) by developing a theory of how subjectivity itself is constituted, (b) by offering a theory of the constitution of the domain of objects by discourse, (c) by rejecting the priority of time, especially of the inner, lived, experiential, and existential time, (d) by highlighting the discontinuity (of *episteme*, of events, of discourse) that makes it impossible for reflection to appropriate all history into its own thinking, and, finally, (e) by rejecting the classic philosophical idea of 'truth' in favor of one that is inseparable from 'power'. If these be among the results of Foucault's researches, it would seem undeniable that they seriously affect philosophy. But are they? I suspect it can be shown that they are not. They are, rather, results of *philosophically* interpreting certain interesting "historical contents"[3] or "a solid body of historical fact"[4] discovered and juxtaposed by him. If that be the case, what we would have on hand is not a case of historical researches exposing philosophy's pretensions, but rather a less interesting case of a certain philosophical interpretation claiming to set aside another on the basis of allegedly factual discoveries. Such a position would still be able to sustain the third alternative, but would render it much less significant.

[3] *P/K*, p. 81.
[4] *P/K*, p. 103.

Foucault as a Philospher 31

In order to render my case regarding the third alternative plausible, but not securely established, let me consider several theses Foucault advances regarding 'power'. My purpose, I repeat, is simply to draw attention to the *nature* of these theses.

THE CONCEPT OF 'POWER': FOUCAULT AND HEGEL

> *[And] for all that I may like to say "I'm not a philosopher, nonetheless if my concern is with truth then I am still a philosopher."*[5]
>
> *Power is neither given, nor exchanged, nor recovered, but rather exercised and . . . it only exists in action.*[6]
>
> *[The] individual is not a pre-given entity which is seized on by the exercise of power. The individual, with his identity and characteristics, is the product of a relation of power. . . .*[7]
>
> *Power must be analyzed as something which circulates. . . . It is never localized here or there. . . . Power is employed and exercised through a net-like organization.*[8]
>
> *Truth isn't outside power, or lacking in power. . . . [T]ruth isn't the reward of free spirits, the child of protracted solitude, not the privilege of those who have succeeded in liberating themselves. Truth is a thing of this world: it is produced only by virtue of multiple forms of constraint.*[9]
>
> *Power is "always already there," . . . one is never outside it, . . . there are no "margins" for those who break with the system to gamble in.*[10] *. . . Power is co-extensive with the social body.*[11]

[5]P/K, p. 66.
[6]P/K, p. 89.
[7]P/K, p. 73–74.
[8]P/K, p. 98.
[9]P/K, p. 131.
[10]P/K, p. 141.

> *Its success is proportional to its ability to hide its own mechanisms. . . . For it, secrecy is not in the nature of an abuse; it is indispensable to its operation.*[12]

Now what kind of concept is this concept of power? I want to suggest that, though clearly not the same, yet it is very similar to the Hegelian concept of *Geist*. The Hegelian *Geist* is always with us, beside us. As a matter of fact, we are in its midst. This is what Hegel says in the context of his critique of Kantian epistemology in the Introduction to the *Phenomenology*.[13] Spirit is not a thing, a substance, "a life-less essence," but "actual" as intersubjective, in the community (which is a network of relationships). It exists, we can say, in action. The individual, in his or her modernistic individuality, is constituted, not pregiven: in this constitution—in the constitution of self-conscious subjectivity—desire, need for recognition, and conflict are necessary moments. Human desire is desire whose object is not a thing, but another desire (recall that, for Foucault, power is action directed to other actions). But the mode of operation of *Geist* is not restricted to exploitation, domination, and repression. *Geist* is also synthesizing and harmonizing—not to be sure, presupposing consent (as power also, for Foucault, does not). The operations of *Geist* are multifarious, irreducible to any single type. *Geist*, as is well known, is what it is through its other. It faces nature as an alien power. The oppositions between consciousness and the unconscious, the known and the unknown, truth and subjectivity, one's own and what is alien, self-consciousness and nature—all these belong to the life of the *Geist*. Clearly enough, I have the conception of *Geist* of the *Phenomenology* in mind, freed from the optimism of reaching Absolute Knowledge—that is, of *Geist* as process, freed from a linear conception of history. Perhaps there is only one major impediment for thus construing the Hegelian *Geist*: the Foucaultian thesis of discontinuities, breaks, and ruptures that prevent us from talking about one historical process realizing a plan of the *Geist*. I shall return to this idea of discontinuity later in this essay. For the present, it needs to be emphasized that (a) the history of spirit, according to the *Phenomenology*, is a series of shapes whose distinctions are not

---

[12]Michel Foucault, *The History of Sexuality, Volume I: An Introduction*, tr. Robert Hurley (New York: Pantheon, 1978), p. 86.
[13]G.W.F. Hegel, *Phenomenology of Mind*, tr. J. B. Baillie (London and New York: Humanities Press, 1966), p. 132.

intended to be obliterated even with Absolute Knowledge; (b) these shapes are, in an important sense, discontinuous (although Hegel thought there is a logically necessitated transition from one to its successor, the sense of *this* necessity is never quite clear, and a certain contingency persists about the series); (c) they all do not line up as succeeding each other in linear time, for that succession does not quite correspond to the actual history; and, finally, (d) a certain circularity characterizes the life of spirit as a whole as well as each phase of it. If we keep this complicated picture in mind, and also recall that the familiar dialectical triad (with a synthesis of opposites) does not fit all Hegelian movements (as Croce, Müller, and Findlay, among others, have well pointed out), then a certain formal affinity between Foucault's 'power' and Hegel's *Geist* becomes apparent, despite his claims to have left Hegel on the wayside. Add to all this the Hegelian "cunning of Reason": Foucault's 'power' also succeeds by "hiding its own mechanism."

The way Foucault (having studied with Hyppolite) saw his relationship to Hegel is best expressed in a telling passage that shows his awareness of "the extent to which Hegel, insidiously perhaps, is close to us . . . to which our anti-Hegelianism is possibly one of his tricks directed against us, at the end of which he stands motionless, waiting for us."[14]

Let me reiterate that my purpose, in this section, is *not* to show how much of a Hegelian Foucault was. It is intended to emphasize that Foucault's fundamental concepts such as 'power' are basically *philosophical* concepts—in the case of 'power', a *speculative* concept—not naturalistic or scientific ones, that the perception that Foucault abandoned philosophy to do positive science in search of facts (and documents) or that he radicalized "naturalization" of philosophy[15] are just mistaken. No positive science of fact can lead to *the sort of thesis* he arrived at (the thesis, namely, that knowledge and power are inseparable). The so-called genealogy is a philosophical thesis that goes beyond any science and in fact is not the result of any scientific discovery. Being a philosophical thesis, it needs to be freed from the pretense of scientificity and to be examined as such. To say, as Foucault said, that the concept of 'power' he put forward is nominalistic, that power is how it works, distributed along the different

[14]Michel Foucault, "The Discourse of Language," tr. Rupert Sawyer, printed as an appendix to *The Archaeology of Knowledge* (New York: Pantheon, 1972).
[15]David Hoy defends such an interpretation in his "Genealogy vs. Rational Reconstruction: Two Conflicting Conceptions of How to Naturalize Philosophy," read at a Temple University conference in September 1987.

centers of power—and not unified in a point of origin, such as the state, the sovereign, or God—would not make the thesis any less philosophical: nominalism is a philosophical, not a scientific, theory by virtue of its pretended positivity and scientificity. As a matter of fact, the Hegelian *Geist* is no less distributive—synchronically and diachronically. One could very well say, *Geist* is how it works. Hegel's discourse, one may add, is more honest in the sense that from the very beginning it abandons the positivist notion of fact, making the notions of facthood, objectivity, and truth relative to each shape of the spirit—thus leaving no neutral observational data against which to measure the large philosophical thesis about 'spirit'. Foucault remains ambivalent on this score.

CONSTITUTION OF SUBJECTIVITY AND TRANSCENDENTAL PHILOSOPHY

> . . . *it is not power but the subject which is the general theme of my research.*[16]

There are three philosophical theses advanced by Foucault to which I now wish to draw attention, in order to reflect on them and bring out their significance far beyond Foucault's own philosophy. These three are:

(A) that domains of objects are constituted by discourse;
(B) that subjectivity itself is constituted;
(C) that the concepts of one time and one history need to be rejected.

Thinking on these three theses will lead me to conclude this essay with some reflections on Foucault on 'transcendental philosophy'.

It is interesting to notice that, of these three theses, A is clearly one that is in the spirit of transcendental philosophy. B is also a thesis that, under a certain construal, is acceptable to the transcendental philosopher. C runs counter to a dominant trend in transcendental philosophy. These remarks bear out that all the three theses are closely related to Foucault's

---

[16]Michel Foucault, "The Subject and Power," *Critical Inquiry* 8 (Summer 1982): 777–795, esp. 778.

continuing concern with, though by no means acceptance of, transcendental philosophy.

(A) The thesis of the *Archaeology* is well known: for each discourse there is no preexistent theme, such as madness, which that discourse simply takes up. On the contrary, it is "the interplay of rules that makes possible the appearance of objects during a given period of time."[17] It is discourse that constitutes a domain of objects. As some have noted, what needs to be demystified, according to Foucault, is the category of 'real', in the sense of an ontological category of reality behind and prior to discourse.[18] In a later essay, Foucault writes: "I wanted to see how these problems of constitution could be resolved within a historical framework, instead of referring them to a constituent object (madness, criminality or whatever)."[19] Phenomenology, especially French, solved it by historicizing the subject. Foucault wants to get rid of the subject—be it a transcendent, ahistorical ego ("an empty sameness throughout the course of history") or a historicized principle as the constituting source. As we shall see, the subject itself is historically constituted. But what then is the principle of constitution? Not, to be sure, history in the familiar, let us say, traditional sense, for the idea of one, continuous, historical process unfolding itself in one time is itself a construction, behind which stands the idea of a transcendental subject. With the pregiven object and the pregiven subject both out, constitution occurs by rules of discourse. But this structuralist theory is soon replaced by the so-called genealogy: all constitution, be it of the subject, of forms of discourse, or of their object domains, is said to be by 'power'.

In view of Foucault's continuing critique of transcendental philosophy and of all theories that trace constitution back to subjectivity, it is understandable that readers would notice his opposition to that tradition. But one is likely to overlook the fact that what he wants to set aside is only one half of that tradition—namely, the priority accorded to subjectivity. The other half he retains, and this is the general theory of constitution. The idea of constitution has its original home in the Kantian-Husserlian tradition. It is incompatible with the naive realism and naturalism that many read into Foucault. Foucault belongs rather to a different tradition,

---

[17]Foucault, *The Archaeology of Knowledge*, p. 15.
[18]Mark Cousins and Athar Hussain, *Michel Foucault* (New York: St. Martin's Press, 1984), p. 261.
[19]*P/K*, p. 117.

stripped of the primacy of subjectivity. 'Power' still occupies the place vacated by subjectivity. Power in effect is the transcendental, as discourse was in the *Archaeology*. Given, however, the nature of the concept of 'power' to which I have drawn attention earlier in this essay, the nature of Foucault's transcendental thinking is all the more impressive. What is noteworthy is that there is a certain 'bad faith' about it. Foucault—granted that his local genealogies are viable stories—lays claim to a universalist thesis about *all* objects, all discourses,[20] all subjectivity, that makes him a universal intellectual, which he at the same time does not want to be.

(B) The radicalization of Foucault's thinking is best illustrated in his attempt to show that subjectivity itself is constituted, so that it cannot be the source of constitution. One must be able to understand the precise nature of this thesis, before one attempts to question its viability. There is a philosophical outlook, shared by many different sorts of philosophers, according to which 'consciousness', 'subjectivity', 'mental', and 'inner' do not stand for any reality, but are rather products of misconstruing or misunderstanding something; that something may be the grammar of one's language, the nature of one's knowledge of oneself, or self-ascription of features. Be that as it may, this is not the sort of thesis Foucault wants to uphold. His attitude towards the principle of subjectivity is far more sophisticated. He is not, to be sure, a behaviorist or a reductionist. Subjectivity is "a constructed entity," but not false or imaginary.[21]

First of all, it is very important to bear in mind that when Foucault rejects subjectivity and consciousness, he rejects them as explanatory concepts. As Garth Gillan puts it, the break with subjectivity is but its elimination as a metatheoretical concept, while the subject remains an important object in the field of history.[22] So he is not denying that there are real subjects acting within history. What he is rejecting is that there is a subject who constitutes history and can provide a principled explanation of history. So the familiar objections to the effect that without subjectivity we could not have agency and a genuine concept of action won't be relevant against Foucault.

In the second place, although Foucault holds that the individual is not

---

[20]Foucault recognizes that his general thesis regarding medicine and psychiatric practice is difficult to extend to theoretical physics and organic chemistry. *P/K*, p. 109.
[21]*P/K*, p. 239.
[22]Charles C. Lemert and Garth Gillan, *Michel Foucault: Social Theory and Transgression* (New York: Columbia University Press, 1982), p. 101.

a pregiven entity but is constituted by relations of power,[23] this thesis about constitution of individuality is not quite the same as the thesis about constitution of the subject.

An important part of Foucault's critique of consciousness is not merely that it is constituted, but that consciousness is not all transparent. This is a point that many others, notably Merleau-Ponty, had pressed against Sartre, who is generally regarded as representative of the view that consciousness is all transparent. In *The Order of Things*, Foucault writes that "'the Other' is that which both escapes consciousness, yet is constitutive to it."[24] The human sciences have been trying to retrieve this Other, and to make it known, as is best exemplified in psychoanalysis. Hegel knew this, although he hoped that in Absolute Knowledge all opacity would be eliminated and all otherness overcome. Kant, in his thesis about the sense representations (imprinted upon the mind by an other), and Husserl, in his thesis about the 'hyle,' also showed awareness of this opacity within the heart of consciousness, but both escaped the consequences of this recognition by restricting 'consciousness' to the *noetic* acts by which synthesis confers meaning. In any case, this is not a criticism that the transcendental-philosophical tradition did not know how to deal with.

If by the subject is meant not merely consciousness but also self-consciousness, then, of all persons, Hegel saw most clearly that self-consciousness is constituted, and constituted by desire, conflict of desires, struggle for recognition, a life-and-death battle, and exercise of power over others, the subjugated. There is no doubt that Foucault owes much to this account, even if he rejects a theory of power as domination.

An account of the constitution of subjectivity, I think, has to be nonreductionist; and the minimum condition that it has to satisfy is that, in its account of the constitution of *the most basic form* of subjectivity, it should be noncircular. With these provisos in mind, let us turn to Foucault's account of constitution as presented in the essay "The Subject and Power."[25] He tells us that his goal is to give a history of the different modes by which human beings are made subjects in our culture. In thus posing the question, he obviously has a very restricted sense of being a subject. A subject is one who is subjected to something by control or

---

[23]*P/K*, p. 74.
[24]Michel Foucault, *The Order of Things: An Archaeology of the Human Sciences*, tr. Alan Sheridan (New York: Pantheon, 1970), p. 322.
[25]*Critical Inquiry* 8 (Summer 1982): 777–795.

dependence; this sense of subjectivity has a close proximity to the idea of subjugation. Struggles against subjugation are said to be directed against forms of subjectivity and submission. This makes perfectly good sense: struggles of a colonized people for freedom, of minority groups against suppression, or the Palestinians on the West Bank for freedom—all are *eo ipso* struggles against a certain form of subjectivity in each case. This entails another side of subjectivity[26] in Foucault's restricted sense: if the subject is a subject insofar as he or she is subjugated, controlled, dependent, his or her specific form of subjectivity is also a sense of identity, a self-knowledge that he or she carries.

Given this sense of 'subject', Foucault goes on to distinguish between three modes of 'objectification' (or, rather, 'subjectification'): (1) There are modes of enquiry such as grammar, philosophy, and linguistics that focus upon, thematize, objectify the speaking subject and modes of enquiry such as economics that focus upon, thematize, objectify the productive subject. (2) The subject is also objectified in what Foucault calls "dividing practices"—practices that divide men into binary oppositions mad/sane, sick/healthy, criminal/good boys. (3) A human being may transform himself or herself into a subject by recognizing himself or herself as a subject of sexuality.

With regard to (1), I must say that it does not satisfy the requirement regarding noncircularity. Even leaving aside the muddle about an *objectification* as constituting *subjectivity* (this is precisely what, Husserl complains, distorts the true nature of subjectivity), it seems to me so clear that scientific thematization of a speaking or producing subject already presupposes prescientific subjectivity. How is the prescientific subjectivity constituted? My suspicion is that Foucault is not concerned with this question; he is concerned with, as stated earlier in this essay, expelling the subject from a metatheoretical role, while leaving it its natural role in prescientific and first-level theories (histories, for example). But this should not give him the satisfaction that he has gotten rid of the constituting subjectivity. Leaving aside the question of what forms of subjective acts go into scientific thematization, we cannot avoid the role of subjectivity in constituting the prescientific world of the speaking and the producing subject.

What Foucault shows is how subjectivity is objectified. Another way of objectification, besides scientific thematization, is dividing it up as either

[26]Ibid., 781.

mad or sane, either sick or healthy, either good or bad. But that such objectification ends up by distorting the nature of subjectivity is precisely what Husserl and Sartre had insisted upon. So, even if Foucault is right, what he regards as a step in the constitution of subjectivity works precisely in the opposite direction—as a step towards the covering up of subjectivity.

The third process is clearly one of subjugation—subjugation, for example, to sexuality. That is why Foucault could regard the subject as an inscription on the fractured body. The asylum, the confessional, the prison, and sexuality *subject* the body to discipline, inscribe power on it, make it self-conscious—thereby giving rise to modern subjectivity. We should recall that, on Foucault's theory, power is not a manifestation of consciousness. I suspect Foucault's *philosophical* thesis, not his historical result, confuses between subjectivity and its distorted forms. Hegel knew better. Foucault holds that the subject is constituted by power, and yet he also holds that power is exercised only over free subjects and only insofar as they are free.[27] There is a dimension of subjectivity underlying 'power', and "we have to promote new forms of subjectivity through the refusal of this kind of individuality."[28]

(C) Finally, I consider the famed thesis about discontinuities and breaks, originally devised (by Bachelard) as a barrier against the claim of subjectivity to reflectively appropriate all history into its own being. Some time ago I argued, against Foucault's thesis about epistemological breaks, that there is no nonarbitrary way of coming up with a series of discontinuous epochs, that if one chose a different leading clue (*Leitfaden*), one could have the ruptures fall at different places (or times).[29] Now I realize that is not contrary to Foucault's own intentions. Reflecting, at one place, on the thesis as presented in *The Order of Things*, Foucault writes: "for me, the whole business of breaks and non-breaks is always at once a point of departure and a very relative thing"; it may well mean "relative to the field of one's enquiry." We can shift the scenery—he goes on to say—and take as starting point something else, change the reference points, and come up with a different story. Does the result depend upon the choice of reference, and the choice of reference on one's conjecture?

---

[27]Ibid., 790.
[28]Ibid., 785.
[29]J. N. Mohanty, *Transcendental Phenomenology: An Analytic Account* (Oxford: Basil Blackwell, 1989), pp. 119–131.

These considerations suggest that my earlier objection does not effectively work against Foucault's position, for Foucault's position amounts to rejecting not only a monolithic 'total' history, a continuous "grand narrative," but also a monolithic discontinuous narrative. The radical consequence of this thesis is that there is no one history, be it continuous or discontinuous, and no one time. Two things are happening at the same time: on the one hand, contrary to a dominant trend of modern philosophy from Kant onwards, Foucault wants to devalue time—even at the cost of seeming to spatialize time.[30] But the real reason underlying this devaluation of time is the realization that there are *times* rather than Time, that the many layers of social formation have their own times,[31] that the concepts of 'history' and 'historicity' themselves are of historical origin (what is the sense of this last occurrence of 'historical'?). I believe, in this respect, Foucault's message is a welcome breath of fresh air in the midst of reigning historicisms. 'History' and 'Time' are themselves constituted out of histories and times. Whether this last thesis eliminates the need for a transcendental turn, or signals the possibility of a different sort of transcendental-constitutive theory, is a question I cannot respond to on this occasion. But one thing seems to me to be clear: one does not understand Foucault unless one understands the nature of his continuing concern with transcendental philosophy.

---

[30]*P/K*, pp. 70, 149–150.
[31]*The Archaeology of Knowledge*, p. 131.

REDEEMING FOUCAULT

Joseph Margolis

THE PARADOX OF TRUTH

There is a paradox at the heart of what is most characteristic of Michel Foucault's entire oeuvre, which at times Foucault was quite blithe about and which, at other times, he found rather disquieting. We may locate it informally in the fact that Foucault took enormous pride in the peculiar accuracy of his own histories, despite the complaint of more academic historians, and that the reliability of the truths he uncovered in unexpected places could not but be hostage to the deep contingency his own theories of truth and history entailed. One is tempted to locate the source of the paradox in his reading of Nietzsche. But there is good evidence to show that it precedes Nietzsche's strong influence on him, also that it does not reach to Nietzsche's deliberately mad view of the utterly delusive nature of the world. In any case, it is instructive in its own right, and its resolution does not require any accommodation of Nietzsche's grand myth.

The paradox is straightforward enough—at least at the start of a certain reflection: truth, Foucault would have us understand, is a *product*, an artifact, of large historical movements enveloping entire societies; yet his own philosophical reflections, his *genealogies*, tell us that this is the truth about truth. He even manages to limn the main lines of the differential rules of truth local to this age and that.

Foucault obviously thought that the paradox was a profound one—possibly ultimate and insoluble. He rightly saw in it a challenge to the transcendental presumptions of Kant and Husserl.[1] But he worried, also rightly, about a challenge that might prove, on any maneuver, to be self-defeating.

There are many places in Foucault's scattered papers and remarks where the paradox comes into view without actually breaching the surface of systematic thought. Here is a particularly risky formulation just a hair away from explicit contradiction:

> Schematically, we can formulate the traditional question of political philosophy in the following terms: how is the discourse of truth, or quite simply, philosophy as that discourse which *par excellence* is concerned with truth, able to fix limits to the rights of power? That is the traditional question. The one I would prefer to pose is rather different. Compared to the traditional, noble and philosophic question it is much more down to earth and concrete. My problem is rather this: what rules of right are implemented by the relations of power in the production of truth? Or alternatively, what type of power is susceptible of producing discourses of truth that in a society such as ours are endowed with such potent effects? . . . We are subjected to the production of truth through power and we cannot exercise power except through the production of truth. *This is the case for every society, but I believe that in ours the relationship between power, right and truth is organized in a highly specific fashion.*[2]

---

[1] A younger student of Foucault's once confided to me that Foucault urged him to center his philosophical studies on the nature of transcendental reasoning—that he, Foucault, had come to realize that he had not yet reconciled his own thought with such constraints. He suggested the issue was of the greatest importance, not one to be dismissed at all.

[2] Michel Foucault, "Two Lectures" (Lecture Two: 14 January 1976), in *Power/Knowledge:*

In a superficial sense, the paradox is easily resolved. That resolution proves superficial because a deeper paradox remains untouched; it is also, however, important because it confirms that the deeper paradox need not entail any incoherence. In fact, the resolution is almost shamefully obvious. In the tired literature of moral theory, for instance, the question is posed whether one ought to do what one believes one ought to do or what one really ought to do.[3] The answer (correct enough) is that, in the first-person setting, there is no operative difference between the two questions; it only arises through an exercise of a temporally deferred critique. Of course, the formal resolution leaves entirely untouched the deeper matter of whether there is an *objective*—perhaps timeless as well as independent—order of moral values to which the "two" questions are directed, so that, with effort, the correct answer regarding *what* one should do could finally be given. Foucault's remark disallows that particular resolution. But its own local paradox can be resolved in a way completely isomorphic with that of the other: thus, should I say what I believe to be true or what really is true? Of course: say what you believe, but be careful.

In an instructive sense, the same question arises for the sociology of knowledge and, more narrowly, for Marx's view of science. Peter Bürger has put the point in an incomparably clear form: "Criticism [on the Marxian model] is not regarded as a judgment that harshly sets one's own views against the untruth of ideology, but rather as the *production* of cognition."[4] This helps to explain the analogy and difference between Marx and Foucault, and begins to suggest the resolution of the deeper paradox—beyond Marx's own flirtation with cognitive privilege, and beyond Foucault's evident inability to reformulate his own effort to universalize what accommodates, but includes more than, the Marxian vision.

Marx himself, in *Grundrisse*, adumbrates (in a thin way at least) Foucault's paradox—for instance, in the following well-known passage:

> Although it is true, . . . that the categories of bourgeois economics possess a truth for all other forms of society, this is to be

---

Selected Interviews and Other Writings, 1972–1977, ed. Colin Gordon, tr. Colin Gordon et al. (New York: Pantheon, 1980), p. 93 (italics added in the last sentence).

[3] See, e.g., Kurt Baier, *The Moral Point of View* (Ithaca: Cornell University Press, 1958), pp. 30–33, for a related discussion.

[4] Peter Bürger, *The Theory of the Avant-Garde*, tr. Michael Shaw (Minneapolis: University of Minnesota Press, 1984), p. 8.

> taken only with a grain of salt. They can contain them in a developed, or stunted, or caricatured form etc., but always with an essential difference. The so-called historical presentation of development is founded, as a rule, on the fact that the latest form regards the previous ones as steps leading up to itself, and, since it is only rarely and only under quite specific conditions able to criticize itself—leaving aside, of course, the historical periods which appear to themselves as times of decadence—it always conceives them one-sidedly. . . . In the succession of the economic categories, as in any other historical, social science, it must not be forgotten that their subject—here, modern bourgeois society—is always what is given, in the head as well as in reality, and that these categories therefore express the forms of being, the characteristics of existence, and often only individual sides of this specific society, this subject, and that therefore this society by no means begins only at the point where one can speak of it *as such;* this holds *for science as well.*[5]

Marx intends his observation to subvert the presumption of "natural," invariant, universally valid categories of thought. Nevertheless, in the same breath, he adds: "In all forms of society there is one specific kind of production which predominates over the rest, whose relations thus assign rank and influence to the others. It is a general illumination which bathes all the other colors and modifies their particularity. It is a particular ether which determines the specific gravity of every being which has materialized with it."[6] One sees here the deep temptation to which Marx often—though not invariably—succumbed: to find in the flux of history an invariant structure of change that enabled him to draw a progressive teleology from the very transience of particular economies. One may also see here Marx's grasp of the natural irony of entrenching the sense of objective order that every economy's habituation irresistibly secures—even that of his own optimism regarding the end of history. The problem is ultimately Hegelian.

It is surely in this second sense—contra the first Marx, perhaps the usual Marx—that Foucault explains, answering the question of the

---

[5] Karl Marx, *Grundrisse: Foundations of the Critique of Political Economy,* tr. Martin Nicolaus (New York: Vintage, 1973), p. 106.
[6] Ibid., pp. 106–107.

relationship of his own view to Marxism and of the difference between his written histories and Marxist histories:

> I wanted to see how these problems of constitution [*producing* "objects"] could be resolved within a historical framework, instead of referring them back to a constituent object (madness, criminality, whatever). But this historical contextualization needed to be something more than the simple relativization of the phenomenological subject. I don't believe the problem can be solved by historicizing the subject as posited by the phenomenologists, fabricating a subject that evolves through the course of history [against the movement from Kant to Husserl to Heidegger, we may conjecture]. One has to dispense with the constituent subject, to get rid of the subject itself, that's to say, to arrive at an analysis which can account for the constitution of the subject within a historical framework. And this is what I would call genealogy, that is, a form of history which can account for the constitution of knowledge, discourses, domains of objects etc., without having to make reference to a subject which is either transcendental in relation to the field of events or runs in empty sameness throughout the course of history.[7]

Truth is the product of *normalisation* all right; but *normalisation* cannot be discerned as an invariant pattern except under the habit of mind of a "particular" *normalisation*. Otherwise, it would produce the contradiction potentially lodged in the deeper paradox we were hinting at a moment ago—which, we may suppose, Marx on occasion succumbed to (certainly, on Foucault's view). Foucault escapes the contradiction, but he nowhere explains how the trick is done. He escapes by falling back to the shallower paradox we resolved a moment ago. But that paradox (with its resolution) has proved, in its turn, not to bear directly at all on the resolution of the deeper one; on the contrary, it has proved to be acceptable to theorists committed to just the sort of transcendental invariance (or universal objectivity) Foucault would dismantle.

Before we try to resolve the deeper puzzle, we should allow its nagging charm to sink in. It is, of course, among other things, the ultimate *reduction* of the project of rational emancipation under the condition of radical

---

[7]Michel Foucault, "Truth and Power," in *Power/Knowledge*, p. 117.

history: for instance, the *reduction* of Jürgen Habermas's recovery of Enlightenment critique. Habermas understands Foucault's challenge thus, though of course he is hardly prepared to admit its success. Foucault's is an attack, he understands, on the resources of "modernity." Effectively, what this comes to (for Habermas) is the repudiation of enunciative discourse altogether—of propositional truth and rational argument. It is true that the problematic of our age may be cast in terms of the relationship between *discourse* (the formal instruments of reference and predication) and the substantive resources of *cognition* (the sources of discerning and confirming truths about the world) formulable in a discursive way *under the constraint of radical history*.[8] But it would be a mistake to deduce, or guarantee, the required cognitive powers from the mere ineliminability of discursive practices. Habermas never quite escapes the blackmail argument that illicit maneuver entails. For example, he believes that Foucault's view of genealogy continues, along Nietzschean lines, the self-defeating paradox of Horkheimer's and Adorno's negative dialectics:

> If they [Horkheimer and Adorno] do not want to renounce the effect of a final unmasking [a totalizing critique] and still want to *continue with critique*, they will have to leave at least one rational criterion intact for their explanation of the corruption of *all* rational criteria. In the face of this paradox, self-referential critique loses its orientation. . . . Foucault, too, in his later work, replaces the model of domination based on repression (developed in the tradition of enlightenment by Marx and Freud) by a plurality of power strategies. These power strategies intersect one another, succeed one another; they are distinguished according to the type of their discourse formation and the degree of their intensity; but they cannot be *judged* under the aspect of their validity, as was the case with consciously working through conflicts in contrast to unconsciously doing so.[9]

---

[8] See Joseph Margolis, "The Limits of Metaphysics and the Limits of Certainty," in Tom Rockmore and Beth Singer, eds., *Antifoundationalism Old and New* (Philadelphia: Temple University Press, 1991) for a more inclusive formulation.

[9] Jürgen Habermas, "The Entwinement of Myth and Enlightenment: Horkheimer and Adorno," in *The Philosophical Discourse of Modernity: Twelve Lectures*, tr. Frederick Lawrence (Cambridge: MIT Press, 1987), pp. 126–127. The wording of the passage on Foucault is somewhat altered from that in *New German Critique* 26 (1982).

Habermas sees this failure as marking the "neoconservatism" of Foucault's political orientation, and it *would* be such if either that was all there was to Foucault's contribution or *nothing more could be developed from it that would leave an intelligible place for genealogy*—for critique under radical history, whether conservative or not. Habermas explicitly opposes the resources of "modernity" to those of Foucault's genealogies: "Doesn't this iceberg ['of arbitrary discourse formations'] begin to demonstrate, under the cynical gaze of Foucault the genealogist, a completely different dynamic than the thought of modernity, with its orientation of contemporary reality, would like to acknowledge—*merely a senseless back-and-forth movement of anonymous processes* of subjugation in which power and nothing but power keeps appearing in ever-changing guises."[10] He draws the inevitable conclusion—that is, the conclusion that both he and Foucault must confront the paradox we earlier acknowledged (though his own convictions, of course, are supposed to free *him*, not Foucault, from the bramble): "Equally instructive is the contradiction in which Foucault becomes entangled when he opposes his critique of power, disabled by the relevance of the contemporary moment, to the analytic of the true in such a way that the former is deprived of the *normative standards* it would have to derive from the latter. Perhaps it is the force of this contradiction that drew Foucault, in this last of his texts, back into a sphere of influence that he had tried to blast open, that of the philosophical discourse of modernity."[11]

What we see here is that the identical puzzle confronts Foucault in his "anti-modern" genealogies and Habermas in his "super-modernism": how, we may ask, does Habermas propose to save the "one rational criterion intact" that Horkheimer and Adorno risked losing; and how does Foucault, under the same circumstance, propose to preserve a reflexive critique without such a recovery?[12] Here, Habermas's argument is no more than a promissory note or a complete sham—since he never explains how to ensure "*the normative standards . . . of the contemporary moment.*" The contem-

---

[10]Jürgen Habermas, "Taking Aim at the Heart of the Present: On Foucault's Lecture on Kant's *What Is Enlightenment?*" in *The New Conservatism, Cultural Criticism and the Historians' Debate*, ed. and tr. Shierry Weber Nicholsen (Cambridge: MIT Press, 1989), p. 177. Cf. Rorty on Foucault, in Richard Rorty, "Habermas and Lyotard on Postmodernity," in Richard J. Bernstein, ed. *Habermas and Modernity* (Cambridge: MIT Press, 1985).

[11]Ibid., pp. 178–179 (italics added).

[12]See Jean-François Lyotard, *The Postmodern Condition*, tr. Geoff Bennington and Brian Massumi (Minneapolis: University of Minnesota Press, 1984).

porary moment, after all, *is* the very moment—the only actual moment of existence—in which we pose the suspicion of a reflexive critique about *whether* we have understood our world, ourselves, our past claims about the world and ourselves, and our present would-be corrections. *If* the contemporary moment did possess an assured normativity, then it would have escaped the historical flux to which our (historicized) doubts apply. On the other hand, *if* Foucault means, by genealogy, "a senseless back-and forth movement of anonymous processes" and nothing more, then Habermas would be entirely justified in rejecting his (and Nietzsche's) line of analysis—without, however, redeeming his own. We are left, therefore, with a great conceptual gap between the work of saving genealogy from mere senseless episodes of power and the work of saving legitimation from the blackmail machine of breaching the productive enclosures of history.

THE RISKS OF RADICAL HISTORY

Can the gap be filled? It is time, of course, to make the effort.

The difference between Foucault and Habermas may be put this way. Foucault risks incoherence in order to secure radical history; he is never tempted by the presumption of assured cognitive invariance. Habermas, on the other hand, risks incoherence precisely because he *does* try to draw invariant norms of rational communication—to draw at least the invariance of a rational approach to cognitive invariance—from the contingencies of history. For Foucault, reason, the capacity to discern what is true and right, is an artifact of serial *normalisation*; for Habermas, it is a capacity to transcend the *discontinuous* contingencies of every contemporary moment, so that, at the limit, we finally do arrive at invariant and exceptionless norms. Foucault stresses, therefore, the incommensurabilities of succeeding *epistemes*; Habermas stresses, rather, the unique asymptotic progress of all efforts at human communication.

There are only two conceptual strategies by which Habermas could possibly recover the required rational criterion under the condition of history: either (1) the totality of the very order of history (historicized knowledge and legitimation) may be effectively discerned at some particular "contemporary moment"; or (2) whatever part of that totality may be discerned at a given "contemporary moment" ensures it against serious legitimative reversal. The slightest reflection shows, of course, that (1) and (2) are essentially the same, hardly more than variant forms of that presuppositionlessness and inclusive totality that Hegel attributes to philosophical knowledge proper.[13]

Habermas, it must be said, attacks the feasibility of Hegel's undertaking—not because it is impossible but rather because (on Habermas's reading) Hegel takes the wrong turn: he attempts to "achieve the goal essential to the self-grounding of modernity [by] thinking the positive element in such a way that it can be overcome by the same principle from which it proceeds—precisely by subjectivity."[14] Hegel, Habermas believes, is merely concerned to reconcile "an *alienated* subjectivity that has broken with the common life," whereas Habermas is entirely ready to correct the matter, to "sketch the philosophical solution for the self-grounding of modernity," "in the universality of an uncoerced consensus arrived at among free and equal persons, [in which] individuals retain a court of appeal that can be called upon even against particular forms of institutional concretization of the common will."[15] Habermas, therefore, actually means to claim for himself the feasibility of Hegel's objective.

But this is as far as he goes. He never demonstrates *when* an "uncoerced consensus" actually occurs, or *how* we should even know that a particular opposition to "institutional concretizations of the common will" successfully escapes the more subtle forms of bias and self-deception. It is hard to believe (but it is nevertheless true) that Habermas relies entirely on the sweet liberal optimism with which he views ordinary communicative intent. There is no escape from historical horizons here. There is no totalized or presuppositionless knowledge looming. Habermas's project cannot but be an utter failure.

The only marvel is that, in a world already chastened by Hegel and Marx and the Frankfurt School and Nietzsche and Heidegger and Peirce (Habermas's favorite)—chastened, that is, by failed presumptions and the exposé of failed presumptions—Habermas's readers should ever have supposed his project to be feasible. In any case, he is a modernist in the strong Enlightenment sense: confident that inquiry moves through history in a way that is normatively justified (legitimated) *through* the horizonal

---

[13]See *Hegel's Logic*, tr. William Wallace (Oxford: Clarendon Press, 1975), p. 1; also, Tom Rockmore, *Hegel's Circular Epistemology* (Bloomington: Indiana University Press, 1986), esp. pp. 85–90.
[14]Habermas, *The Philosophical Discourse of Modernity*, pp. 29–30.
[15]Ibid., pp. 29, 31, 40.

shifts of history itself. It need not, therefore, aspire (he thinks) to the excesses of Kantian transcendental reasoning. Magically, it preserves its universal validity though it remains inseparable from whatever of unreason (or the distortion of would-be reason) lies embedded in the practices of actual life.

That his vision *is* a magical one—no more than magical—is all but conceded by Habermas himself:

> In argumentation, critique is constantly entwined with theory, enlightenment with grounding, even though discourse participants always have to suppose that only the unforced force of the better argument comes into play under the unavoidable communication presuppositions of argumentative discourse. But they know, or they can know, that even this idealization is only necessary because convictions are formed and confirmed in a medium that is not "pure" and not removed from the world of appearances. . . .[16]

Rightly read, this signifies that communicants can never *know* that the would-be universal rules they abide by actually function to lead them to that communicative reason in the sky they long to share. Habermas has, therefore, produced a curious theory: he believes we can know what universal rationality would require of us ideally, without ever knowing what, precisely, *that* would entail *in* science, *in* morality, *in* logic, *in* interpretation, *in* practical life; and he believes we are rationally obliged *to* commit ourselves to such rules in spite of such insuperable ignorance and in spite of the apparent success of discursive communication that neither knows nor subscribes to his universal rules.[17]

One may reasonably claim, therefore, that he has not rightly understood the irony (or failure) of Hegel's project: *nothing* depends on the mere shift from "subjectivity" to "uncoerced consensus"; it is, rather, the presumption of escaping the preformative and fragmentary shaping of our reason that marks the failure of what Habermas would redeem, *not* the shift he supposes. For example, there is no reason in the world why "the unforced force of the better argument" is anything more than a purely *local*

---

[16]Ibid., p. 130.
[17]See Jürgen Habermas, *The Theory of Communicative Action*, Vol. 1, tr. Thomas McCarthy (Boston: Beacon Press, 1984), Ch. 1; "What Is Universal Pragmatics?" in *Communication and the Evolution of Society*, tr. Thomas McCarthy (Boston: Beacon Press, 1979).

appraisal, not transitive or universalizable over history, over conceptual discontinuity, over incommensurability, even over the least uncertainty. Habermas's optimism is no more than Peirce's, which is no more than Hegel's shorn even of their failed gymnastics. It is also a failure Foucault could grasp at once. Precisely this sort of critique of Habermas, in fact, confirms the initial plausibility of Foucault's thesis.

POSTMODERNISM AND POSTSTRUCTURALISM

But *is* Foucault consistent? And *is* his thesis adequate?

Habermas misunderstands Foucault profoundly. Here is what he says—perhaps the best introduction to what we should avoid in theorizing about Foucault:

> Foucault's genealogy of the human sciences enters on the scene in an irritating double role. On the one hand, it plays the *empirical role* of an analysis of technologies of power that are meant to explain the functional social context of the science of man. Here power relationships are of interest as conditions for the rise of scientific knowledge and as its social effects. On the other hand, the same genealogy plays the *transcendental role* of an analysis of technologies of power that are meant to explain how scientific discourse about man is possible at all. Here the interest is in power relationships as constitutive conditions for scientific knowledge. These two epistemological roles are no longer divided into two competing approaches that are merely related to the same object, the human subject in its life-expressions. Instead, genealogical historiography is supposed to be both at once—functionalist social science and at the same time historical research into constitutive conditions.[18]

Effectively, what Habermas has done is construe Foucault as if he were an ordinary *modernist* who, unaccountably, subverts his own endeavor by insisting on the paradoxes of "power"—hence, plays *postmodernist* to his own modernism.

But this won't do at all. Foucault is not a postmodernist—in Lyotard's sense. It is true that Lyotard begins *The Postmodern Condition* by remarking:

[18]Habermas, *The Philosophical Discourse of Modernity*, pp. 273–274.

"Our working hypothesis is that the status of knowledge is altered as societies enter what is known as the postindustrial age and cultures enter what is known as the postmodern age. . . . The nature of knowledge cannot survive unchanged within the context of general transformation."[19] Both Habermas and Foucault could easily accept this much—as also, of course, could Hegel and Marx, neither of whom may be called a flaming postmodern. Foucault does not object to legitimation, but he is neither a modernist (like Habermas) nor a postmodernist (like Lyotard): he is what, by a distinction of art, has come to be called a *poststructuralist*.

Lytoard has defined the postmodernist's objective in what has become the *philosophically* standard sense of the term—there being no reason to suppose that its various uses will not remain conceptually polymorphous:

> to the extent that science does not restrict itself to stating useful regularities and seeks the truth, it is obliged to legitimate the rules of its own game. It then produces a discourse of legitimation with respect to its own status, a discourse called philosophy. I will use the term *modern* to designate any science that legitimates itself with reference to a metadiscourse of this kind making an explicit appeal to some grand narrative, such as the dialectics of Spirit, the hermeneutics of meaning, the emancipation of the rational or working subject, or the creation of wealth. . . . Simplifying to the extreme, I define *postmodern* as incredulity toward metanarratives.[20]

Of course, as it happens, Lyotard is *also* a poststructuralist, particularly in developing his notion of the *différend*.[21]

It is worth a small detour to have Lyotard's version of poststructuralism before us as well: it will make it easier to identify Foucault's intended distinction. Lyotard favors a legal model:

> The plaintiff lodges his or her complaint before the tribunal, the accused argues in such a way as to show the inanity of the accusation. Litigation takes place. . . . A case of differend be-

---

[19]Lyotard, *The Postmodern Condition*, pp. 3–4.
[20]Ibid., pp. xxiii–xxiv.
[21]See Jean-François Lyotard, *The Differend: Phrases in Dispute*, tr. Georges Van Den Abbeele (Minneapolis: University of Minnesota Press, 1988).

tween two parties takes place when the "regulation" of the conflict that opposes them is done in the idiom of one of the parties while the wrong suffered by the other is not signified in that idiom."[22]

The postmodernist opposes second-order legitimation of any kind. The poststructuralist disallows altogether the *relevance* of a distinction between first-order and second-order legitimative discourse; but he need not (indeed, he cannot) disallow what passes for legitimative discourse. His point is, rather, to expose *the discursive suppression of the "other" in all forms of linguistic (though not merely linguistic) practice.* Lyotard's illustration of the *différend* suggests only the deliberate suppression, the outlawing, of the known discursive practice of this or that particular "other"; but the rest of his account confirms that he is also interested in the pretense that the prevailing forms of discourse, "normal" discourse, are (somehow) universally competent for all possible distinctions that *are yet to come*, that *have not yet been* formulated. The "other" signifies a deep suspicion, at once linguistic and political, regarding the entrenched normality of first-order discourse and the rational adequacy of would-be second-order legitimation.

The "political" significance of all this lies with what Lyotard calls "terrorism": "What their 'arrogance' means [that is, the confidence and efficiency of social technocrats] is that they identify themselves with the social system conceived as a totality in quest of its most performative unity possible."[23] It raises "all language games to self-knowledge," and it "eliminate[s], or threaten[s] to eliminate, a player from the language game one shares with him."[24] Poststructuralism extends the critique and changes its terms by representing (in the political sense) even the unknown "other" victimized merely by the efficiency of normalizing terror.

Foucault offers, then, one of the most ramified versions of poststructuralism. Lyotard is both a postmodernist and a poststructuralist. Richard Rorty is perhaps a postmodernist who is not a poststructuralist, despite his demurrer.[25] And Foucault (like Derrida, though in an altogether different way) is a poststructuralist who is not a postmodernist.

One further example may help us here. When, in pursuing feminist

---

[22]Ibid., p. 12.
[23]Lyotard, *The Postmodern Condition*, p. 63.
[24]Ibid., pp. 62, 63.
[25]See esp. Richard Rorty, *Contingency, Irony, and Solidarity* (Cambridge: Cambridge University Press, 1989).

concerns in the poststructuralist manner, Luce Irigaray worries the question (which a man may sinisterly address to a woman) "*Are* you a *woman?*" she says, among other things: "I don't think that a woman—unless she has been assimilated to masculine, and more specifically phallic, models [Irigaray is writing in opposition to Freud's and Lacan's 'phallocentrism' and 'patriarchal' discourse]—would ask me that question. Because 'I' am not 'I,' I *am* not, I am not *one* [not specifiable as a female individual conformably with the normalizing terror of Freudian psychology: I am really an 'other']." She adds: "Of course, if I had answered: 'My dear sir, how can you have such suspicions? It is perfectly clear that I am a woman,' I should have fallen back into the discourse of a certain 'truth' and its power. And if I were claiming that what I am trying to articulate, in speech or writing, starts from the *certainty* that I am a woman, then I should be caught up once again within 'phallocratic' discourse. I might well attempt to overturn it, but I should remain included within it. Instead, I am going to make an effort—for one cannot simply leap outside that discourse—to situate myself at its borders and to move continuously from the inside to the outside."[26] Irigaray specifically links "the repressed feminine" to "something 'other'"—which is open to the opposing modes of discourse that would suppress or recover the "feminine."[27]

What all this shows, what is distorted mercilessly in Habermas's summary of Foucault's work, is that the recovery of the "other" requires a parasitic use of language that is never merely discursive, though it will appear to be.

LEGITIMATION AND GENEALOGY

So Habermas gets Foucault dreadfully wrong. Foucault does introduce "empirical" and "transcendental" discourse all right. He *uses* it, aware that, in doing so, *he* is normalizing the distinctions and claims he introduces. But he introduces it to subvert it. He functions then and there as what he calls a "genealogist," which is to say, as a poststructuralist who works by that sort of parasitic insinuation—neither "empirical" nor "transcendental,"

---

[26]Luce Irigaray, *This Sex Which is Not One*, tr. Catherine Porter with Carolyn Burke (Ithaca: Cornell University Press, 1985), pp. 120–122.
[27]Ibid. pp. 121, 123.

since both are forms of normalizing "power" (or "terror" or "violence")—that recovers, in history, the possibility of the "other" within every such "discursive regime." It was apparently his own failure to grasp this, during the writing of *The Order of Things*, that Foucault, at his most earnest, criticizes: "what was lacking here was this problem of the 'discursive regime', of the effects of power peculiar to the play of statements. I confused this too much with systematicity, theoretical form, or something like a paradigm."[28] In short, Habermas takes as gospel just what Foucault renounces in his mature reflection.

It is for the same reason that Foucault rejects the thought that what he is exposing is mere "ideology"; for, "like it or not, [ideology] always stands in virtual opposition to something else which is supposed to count as truth," whereas Foucault's own problem requires "seeing historically how effects of truth are produced within discourses which in themselves are neither true nor false."[29] There you have, at one stroke, Foucault's shallow resolution of the shallower paradox (we introduced at the very beginning of our analysis) *and* the evidence that Foucault does not quite manage to extricate himself from the profounder paradox. Habermas, then, did not charge him with the "right" mistake, but only with the "wrong" one he himself mistakenly "corrects."

There is of course a sense in which "discourses . . . in themselves are neither true nor false," that is, a sense in which speech and writing are merely *events* or *artifacts*. It is, however, an irrelevant sense here, in that it is true of *whatever* may be true or false—claims, judgments, assertions that this or that is true. It is not irrelevant for identifying a site of "power," of effective consequences. But then ideologies "in themselves are [also] neither true nor false." In fact, in "The Discourse on Language," Foucault actually counts "the opposition between true and false" as one of "three great systems of exclusion governing discourse [exclusion of the 'other']—prohibited words, the division of madness and the will to truth."[30] So he cannot now think that the distinction between "events" and "*énoncé*" would support the distinction between the critique of ideology and the genealogy of discourse. Much more is needed.

There is a direct parallel between Foucault's and Marx's insistence on

---

[28]Foucault, 'Truth and Power,' p. 113.
[29]Ibid., p. 118.
[30]Michel Foucault, 'The Discourse on Language," tr. Rupert Sawyer, bound with *The Archaeology of Knowledge*, tr. A. M. Sheridan Smith (New York: Pantheon, 1972), pp. 217, 218.

the "production" of discourse or cognition. We have noted it before. But Foucault develops the notion in a way quite different from Marx's, although there is an incipient "poststructuralist" tendency in Marx as well. In any case, the notion of production indissolubly links "event" and "*énoncé*": "I am supposing [says Foucault] that in every society the production of discourse is at once controlled, selected, organized and redistributed according to a certain number of procedures, whose role is to avert its powers and its dangers, to cope with chance events, to evade its ponderous, awesome materiality. In a society such as our own we all know the rules of *exclusion*. The most obvious and familiar of these concerns what is *prohibited*."[31]

Our own solution of the shallow paradox, you will remember, was straightforward enough: the cognitive point at which a speaker innocently makes a first-order claim and the point at which he theorizes (in a second-order sense) that *that* claim falls within the *production* of discourse of some particular economy or regime of power cannot, logically, be the same; at the first point, he says something he believes to be true *sans phrase* that, at the second, he believes to he "true" only relative to the "discursive regularities" of his own society; but, at the second point, he *does* believe that certain discursive regularities *are* (truly) in force (and are not always in force for every society and every age). That much at least may be conceded to Habermas. *But even that cannot be conceded, in accord with Foucault's developed view, without invoking the disruptive notion of genealogy, which is itself neither empirical nor transcendental in the usual sense.* Of course, to speculate on the genealogy of his own discourse *and* to go on with "the opposition between true and false" require an ulterior second-order stance regarding the second-order stance with which he locates his original first-order claim. For, in an obvious sense, the "will to truth" cannot really be abandoned by any viable society. What then?

Foucault's originality lies in this: that he construes the second-order legitimation of a discursive regime as itself subject to the effective "power" that installs or produces that very regime. He therefore opposes the conceptual optimism—at once Hegelian and (more obliquely) structuralist—that there *is*, in principle and in practice, a cognitive stance at the point of which "historical consciousness" ("the founding function of the subject") may exercise its art so that the dispersed "time [of encountered events may be] conceived in terms of totalization and

---

[31]Ibid., p. 216.

revolutions [would] never [be] more than moments of consciousness."[32] What is needed is a conceptual instrument by the use of which *no* second-order legitimation could ensure (or claim to ensure) that it was formulated either at the point of totalized historical consciousness (the fatal move Habermas borrows from Hegel) or at some point reliably assured of being an asymptotic advance toward such a totalized consciousness (the fatal move Habermas borrows from Peirce, borrowing from Hegel). That instrument is the notion of genealogy. Foucault shapes it but does not quite explain its logical role or how we may escape the deeper paradox.

The answer is elementary. There *are* perceived invariances within the space of any viable discursive regime—empirical, first-order, contingent, "indicative," *produced* invariances, we may say. But there are no legitimative invariances, no second-order invariances, exceptionless or normative or necessary, in virtue of which truth, validity, rationality, rightness and the like hold in a way that may be totalized for all the dispersed events of discourse itself. Furthermore, *that* very pronouncement is *not* a second-order (invariant) truth but a genealogical insinuation, a risked stance of doubt, a bet, an attitude of life habituated from every local genealogical disruption of every presumed (universal) legitimacy of this or that discursive regime. It cannot be a transcendental truth claim, on pain of contradiction. *It is a commitment to the "other,"* to what is not merely distributively "excluded" here and now (madmen, or women, for instance) but to what we can never assure ourselves we will not have excluded by the exclusionary rules of whatever discourse we do enter (the possible worlds of discourse—and of differential power—that *some* future cohort *might* have occupied). "Empirical" and "legitimative" discourse—Habermas deliberately tags Foucault's view as "transcendental," to force the contradiction on him that he avoids—cannot fail to be tainted by just *that* limitation.

Foucault gradually grasps his own undertaking—through what he regards as the serious limitation, possibly the failing, of *The Archaeology of Knowledge* and *The Order of Things*: he places all second-order legitimation under the condition of radical history. The "other," then, is what all regularizing histories must exclude. It is only remotely related to the mark of the "other" that Derrida draws from Levinas, both because Levinas

---

[32]Foucault, *The Archaeology of Knowledge*, p. 12. Even here, then, part (but only part) of what genealogy requires is supplied.

impossibly *addresses* the "other" that *discourse cannot address* and because Derrida treats the "other" as merely "that" which no totalized ontology can capture.[33]

In Foucault, the legitimating invariances of every age are exposed as artifacts by the continual irruptions of historical currents (that give form to new discursive regimes). We find them as in *The History of Sexuality* and in *Discipline and Punish*, by our own "empirical" and "transcendental," inquiries. In pursuing them, we realize that we cannot stop the process. We guess that others will come after us who will see a different order in the "dispersed" succession of *epistemes*. But we will see a unity. There is never—as Habermas has it—"merely a senseless back-and-forth movement of anonymous processes of subjugation in which power and nothing but power keeps appearing in ever-changing guises." There is always the work of the "will to truth," which constructs, within its own legitimating space, some narrative of meaning that recovers its own constructed past. Habermas requires the threat of utter chaos, in order to demonstrate the need for a "modernist" (that is, a Kantian) legitimation (despite his protests to the contrary). There is no such chaos in Foucault's account, only the bewildering proliferation of serially competing forms of order—until, that is, we realize the radical transience of our own order, which (living within which) we cannot abandon, even where we would attack it.

It is the resolution of the shallow paradox that saves us. For we cannot choose what we cannot choose. What we do choose is meant to make legitimated sense within the only discourse we acquire. Foucault was never reconciled to that resolution, for he "saw" the contingency, the danger, of *every* construction of the human "subject."

Perhaps he didn't understand what he himself discerned. In his very last interview, opposing the skeptic's transcendental zeal, he still declares:

---

[33]See Jacques Derrida, "Violence and Metaphysics: An Essay on the Thought of Emmanuel Levinas," in *Writing and Difference*, tr. Alan Bass (Chicago: University of Chicago Press, 1978), p. 83: "This hollow space is not an opening among others. It is opening itself, the opening of opening, that which can be enclosed within no category or totality, that is, everything within experience which can no longer be described by traditional concepts, and which resists every philosopheme." See also Emmanuel Levinas, *Totality and Infinity*, tr. Alphonso Lingis (Pittsburgh: Duquesne University Press, n.d.), p. 269: "Being is produced as multiple and as split into same and other; this is its ultimate structure. It is society, and hence it is time. We thus leave the philosophy of Parmenidean being. Philosophy itself constitutes a moment of this temporal accomplishment, a discourse always addressed to another. . . . Transcendence is time and goes unto the other. But the Other is not a term: he does not stop the movement of Desire."

"there is no subject." Moral and political commitment remains unavoidable, but he still affirms: "The search for a norm of morality acceptable to everybody, in the sense that everyone should submit to it, strikes me as catastrophic." He does not waver here. He does not explain himself, but he does not restore an essential moral agent:

> It is experience which is the rationalization of a process, itself provisional, which results in a subject, or rather, in subjects. I will call subjectivation the procedure by which one obtains the constitution of a subject, or more precisely, of a subjectivity which is of course only one of the given possibilities of organization of a self-consciousness.[34]

But perhaps we have learned more than Foucault dared to say in his own voice. Genealogy yields no criteria *for* thought or action; it offers only an attitude of life *in* every commitment. When we act or judge, we must do so *as we believe*. We favor legitimating such action in favoring such action; but we also guess, genealogically, that we cannot make that belief stick—universally, invariantly, necessarily, normatively, in any totalized way. For some, that will be enough; for others, it will be permanently disquieting.

---

[34] Michel Foucault, 'The Return of Morality,' tr. Thomas Levin and Isabelle Lorenz, in *Politics, Philosophy, Culture: Interviews and Other Writings, 1977–1984*, ed. Lawrence D. Kritzman, tr. Alan Sheridan et al. (New York: Routledge, 1988), pp. 253–254.

Part III

THE SELF AND ITS SEX

FOUCAULT AND THE PROBLEM OF SELF-CONSTITUTION

Mark Poster

The question of the subject or the self has been a central issue of contention for intellectual movements in the twentieth century. Psychoanalysis, surrealism, existentialism, structuralism, and most recently poststructuralism have sought to differentiate themselves from prevailing positions by putting into question their formulations on the self. The point of disagreement to some extent has been remarkably consistent: the position under attack is said to present a doctrine of the self that is too centered, too unified, too rationalist, in short, too Cartesian. The flight from the Cartesian position on the self is characterized by a cycle of repetition. The new position misrecognizes the one under attack as the Cartesian position. Structuralists identified existentialists as Cartesians even though the latter took their position by attacking neo-Kantians as Cartesians. From Sartre contra Brunschvicg to Lévi-Strauss contra Sartre to Derrida contra Lacan the rush continues to the position of the decentered self.

In Foucault's case the issue of the decentered self becomes very complicated. His earliest works (a translation of Binzwanger, *Psychology and Mental Illness, Madness and Civilization*) contained definite existentialist themes. The authenticity of madness (a form of decentering) was defended against rationalist claims (a form of Cartesianism). With *The Order of Things* Foucault dramatically shifted to the structuralist position with pronouncements about the death of man, the end of the subject, and so forth. Without completely identifying with structuralism, Foucault studied the limitations of rationalist sciences in works on asylums (*The Birth of the Clinic*) and prisons (*Discipline and Punish*). He brilliantly dissected what he called "technologies of power" that were authorized by the sciences of medicine and criminology. In these disciplines individual subjects became cases, ruled by the normalizing power of the Cartesian scientific gaze. In these works Foucault questioned the centered, authorial, scientific subject, undermining its claims of transcendent objectivity by demonstrating the connection of science to power, the roots of truth in the soil of politics. Far from neutral statements of truth, the discourses of science emerge fully implicated in practices of domination. Foucault's strategy of dispersing the centered subject among discursive practices that generate "technologies of power" continued through the 1970s and *The History of Sexuality*, Volume I, entitled "The Will to Truth."

When Volumes II and III of *The History of Sexuality* appeared in 1984 shortly before his death, Foucault's problematic of the self had considerably shifted. From the dispersal of the subject in discourse he moved to the issue of the "constitution of the self" in discourse. A centered self once again became a possibility, only now the self was understood in historical-social terms, not in ontological ones. Position 1 of the 1960s (which Foucault was later to call "archaeology") was a critique of the self as rationalist by a strategy of *reversal*: madness vs. reason. Position 2 of the 1970s (which Foucault was to call "genealogy") was a critique of the self as centered consciousness by a strategy of *displacement*: the locus of intelligibility shifted from subject to structure. Position 3 of the 1980s (which Foucault was to call "ethics") was a hermeneutics of the self using a strategy of *historicism*: the emphasis fell on the activity of self-constitution in discursive practices.[1]

---

[1] There are a number of interesting studies of Foucault's intellectual career, each

In this last phase of Foucault's theory of the subject one senses a return of sorts to the problematic of Sartre and the existentialists. In place of the hermeneutic of suspicion in Positions 1 and 2 there is an affirmative effort to comprehend a process of self-constitution, a genuine search for an ethics. In *Being and Nothingness* (1943) and *Critique of Dialectical Reason* (1960) Sartre carried out a similar quest. The existential Marxist attempted to locate a ground for the freedom of self-creation or, in Foucault's terms, self-constitution. Sartre's project was both a decentering and recentering of the subject.[2] In *Being and Nothingness* self-creation was centered in the capacity to give meaning, very similar to Nietzsche's concept of values created by the will-to-power of the individual. Sartre associated the capacity of self-creation with time, nothingness, contingency, excentricity, alterity—all the negative attributes of the human condition as defined by what is now called the Western philosophical tradition. Sartre's reversal of that tradition recentered the subject in the most ephemeral aspects of being that, at the same time, claimed to be more primordial and at a deeper level of the self than Platonic reason. Sartrean freedom, developed in *Being and Nothingness* and extended in *Critique of Dialectical Reason*, was the theological power of the creation of the self *ex nihilo*.

From the vantage point of Foucault's Position 3, there is one chief difficulty with Sartre's position: it claims to define self-constitution for all humanity. Sartre's texts operate at the ontological level, sketching the contours of *l'être humain* with the indelible ink of the philosopher, the absolute author, the universal intellectual. In this sense, an important part of the rationalist tradition is preserved and reinforced in the pages of the existentialist. Reason is reestablished as the ground of truth in Sartrean discourse because the manifesto of freedom in finitude is made from the

---

interpreting it somewhat differently. Here are some suggestions: Charles C. Lemert and Garth Gillan, *Michel Foucault: Social Theory and Transgression* (New York: Columbia University Press, 1982); Pamela Major Poetzl, *Michel Foucault's Archaeology of Western Culture* (Chapel Hill: University of North Carolina Press, 1983); Hubert Dreyfus and Paul Rabinow, *Michel Foucault: Beyond Structuralism and Hermeneutics* (Chicago: University of Chicago Press, 1982); Barry Smart, *Foucault, Marxism and Critique* (London: Routledge and Kegan Paul, 1983); John Rajchman, *Michel Foucault: The Freedom of Philosophy* (New York: Columbia University Press, 1985); Mark Cousins and Athar Hussain, *Michel Foucault* (New York: St. Martin's Press, 1984); Karlis Racevskis, *Michel Foucault and the Subversion of Intellect* (Ithaca: Cornell University Press, 1983); Mark Poster, *Foucault, Marxism and History* (New York: Basil Blackwell, 1985).

[2] I have described this process in *Existential Marxism in Postwar France* (Princeton: Princeton University Press, 1976) as an attempt to supplement Marxism with a theory of the subject.

absolute pulpit of the philosophical subject. Sartre asserts the situated, limited nature of meaning, the particularity of self-creation, while speaking from the transcendent, unlimited locus of reason. Everything in *Being and Nothingness* works to give the impression that the truth it enunciates is absolute. Or so at least things appeared to Foucault.

In the 1960s Sartre and Foucault debated the question of the subject in *La Quinzaine littéraire*.[3] Foucault returned to Sartre's concept of the self in an interview with Gérard Raulet where he applauded the Nietzschean quality of an early essay by Sartre published in a high school journal in 1925 entitled "The History of the Truth."[4] The best discussion by Foucault of the difference between Sartre's concept of the self and his own came in an interview in 1983. He agrees that in many ways his ideas and Sartre's have common parentage in Nietzsche's notion that the self is not given or fixed but created by each individual. Foucault locates in Sartre's concept of authenticity, however, traces of a fixed self, a center, a core: "through the moral notion of authenticity he turns back to the idea that we have to be ourselves—to be truly our true self."[5] Because we have no "true self" Foucault asserts that "we have to create ourselves as works of art."[6] Sartre looks for the quality of authenticity or bad faith in the relation a person has with his or her self; Foucault wants to study the discursive practices by which the self establishes the "truth" of itself in the relation it has with itself.

Foucault is correct to object to omniscient voices, universalizing postures, absolute grounds that are strewn throughout Sartre's texts. But he ignores aspects of Sartre's writing that go in the other direction, toward undoing the universal subject. First, Sartre's philosophical texts introduce scenes from daily life: Pierre the waiter, the woman on a date, and the man at the keyhole in *Being and Nothingness*; reading a newspaper, waiting for a bus, and participating in the French Revolution of 1789 in *Critique of Dialectical Reason*. At one level these are merely examples serving philosophical points; at another they are Sartre's philosophy. The little dramas ubiquitously incorporated in the philosophical text obtrude the contin-

---

[3] The responses and counterresponses are found in No. 5 (May 16, 1966), p. 14; No. 14 (October 1966), p. 4; and No. 46 (March 1, 1968), p. 20.

[4] "Structuralism and Post-Structuralism: An Interview with Michel Foucault," tr. Jeremy Harding, *Telos* 55 (Spring 1983): 204.

[5] "How We Behave," interview with Michel Foucault in *Vanity Fair* (November 1983), p. 565.

[6] Ibid.

gency of daily life into the voice of reason, the absolute epistemological subject. Their presence signifies the failure of reason's self-sufficiency, the dead end of presuppositionless thought. The fiction of Pierre the waiter makes the truth of self-creation just a bit less than universal.

Perhaps more significantly, Sartre undermines the universality of his claims in *Critique of Dialectical Reason* by presenting a phenomenology of the discursive subject that resonates in Foucault's Position 3. Sartre here argues that the author *must* totalize the field and *must* do so from a situated position.[7] The author addresses the universal precisely because he or she is a situated subject. Only in the finitude of a place does a perspective on the totality emerge. Looking out from a balcony while on vacation, the (bourgeois) intellectual perceives two workmen on either side of a wall oblivious to each other. The intellectual's view unifies or totalizes the field, introducing a meaning to the entire scene where otherwise there would be none.[8] This totalization of the field, however, is not the only one possible: from another balcony opening onto the same street scene, Simone de Beauvoir might retotalize the field. Perceiving Sartre observing the workmen, she might intervene with a new meaning, one that notes the unity in difference of men, the commonality of Sartre and the workmen, and the relative privilege of all in comparison with women. Behind her a black servant, having visual access to the street, Sartre, and de Beauvoir, might retotalize the field again, this time introducing a meaning about the unity in difference of whites, be they workmen, intellectuals, or women. Like Bakhtin's notion of the dialogic, Sartre's insistence on totalization gives priority to the infinite polysemy of self-creation.

Even granting Sartre these fissures in the rampart of universalism, Foucault's case can still be made. Sartrean self-creation remains rooted in the Western philosophical tradition, or more narrowly the Enlightenment tradition, by its persistent quest for the unity of intelligibility. Sartre struggles, in *Critique of Dialectical Reason*, not to underscore the anti-universalist limits of reason but to locate a spot of ultimate totalization, a place from which the situated perspective of the intellectual is harmonious with the collective destiny of mankind. He attempts this in an extended analysis of the Russian Revolution of 1917 where the conditions for the possibility of dialectical reason are attached to the spiraling totalizations

---

[7]Jean-Paul Sartre, *Critique of Dialectical Reason, Volume 1: Theory of Practical Ensembles*, tr. Alan Sheridan-Smith (London: New Left Books, 1976), p. 45.
[8]Ibid., p. 100.

of the class struggle. Sartre tightly grasps the straw of the proletariat as the group subject that contains the potential to create a meaning for mankind, one that self-consciously recognizes the historicity of the freedom of self-creation but one that nonetheless truly totalizes human experience. The pathos of Sartre's text is the impossibility of this totalization and the equal impossibility of Sartre to give it up. For on the other side of this totalization lies the frightening nothingness that the philosophical subject is not transcendent but rooted in power, that dialectical reason is not a condition for the possibility of human freedom.

The issue of universality goes back beyond Hegel to the Enlightenment definition of reason. For Foucault the transition from Position 2 to Position 3 was effected by a reexamination of the Enlightenment. In his important essay "What Is Enlightenment?" Foucault made a final effort to redefine the limits of reason in relation to the question of self-constitution.[9] So important did he regard the interpretation of the Enlightenment that he urged the formation of groups to study it. He defined modern thought as the effort to answer the question "what is enlightenment?"[10] Whereas Positions 1 and 2 presented strong critiques of the Enlightenment, Foucault now reversed himself. There was for him something in the Enlightenment that the methods of archaeology and genealogy did not confront, some "attitude" of the Enlightenment that had to be preserved. This attitude concerned the nature of the subject. Foucault's formulation is worth repeating:

> I have been seeking, on the one hand, to emphasize the extent to which a type of philosophical interrogation—one that simultaneously problematizes man's relation to the present, man's historical mode of being, and the constitution of the self as an autonomous subject—is rooted in the Enlightenment. On the other hand, I have been seeking to stress that the thread that may connect us with the Enlightenment is not faithfulness to doctrinal elements, but rather the permanent reactivation of an attitude—that is, of a philosophical ethos that could be described as a permanent critique of our historical era.[11]

---

[9]"What Is Enlightenment?" in *The Foucault Reader*, ed. Paul Rabinow (New York: Pantheon, 1984), pp. 32–50. This essay was presented as a lecture in Berkeley in 1984.
[10]Ibid., p. 32.
[11]Ibid., p. 42.

This passage needs to be examined carefully because it contains the core of Foucault's Position 3.

The passage concerns an "ethos," a personal position that Foucault is committing himself to in sharp contrast to his authorial stance in Positions 1 and 2. What characterizes Foucault's authorial voice in earlier books is flight. Until the 1980s Foucault's authorial voice shifted, feinted, maneuvered in and around his own pages so as to avoid being fixed by the reader's gaze and by the panoptical stare of the public. During the period of Position 1, Foucault's authorial flight was associated with the structuralist attack on phenomenology: a text was to be read, the structuralists argued, not as a sum of the author's intentions, but as the play of signifiers operating at the textual level. Of course this positioned the voice of structuralist authors in an epistemological nowhere, like a hidden god absent from the world of the book. Foucault took a similar position[12] but, to be consistent, refused even to group himself with the structuralists. That would define his voice too clearly.

During the 1970s, the phase of Position 2, Foucault's authorial voice did not change but his reasons for so positioning himself did change. At stake now was not so much the anti-phenomenological stance but the dynamics of politics. In *The Archaeology of Knowledge* he anticipates the annoyance the reader has with his absence:

> Are you going to change yet again, shift your position according to the questions that are put to you, and say that the objections are not really directed at the place from which you are speaking? Are you going to declare yet again that you have never been what you have been reproached with being? Are you already preparing the way out that will enable you in your next book to spring up somewhere else and declare as you're now doing: no, no, I'm not where you are lying in wait for me, but over here, laughing at you?

Foucault provides the following response to the imaginary irked reader:

> What, do you imagine that I would take so much trouble and so much pleasure in writing, do you think that I would keep so

---

[12]See "What Is an Author?" in *Language, Counter-Memory, Practice: Selected Essays and Interviews*, ed. Donald Bouchard, tr. Donald Bouchard and Sherry Simon (Ithaca: Cornell University Press, 1977), pp. 113–138.

> persistently to my task, if I were not preparing—with a rather shaky hand—a labyrinth into which I can venture, in which I can move my discourse, opening up underground passages, forcing it to go far from itself, finding overhangs that reduce and deform its itinerary, in which I can lose myself and appear at last to eyes that I will never have to meet again. I am no doubt not the only one *who writes in order to have no face. Do not ask who I am and do not ask me to remain the same; leave it to our bureaucrats and our police to see that our papers are in order.*[13]

In this extraordinary passage Foucault sees himself as Slothrop in the paranoid vision of Pynchon's *Gravity's Rainbow*. In the bizarre politics of the twentieth century, invisible forces are at work everywhere, controlling everything. The function of defining the self of the author is therefore repressive; to define the individual is to make him or her into a case, to control in order to study, to objectify for scientific ends. These are the normalizing functions associated with technologies of power, power that is everywhere in society, not merely confined to the state.

As he moved into Position 3, Foucault realized that authorial absence, while justified on epistemological or political grounds, was damaging to the self of the author and therefore ultimately was inadequate both politically and epistemologically. Foucault had long been concerned with the question of maturity. He typically attacked the positions of others for their lack of maturity. In *The Archaeology* again he denounced conventional historians as those who "refuse to grow up,"[14] limiting themselves to discovering filiations in texts rather than probing to deeper archaeological layers. Maturity became a major preoccupation of Position 3 in "What Is Enlightenment?"[15] The mature self was now defined as one with an enlightened attitude, with an ethos of autonomy. Having traced Foucault's positions on the author and on maturity, we may now confront the passage quoted above from "What Is Enlightenment?"

The Enlightenment offers contemporary thinkers no doctrines, no formulated ideas; today these are for the most part elements of liberal ideology. Instead, it presents a historically unique standpoint in which the

---

[13]*The Archaeology of Knowledge and the Discourse on Language*, tr. A. M. Sheridan Smith (New York: Pantheon, 1972), p. 17 (emphasis added).
[14]Ibid., p. 144.
[15]See Hubert Dreyfus and Paul Rabinow, "What Is Maturity?" in *Foucault: A Critical Reader*, ed. David Hoy (New York: Basil Blackwell, 1986), pp. 109–122.

development of the individual self is associated with a confrontation with the present. The individual recognizes that personal identity cannot be separated from the fate of humanity and this fate is understood as historically constituted. In this sense maturity designates the insight of the individual's connectedness with the world. On that basis and on that basis alone, Foucault argues, the self may be constituted as autonomous. Maturity means understanding that we cannot escape our heritage from the Enlightenment: "We must try to proceed with the analysis of ourselves as beings who are historically determined, to a certain extent, by the Enlightenment."[16] Foucault was now willing to swallow a bitter pill in order to grow up: his identity as author in flight had to be rejected. The man who defined himself against the Enlightenment, against "reason," against humanism, against "man," who defined himself therefore in decentered flight from authorial presence, from the stable ego, the solid subject standing firmly behind his texts, this man now reversed himself once more, only this time in order to accept the parentage of the philosophes.

The philosopher who accepts his status as child of the Enlightenment thereby attains maturity and on that basis lays the foundation for a critical attitude. The new ethos, manifesting a reconciliation with one's intellectual family, also insists on finitude, on facing the problem of self-constitution and the problem of the social critique of the present as preeminently historical problems. Foucault writes: "criticism is no longer going to be practiced in the search for formal structures with universal value, but rather as a historical investigation into the events that have led us to constitute ourselves and to recognize ourselves as subjects of what we are doing."[17] Accepting his own finitude, his own historicity, his own debt to the Enlightenment, Foucault proposes that philosophers commit themselves and take responsibility for that commitment. The subject becomes an active agent, a point of intelligibility, a self that constitutes itself in relation to history. The question may be raised at this point if Foucault is merely returning to the positions of Sartre or even Habermas.

The place of the subject in the history of social theory may be outlined as follows: liberalism treats the subject as an autonomous, rational, often presocial individual, wary of its rights in relation to other individuals; Marxism treats the subject as a collective agent in contest with other

[16]"What Is Enlightenment?" p. 43.
[17]Ibid., pp. 45–46.

collective agents. In both cases the subject is the ground of history. By the late twentieth century both positions have become unconvincing, liberalism's subject as citizen and entrepreneur and Marxism's subject as revolutionary proletariat no longer work as characters in the play of human time. In Germany intellectuals of the Frankfurt School like Adorno, acknowledging the bleak situation, retreated to the defense of critical theory.[18] In France structuralists like Althusser theorized history without agents. Starting in the 1970s there has been, in both countries, an effort to reconstruct a theory of the subject as agent of change.

In Germany this effort has centered on the work of Jürgen Habermas. His intricate, encompassing social systematics preserves critique by resurrecting the Enlightenment subject as the autonomous individual. Habermas's subject differs from Marxism by privileging communications over labor. In the massive *Theory of Communicative Action* Habermas deduces the social conditions for free public speech and regards them as the precondition of democracy.[19] If the conditions of "the ideal speech situation" are fulfilled, the subject emerges as a rational, autonomous agent. Habermas's subject is not quite the Enlightenment subject: in a Hegelian turn, he historicizes the individual in terms of moral development. Habermas relies on the theory of cognitive development of Piaget and Kohlberg to support the claim that the human race has evolved to a point where moral maturity is possible.[20] If in addition the conditions of public speech are altered to support the "universal pragmatics" of language, then freedom will be realized.

From this standpoint Habermas has been appalled by French poststructuralism. In essay after essay he attacked Foucault, Derrida, Lyotard, and all the defenders of "postmodernity" on the ground that they abandon the Enlightenment and fall into irrationalism and reactionary politics. When the French took positions against rationalism that appeared identical with the pessimism of Adorno and Horkheimer in *Dialectic of Enlightenment*, Habermas was careful to distinguish between the latters' anti-scientism, which was "recuperable," and the pessimism of the French, which was not.[21] Becoming more and more agitated by the growing

---

[18]Theodor Adorno, *Negative Dialectics*, tr. E. B. Ashton (New York: Seabury, 1973).
[19]Jürgen Habermas, *The Theory of Communicative Action, Volume 1: Reason and the Rationalization of Society*, tr. Thomas McCarthy (Boston: Beacon Press, 1984).
[20]*Communication and the Evolution of Society*, tr. Thomas McCarthy (Boston: Beacon Press, 1979), pp. 69–94.
[21]"Modernity versus Postmodernity," *New German Critique* 22 (Winter 1981): 3–18, and

influence of the French postmodern thesis, Habermas devoted an entire book to the topic.²²

But does Foucault in Position 3 deserve this criticism? Habermas was apparently unaware of any change in Foucault's theory of the self until after the latter's death. In a short piece devoted to Foucault's "What Is Enlightenment?" Habermas was taken aback by Foucault's reevaluation of the Enlightenment: "Up to now, Foucault traced [the] will-to-knowledge in modern power-formations, only to denounce it. Now, however, he presents it in a completely different light, as the critical impulse worthy of preservation and in need of renewal. This connects his own thinking to the beginnings of modernity."²³ Foucault had changed sides going over to the camp of modernity against the camp of postmodernity. Habermas interprets the change as Foucault's admission of the failure of all his previous work, which betrayed a contradictory effort to base a critique of power on a critique of "truth." Habermas concludes: "Perhaps the force of this contradiction caught up with Foucault in this last of his texts, drawing him again into the circle of the philosophical discourse of modernity which he thought he could explode."²⁴

Habermas comes to this conclusion only by eliding the difference between his own concept of the subject and Foucault's. Habermas conserves, as Foucault does not, the Enlightenment concept of the rational subject both as the field of history and as the epistemological point of theory. Foucault, as theoretical subject, confronts the present as difference from and rupture with the past. Habermas, as theoretical subject, transcends the present in a totalization of the past. Habermas derives the individual from the vantage point of the truth value of his historical totalization; Foucault, on the contrary, urges an attitude *that has no truth value* but nonetheless an attitude through which the theorist constitutes his or her self in the present. The difference between the two is crucial: Habermas reconstitutes the Enlightenment subject, the rational, autonomous individual; Foucault constitutes himself as discursive subject by coming to terms with his historical situation.

"The Entwinement of Myth and Enlightenment," *New German Critique* 26 (Spring/Summer 1982): 13–30.
  ²²*Der philosophische Diskurs der Moderne: Zwolf Vorlesungen* (Frankfurt: Suhrkamp, 1985).
  ²³Jürgen Habermas, "Taking Aim at the Heart of the Present," in *Foucault: A Critical Reader*, p. 107.
  ²⁴Ibid., p. 108.

The status of theory is very different in the two positions. For Habermas, theory is grounded in the truth of a totalization: because of the current position of humanity the theorist may define truth or rationality as the ideal speech situation; all other positions may be denounced as reactionary or irrational. For Foucault, self-constitution is established as a relative position against the dominance of scientific discourses or practices that claim to ground themselves in the truth. Not only is the status of theory at odds between the two thinkers. They differ also over the nature of the social field. For Habermas, the social is the arena of the emergence of rationality; for Foucault, it is a multiplicity of technologies of power that claim rationality for themselves but that are to be opposed on the basis of a self-constitution that seeks "to give new impetus . . . to the undefined work of freedom."[25]

Another way to define Foucault's late position on the subject is to raise the question of universality. The danger of the return to the Enlightenment is the danger of ethnocentrism. The Enlightened philosophes in the eighteenth century (and Habermas today) universalize their position. The European intellectual, having discovered reason, speaks for all humanity. It bears reminding that the sense of innocence with which the philosophes read the "self-evident" truths of reason was, regardless of their intentions, concurrent with and inevitably an aid to the brutal spread of European power throughout the world. Today that power has been transferred both east and west to the elephantine children of European culture, while Europeans may now more readily accept the relativity of their intellectual products. The issue, then, is how can the activity of self-constitution through rational critique of the present avoid giving universal status to the subject?

After World War II Sartre recognized the limits of the disengaged intellectual, maturing to a position of commitment. Like Foucault in Position 3, Sartre saw the necessary relation between self-constitution and political engagement. The existentialist, however, did not hesitate to universalize. In *What Is Literature?* he spoke of commitment: "Every day we must take sides: in our life as a writer, in our articles, in our books." The result was a literature that "manifests the totality of the human condition as a free product of a creative activity. . . ."[26] The constitution of the

---

[25]"What Is Enlightenment?" p. 46.
[26]Jean-Paul Sartre, *What Is Literature?*, tr. Bernard Frechtman (New York: Washington Square Press, 1966), p. 192.

situated, engaged self of the writer authorizes a universal voice. The closer the intellectual approached the conditioned finitude of politics, the more transcendent the constituted subject became. Sartre's argument was novel in its day only because the "universal" values of scientific truth and literary beauty had been associated, in bourgeois ideology, with ahistorical transcendence. Sartre reversed the poles: engagement was now the path to universality.

Some commentators contend that Foucault is largely successful in avoiding universalist arrogance as well as its relativist opposite because he advocates cosmopolitanism as the attribute of the engaged ethos.[27] Foucault treats the issue in terms of the "generality" of the discourse that emerges from engaged self-constitution. The questions posed by the philosopher are not, he assures us, based on a total, systematic grasp of the present conjuncture. Against Sartre who argued that the philosopher must totalize the present in developing his or her problematic, Foucault insists on its particularity. Topics such as insanity, labor, and prisons derive their exigency from the power they impose in the present on the constituting self. The only guarantee invoked by Foucault that these topics have importance beyond the individual's singular preoccupations is the fact "that they have continued to recur up to our time. . . ."[28] The mere persistence of the themes, a watered-down version of Nietzsche's eternal return of the same, enhances them with "generality." Generality, then, derives not from the force of the issue in the present but, for Foucault, from its historic repetition.

Foucault seriously errs in this discursive move. By relying on the past to avoid solipsism, his position loses its grounding in the present and therefore its potential as a political intervention against dominant discourses. In this respect Sartre's totalizing position is more to the point. Critical discourses on prisons, sexuality, and so forth contribute to the undoing of particular structures of domination not because of the historic generality of the issue but because these structures are today prevalent and oppressive. Foucault's cosmopolitanism unnecessarily retreats from engagement at the crucial moment. He shies away from making the decisive connection of his late concerns with sexuality and the welfare state with the force of these problematics in the present. The reason Foucault's writing on sexuality appeals to others to be read is not because the issue

[27]Dreyfus and Rabinow, *Michel Foucault*.
[28]"What is Enlightenment?," p. 49.

has been raised before but because, without aspiring to the status of a totalization, it nonetheless has weight today.

Another problem in Foucault's return to the Enlightenment concerns the vagueness of the term "self-constitution." In *Being and Nothingness* Sartre spoke of self-creation as the process of consciousness in which values or meanings are inserted into the world. The ego or self is the sum of projects, of foisting meanings upon nothingness. Sartre qualified the process of self-creation with categories of the situation, being-for-others, being-with-others, and so forth in an effort to avoid solipsism. Yet the radical freedom of the self to make itself mitigated the force of these alterities. In *Critique of Dialectical Reason* Sartre moved closer to a balanced relation of self and world, but the self remained centered in evanescent consciousness. When Foucault returned to the problematic of the subject in Position 3, he relied on the theme of language rather than consciousness.

Foucault introduces the problem of self-constitution in *The Use of Pleasure*, Volume II of *The History of Sexuality*. In the eight years that separated Volume I from Volume II, Foucault had shifted emphasis: from a concern with the power effects of discursive practices he moved on to look at the way the subject responds to them. In his first use of the term "self-constitution," Foucault writes:

> It seemed appropriate to look for the forms and modalities of the relation to self by which the individual constitutes and recognizes himself *qua* subject. After first studying the games of truth in their interplay with one another, as exemplified by certain empirical sciences in the seventeenth and eighteenth centuries, and then studying their interaction with power relations, as exemplified by punitive practices—I felt obliged to study the games of truth in the relationship of self with self and the forming of oneself as a subject. . . .[29]

The question of the subject makes its appearance as a continuation of earlier work rather than as a break with it. Foucault returns to a prestructuralist problematic from the position of a poststructuralist. How successful is this self-described continuity?

---

[29]*The History of Sexuality, Volume II: The Use Of Pleasure*, tr. Robert Hurley (New York: Pantheon, 1985), p. 6 (French edition 1984).

If Sartre understood self-constitution as the inner experience of consciousness, Foucault attempts to grasp the process as part of the play of social codes, normative discourses, systems of knowledge. One can only applaud Foucault's courage in facing such a difficult task, one that he called "a hermeneutics of the self." And one is saddened by knowing that we will never have the fruits of his insight on this question beyond what he has already given us, that is, up to the end of the Hellenistic period.[30] Just as frustrating to me is Foucault's refusal to relate his project to the present. His discussion in the opening pages of *The Uses of Pleasure* concerns the nature of the shift from Position 2 to Position 3, asking the reader's pardon for the delay of publication that necessarily ensued. The reasons he gives for the change concern the importance of the question being posed, not its specific problematization in the present. One could well ask if the question of self-constitution does not in fact derive its urgency and force from its problematization in the present, and if that in turn is what raises the issue of its historical transformations.

Foucault sets the issue of self-constitution in the context of morality. He identifies three types of moral "self-activity": codes of behavior, forms of subjectivation or "the forming oneself as an ethical subject," and last, the heart of the issue, self-constitution, or, in his words:

> a history of the way in which individuals are urged to constitute themselves as subjects of moral conduct would be concerned with the models proposed for setting up and developing relationships with the self, for self-reflection, self-knowledge, self-examination, for the decipherment of the self by oneself, for the transformations that one seeks to accomplish with oneself as object.[31]

The first two types of moral self-activity are of less importance to Foucault because, he contends, they did not change drastically in the course of Western history. Moral codes and their imposition on individuals are not the main problem. The third type, self-constitution, on the contrary, is the area of significant change.

For the purposes of this essay the changes Foucault traces in Volumes II and III are of less interest than is the category of self-constitution. When

---

[30] Volume IV of *The History of Sexuality*, *The Confessions of the Flesh*, on the early Christian period may appear at some time, though it was left incomplete by Foucault.
[31] *The Use of Pleasure*, p. 29.

and how do individuals constitute themselves? Foucault names as among his examples of self-constitution Greek discourses on the art of living, the Christian confessional, and the psychoanalytic therapy session. One may ask, however, when is one *not* in a situation of self-constitution? At any moment of daily life the individual may regard his or her self as an object of moral judgment such that his or her ethical being is in question. The only criterion Foucault would seem to have established for self-constitution is that there exist elaborated and systematized social codes, continuous practices, enduring conventions, and that these serve to demark moral questions. But there are a multiplicity of these "institutions" in every society, not only one context—for instance, therapy sessions—in which the events of self-constitution occur.

Foucault isolates sex as the nub of the question without, however, giving much attention to that selection. For him, Western culture prescribes the moral "truth" of the individual in his or her sexuality. But are there not business and military codes that may equally serve as the center of the discussion? Are not the entrepreneur and worker enmeshed in codes and practices in which they constitute themselves as subjects in terms of morals or values?

Could it be said that Foucault selected sexual activity as the venue of self-constitution because for him, a gay person, it was the center of his own self-constituting action? Indeed, does not the emergence in the 1970s and 1980s of political movements and subcultures that question traditional forms of self-constitution through sex—the women's movement, the gay and lesbian movements—form the "generality" of Foucault's inquiry? I raise the question not for *ad hominem* reasons but rather because the issue of the present troubles Foucault's position on the self. While the selection of sex as the arena of self-constitution may be justified on grounds of both historic and present-day importance, it cannot serve to rule out other topics and it does not successfully delimit the question of self-constitution.

In relation to the present situation, perhaps more important than the issue of sex is that of self-constitution. I contend that self-constitution is undergoing radical changes in the late twentieth century, and that Foucault's interpretive genius is manifested in raising that issue. For the dominant groups, that is to say, men, capitalist culture confines self-constitution to the activity of work. Hence the rise of sexual counter-moralities threatens that culture. But another aspect of the category of self-constitution opens up different topics for attention.

This other aspect is language. Foucault's theme of self-constitution gives prominence to language to a greater degree and in a more heuristic manner than other social theorists. The arts of living, the confessional, and the therapy session do not simply privilege sex: they are all *discursive* practices. The individual wrestles with self-constitution through the manipulation of symbols, through carefully elaborated and systematized rules of formation, enunciative statements, and so forth. Military and industrial practices also included codes, but soldiery was proven in battle and work was judged by economic performance. In both cases action rather than discourse was crucial. As I see it, late twentieth-century culture is distinct in that (1) it gives prominence to language and (2) it enacts drastic changes in the structure of language. In what I call the Mode of Information, new language experiences pervade everyday life—electronically mediated language experiences in which the individual is structured to constitute the self and to do so in drastically new ways.

Electronically mediated language structures self-constitution in a double sense. The individual must constitute his or her self as a consumer; in this way the Mode of Information strengthens the hegemonic forces. But the individual must also play with the very process of self-constitution; in this respect the Mode of Information undermines the cultural basis of dominant structures. The constitution of self as consumer deserves much attention: the individual continually tests his or her worth against images of the good or the desirable. But the other sense of self-constitution in the Mode of Information is equally salient. Watching TV (especially ads), being monitored by computerized data bases, participating in computer conferencing or even using computers—all of these experiences enact discursive practices that are asynchronous, that heighten the self-referentiality of language, that undermine the earlier stability of the subject, the sense of having a continuous identity rooted in time, in space, and in relations with others and things. These discursive practices upset the stability of ego continuity. The anonymity of high tech "conversations" elicits a play of multiple self-identifications.

The Mode of Information is the "generality" of Foucault's problematic of self-constitution, or at least it is one possible such "generality." Electronically mediated languages constitute a new social region distinct from but overlapping with the capitalist economy, the welfare state, and the nuclear family. Structurally distinct from face-to-face interactions and from printed communications, they emerge into technically advanced societies undermining the boundary between public and private space. Enlightened and unenlightened subjects alike must take them into account. In a new way they define the self as a locus of truth. Data banks designate the truth of the individual as credit risk, as political subversive, as criminal, as customer, client, agent, friend, parent, and lover. Television ads shape the truth of the individual as consumer or commodity, as one whose personality is Calvin Klein, who is the classiness of Members Only jackets, or the sleekness of a Camaro, the compassion and caring of one who uses AT&T "to reach out and touch someone." In these and so many other ways, the subject becomes his or her own object of knowledge through electronically mediated exchanges.

If Weber is right that bureaucracies are iron cages of oppression, if Marx is right that capitalism alienates and exploits creative energies, if Freud is right that the nuclear family twists libido into neurosis, then we need also to account for the discursive effects on the subject who constitutes his or her self in the Mode of Information.[32]

---

[32] I give an extensive analysis of this problem in *The Mode of Information* (Chicago: University of Chicago Press, 1990).

SEXUAL INVERSIONS

Judith Butler

In honor and memory of Linda Singer

Some might say that the scandal of the first volume of Foucault's *History of Sexuality* consists in the claim that we did not always have a sex. What can such a notion mean? Foucault proposes that there was a decisive historical break between a socio-political regime in which sex existed as an attribute, an activity, a dimension of human life, and a more recent regime in which sex became established as an identity. This particularly modern scandal suggests that for the first time sex is not a contingent or arbitrary feature of identity but, rather, that there can be no identity without sex and that it is precisely through being sexed that we become intelligible as humans. So it is not exactly right to claim we did not always *have* a sex. Perhaps the historical scandal is that we *were* not always our sex, that sex did not always have the power to characterize and constitute identity with such thoroughgoing power. (Later there will be occasion to ask after the exclusions that condition and sustain the Foucaultian "we," but for now we will try on this "we," if only to see where it does not fit.) As Foucault points out, sex has come to characterize and unify not only biological functions and anatomical traits but sexual activities as well as a kind of psychic core that gives clues to an essential, or final meaning to, identity. Not only is one one's sex, but one has sex and, in the having, is supposed to show the sex one "is" even as the sex one "is" is psychically deeper and more unfathomable than the "I" who lives it can ever know. Hence this "sex" requires and secures a set of sciences that can mediate endlessly on that pervasive indecipherability.

What conditioned the introduction into history of this notion of sex that totalizes identity? Foucault argues that during the course of the eighteenth century in Europe famines and epidemics start to disappear and that power, which had previously been governed by the need to ward off death, now becomes occupied with the production, maintenance, and regulation of *life*. It is in the course of this regulatory cultivation of life that the category of sex is established. Naturalized as heterosexual, it is designed to regulate and secure the reproduction of life. Having a true sex with a biological destiny and natural heterosexuality thus becomes essential to the aim of power, now understood as the disciplinary reproduction of life. Foucault characterizes early modern Europe as governed by *juridical* power. As juridical, power operates negatively to impose limits, restrictions, and prohibitions; power reacts defensively, as it were, to preserve life and social harmony over and against the threat of violence or natural death. Once the threat of death is ameliorated, as he claims it is in the eighteenth century, those juridical laws are transformed into instances of *productive* power, in which power effectively *generates* objects to control, in which power elaborates all sorts of objects and identities that guarantee the augmentation of regulatory scientific regimes.[1] The category of "sex" is constructed as an "object" of study and control, which assists in the elaboration and justification of productive power regimes. It is as if once the threat of death is overcome, power turns its idle attention to the construction of objects to control. Or, rather, power exerts and articulates its control through the formation and proliferation of objects that concern the continuation of life. (Later I will briefly examine the way in which the term "power" operates in Foucault's

---

[1] See Michel Foucault, *The History of Sexuality, Volume I: An Introduction*, tr. Robert Hurley (New York: Pantheon, 1978), pp. 85–91. This text was originally published as *La Volonté de savoir* (Paris: Editions Gallimard, 1976).

text, its susceptibility to personification and the interrelations of the juridical and productive modalities.)

I want to raise two kinds of questions in this essay, one concerning the problematic history Foucault tries to tell, and why it cannot work in light of the challenge of the recent emergence of the epidemic of AIDS, and a second, subordinate here, concerning the category of sex and its suppression of sexual difference. To be sure, Foucault could not have known in 1976 when he published the first volume of *The History of Sexuality* that an epidemic would emerge within the very terms of late modern power that would call the terms of his analysis into question. "Sex" is constructed not only in the service of life or reproduction but, what might turn out to be a logical corollary, in the service of the regulation and apportionment of death. In some recent medico-juridical discursive efforts to produce sex, death is installed as a formative and essential feature of that sex. In some recent discourse, the male homosexual is figured time and again as one whose desire is somehow structured by death, either as the desire to die or as one whose desire is inherently punishable by death (Mapplethorpe); paradoxically and painfully, this has also been the case in the postmortem figuration of Foucault himself. Within the medico-juridical discourse that has emerged to manage and reproduce the epidemic of AIDS, the juridical and productive forms of power *converge* to effect a production of the homosexual subject as a bearer of death. This is a matrix of discursive and institutional power that adjudicates matters of life and death through the construction of homosexuality as a category of sex. Within this matrix, homosexual sex is "inverted" into death, and a death-bound desire becomes the figure for the sexual invert. One might ask here whether lesbian sexuality even qualifies as sex within hegemonic public discourse. "What is it that they do?" might be read as "Can we be sure they do anything at all?"

For the most part, I will concentrate on the question of how Foucault's historical account of the shift in power calls now to be rewritten in light of the power/discourse regime that regulates AIDS. For Foucault, the category of "sex" emerges only on the condition that epidemics are over. So how are we now, via Foucault, to understand the elaboration of the category of sex within the very matrix of this epidemic?

Along the way, I will ask about the adequacy of this notion of "sex" in the singular. Is it true that "sex" as a historical category can be understood apart from the sexes or a notion of sexual difference? Are notions of "male" and "female" similarly subjected to a monolithic notion of sex, or is there

here an erasure of difference that precludes a Foucaultian understanding of "the sex which is not one."[2]

LIFE, DEATH, AND POWER

In the final section of the first volume, the "Right of Death and Power over Life," Foucault describes a cataclysmic "event" that he attributes to the eighteenth century: "nothing less than the entry of life into history."[3] What he means, it seems, is that the study and regulation of life becomes an object of historical concern, that is, that life becomes the site for the elaboration of power. Before this unprecedented "entry" of life into history, it seems that history and, more important, power were concerned with combatting death. Foucault writes:

> the pressure exerted by the biological on the historical had remained very strong for thousands of years; epidemics and famine were the two great dramatic forms of this relationship that was always dominated by the menace of death. *But through a circular process*, the economic—and primarily agricultural—development of the 19th century, and an increase in productivity and resources even more rapid than the demographic growth it encouraged, allowed a measure of relief from those profound threats: despite some renewed outbreaks, the period of great ravages from starvation and plague had come to a close before the *French Revolution*; death was ceasing to torment life so directly. But at the same time, the development of the different fields of knowledge concerned with life in general, the improvement of agricultural techniques, and the observations and measures relative to man's life and survival contributed to this relaxation: a relative control over life averted some of the imminent risks of death.[4]

There are of course several reasons to be suspicious of this kind of

---

[2] See Luce Irigaray, *The Sex Which is Not One*. tr. Catherine Porter with Carolyn Burke (Ithaca: Cornell University Press, 1985).
[3] *History of Sexuality*, p. 141.
[4] Ibid., p. 142.

epoch-making narrativizing. It appears that Foucault wants to make a historical shift from a notion of politics and history that is always threatened by death, and guided by the aim of negotiating that threat, to a politics that can to some extent *presume* the continuation of life and, hence, direct its attention to the regulation, control, and cultivation of life. Foucault notes the Eurocentrism in his account, but it alters nothing. He writes:

> it is not that life has been totally integrated into techniques that govern and administer it; it constantly escapes them. Outside the Western world, famine exists, on a greater scale than ever; and the biological risks confronting the species are perhaps greater, and certainly more serious, than before the birth of microbiology.[5]

Foucault's historical account can perhaps be read only as a wishful construction: death is effectively expelled from Western modernity, cast *behind* it as a historical possibility, surpassed or cast *outside* it as a non-Western phenomenon. Can these exclusions hold? To what extent does his characterization of later modernity require and institute an exclusion of the threat of death? It seems clear that Foucault must tell a phantasmatic history in order to keep modernity and productive power free of death and full of sex. Insofar as the category of sex is elaborated within the context of productive power, a story is being told in which sex, it seems, surpasses and displaces death.

If we accept the historically problematic character of this narration, can we accept it on logical grounds? Can one even defend against death without also promoting a certain version of life? Does juridical power in this way entail productive power as its logical correlate? "Death," whether figured as *prior* to modernity as that which is warded off and left behind or as a threat *within* premodern nations *elsewhere*, must always be the death, the end, of a specific way of life; and the life to be safeguarded is always already a normatively construed *way* of life, not life and death pure and simple. Does it make sense, then, to reject the notion that life entered into history as death took its exit from history? On the one hand, neither one ever entered or departed, since the one can only appear as the immanent possibility of the other; on the other hand, life and death might be construed as the incessant entering and departing that characterizes any

[5]Ibid., p. 143.

field of power. Perhaps we are referring neither to a historical shift nor to a logical shift in the formation of power. For even when power is in the business of warding off death, that can only be in the name of some specific form of life and through the insistence on the right to produce and reproduce that way of life. At this point, the distinction between juridical and productive power appears to collapse.

And yet this shift must make sense for Foucault to argue convincingly that "sex" enters history in later modernity and becomes an object that productive power formulates, regulates, and produces. When sex becomes a site of power, it becomes an object of legal and regulatory discourses; it becomes that which power in its various discourses and institutions *cultivates* in the image of its own normative construction. There is no "sex" to which a supervening law attends; in attending to sex, in monitoring sex, the law constructs sex, producing it as that which calls to be monitored and *is* inherently regulatable. There is a normative development to sex, laws that inhere in sex itself, and the inquiry that attends to that lawlike development postures as if it merely discovers in sex the very laws that it has itself installed at the site of sex. In this sense, the regulation of "sex" finds no sex there, external to its own regulation; regulation produces the object it comes to regulate; regulation has regulated in advance what it will only disingenuously attend to as the object of regulation. In order to exercise and elaborate its own power, a regulatory regime will generate the very object it seeks to control.

And here is the crucial point: it is not as if a regulatory regime first controls its object and then produces it or first produces it in order then to control it; there is no temporary lag between the production and the regulation of sex; they occur at once, for regulation is always generative, producing the object it claims merely to discover or to find in the social field in which it operates. Concretely, this means that we are not, as it were, (merely) discriminated against on the basis of our sex. Power is more *insidious* than that: either discrimination is built into the very formulation of our sex, or enfranchisement is precisely the formative and generative principle of someone else's sex. And this is why, for Foucault, sex can never be liberated *from power*: the formation of sex is an enactment of power. In a sense, power works on sex more deeply than we can know, not only as an external constraint or repression but as the formative principle of its intelligibility.

Here we can locate a shift or inversion at the center of power, in the very structure of power, for what appears at first to be a law that imposes itself upon "sex" as a ready-made object, a juridical view of power as constraint or *external* control, turns out to be—all along—performing a fully different ruse of power; silently, it is *already productive* power, forming the very object that will be suitable for control and then, in an act that effectively disavows that production, claiming to discover that "sex" outside of power. Hence the category of "sex" will be precisely what power produces in order to have an object of control.

What this suggests, of course, is that there is no historical shift from juridical to productive power but that juridical power is a kind of dissimulated or concealed productive power from the start and that the shift, the inversion, is within power, not between two historically or logically distinct forms of power.

The category of "sex," which Foucault claims is understandable only as the result of a historical shift, is actually, as it were, produced in the midst of this shift, this very shiftiness of power that produces in advance that which it will come to subordinate. This is not a shift from a version of power as constraint or restriction to a version of power as productive but a production that is *at the same time* constraint, a constraining in advance of what will and will not qualify as a properly sexed being. This constraining production works through linking the category of sex with that of identity; there will be two sexes, discrete and uniform, and they will be expressed and evidenced in gender and sexuality, so that any social displays of nonidentity, discontinuity, or sexual incoherence will be punished, controlled, ostracized, reformed. Hence, by producing sex as a category of identity, that is, by defining sex as one sex or another, the discursive regulation of sex begins to take place. It is only after this procedure of definition and production has taken place that power comes to posture as that which is external to the object—"sex"—that it finds. In effect, it has already installed control in the object by defining the object as a self-identical object; its self-identity, presumed to be immanent to sex itself, is precisely the trace of this installation of power, a trace that is simultaneously erased, covered over, by the posturing of power as that which is external to its object.

What propels power? It cannot be human subjects, precisely because they are one of the occasions, enactments, and effects of power. It seems, for Foucault, that power seeks to augment itself within modernity just as life sought to augment itself prior to modernity. Power acts as life's proxy, as it were, taking over its function, reproducing itself always in excess of any need, luxuriating in a kind of self-elaboration that is no longer hindered by the immanent threat of death. Power thus becomes the locus of a certain displaced vitalism in Foucault; power, conceived as productive, is the form life takes when it no longer needs to guard itself against death.

SEX AND SEXUALITY

How does this inversion from early to late modern power affect Foucault's discussion of yet another inversion, that between *sex* and *sexuality*? Within ordinary language we sometimes speak, for instance, of being a given sex, and having a certain sexuality, and we even presume for the most part that our sexuality in some way *issues* from that sex, is perhaps an *expression* of that sex, or is even partially or fully *caused* by that sex. Sexuality is understood to come from sex, which is to say that the biological locus of "sex" in and on the body is somehow conjured as the originating source of a sexuality that, as it were, flows out from that locus, remains inhibited within that locus, or somehow takes its bearings with respect to that locus. In any case, "sex" is understood logically and temporally to *precede* sexuality and to function, if not as its primary cause, then at least as its necessary precondition.

However, Foucault performs an *inversion* of this relation and claims that this inversion is correlated with the shift from early to late modern power. For Foucault, "it is apparent that the deployment of sexuality, with its different strategies, was what established this notion of 'sex'."[6] Sexuality is here viewed as a discursively constructed and highly regulated network of pleasures and bodily exchanges, produced through prohibitions and sanctions that quite literally give form and directionality to pleasure and sensation. As such a network or regime, sexuality does not emerge from bodies as their prior cause; sexuality takes bodies as its instrument and its object, the site at which it consolidates, networks, and extends its power. As a regulatory regime, sexuality operates primarily by *investing bodies with the category of sex*, that is, making bodies into the *bearers of a principle of identity*. To claim that bodies are one sex or the other appears at first to be a purely *descriptive* claim. For Foucault, however, this claim is itself a *legislation* and a *production* of bodies, a discursive demand, as it were, that

[6] Ibid., p. 154.

bodies become produced according to principles of heterosexualizing coherence and integrity, unproblematically as either female or male. Where sex is taken as a principle of identity, it is always positioned within a field of two mutually exclusive and fully exhaustive identities; one is either male or female, never both at once, and never neither one of them. Foucault writes:

> the notion of sex brought about a fundamental reversal; it made it possible to invert the representation of the relationships of power to sexuality, causing the latter to appear, not in its essential and positive relation to power, but as being rooted in a specific and irreducible urgency which power tries as best it can to dominate; thus the idea of "sex" makes it possible to evade what gives "power" its power; it enables one to conceive power solely as law and taboo.[7]

For Foucault, sex, whether male or female, operates as a principle of identity that imposes a fiction of coherence and unity on an otherwise random or unrelated set of biological functions, sensations, pleasures. Under the regime of sex, every pleasure becomes symptomatic of "sex," and "sex" itself functions not merely as the biological ground or cause of pleasure but as that which determines its directionality, a principle of teleology or destiny, and as that repressed, psychical core that furnishes clues to the interpretation of its ultimate meaning. As a fictional imposition of uniformity, sex is "an imaginary point" and an "artificial unity," but as fictional and as artificial, the category wields enormous power.[8] Although Foucault does not quite claim it, the science of reproduction produces intelligible "sex" by imposing a compulsory heterosexuality on the description of bodies. One might claim that sex is here produced according to a heterosexual morphology.

The category of "sex" thus establishes a principle of intelligibility for human beings, which is to say that no human being can be taken to be

---

[7]Ibid., p. 155.
[8]Foucault writes: "It is through sex—in fact an imaginary point determined by the deployment of sexuality—that each individual has to pass in order to have access to his own intelligibility (seeing that it is both the hidden aspect and the generative principle of meaning), to the whole of his body (since it is a real and threatened part of it, while symbolically constituting the whole), to his identity (since it joins the force of a drive to the singularity of a history)." Ibid., pp. 155–156.

human, can be recognized *as* human, unless that human being is fully and coherently marked by sex. And yet it would not capture Foucault's meaning merely to claim that there are humans who are marked by sex and thereby become intelligible. The point is stronger: to qualify as legitimately human, one must be coherently sexed. The incoherence of sex is precisely what marks off the abject and the dehumanized from the recognizably human.

Luce Irigaray would clearly take this point further and turn it against Foucault. She would, I think, argue that the only sex that qualifies as a sex is a masculine one, which is not marked as masculine but parades as the universal and thereby silently extends its dominion. To refer to a sex that is not one is to refer to a sex that cannot be designated univocally as sex but is outside identity from the start. Are we not right to ask, which sex is it that renders the figure of the human intelligible, and within such an economy, is it not the case that the feminine functions as a figure for unintelligibility? When one speaks of the "one" in language—as I do now—one makes reference to a neuter term, a purely human term. And though Foucault and Irigaray would agree that sex is a necessary precondition for human intelligibility, Foucault appears to think that any sanctioned sex will do, whereas Irigaray would argue that the only sanctioned sex is the masculine one—that is, the masculine that is reworked as a "one," a neuter, a universal. If the coherent subject is always sexed as masculine, then it is constructed through the abjection and erasure of the feminine. For Irigaray, masculine and feminine sexes are not similarly constructed as sexes or as principles of intelligible identity; in fact, she argues that the masculine sex is constructed as the only "one," and that it figures the feminine other as a reflection only of itself; within that model, then, both masculine and feminine reduce to the masculine, and the feminine, left outside this male autoerotic economy, is not even designatable within its terms or is, rather, designatable as a radically disfigured masculine projection, which is yet a different kind of erasure.[9]

---

[9]In this sense, the category of sex constitutes and regulates what will and will not be an intelligible and recognizable human existence, what will and will not be a citizen capable of rights or speech, an individual protected by law against violence or injury.

The political question for Foucault, and for those of us who read him now, is *not* whether "improperly sexed" beings should or should not be treated fairly or with justice or with tolerance. The question is whether, if improperly sexed, such a being can even be a being, a human being, a subject, one whom the law can condone or condemn. For Foucault has outlined a region that is, as it were, outside of the purview of the law, one that excludes

This hypothetical critique from an Irigarayan perspective suggests something problematic about Foucault's constructivism. Within the terms of productive power, regulation and control work through the discursive articulation of identities. But those discursive articulations effect certain exclusions and erasures; oppression works not merely through the mechanism of regulation and production but by foreclosing the very possibility of articulation. If Foucault claims that regulation and control operate as the formative principles of identity, Irigaray in a somewhat more Derridean vein would argue that oppression works through other means as well, through the *exclusion* and *erasure* effected by any discursive formation, and that here the feminine is precisely what is erased and excluded in order for intelligible identities to be produced.[10]

CONTEMPORARY IDENTITY IN THE AGE OF EPIDEMIC

This is a limitation of Foucault's analysis. And yet he offers a counter-warning, I think, to those who might be tempted to treat femaleness or the feminine as an identity to be liberated. To attempt that would be to repeat the gesture of the regulatory regime, taking some aspect of "sex" and making it stand synecdochally for the entirety of the body and its psychic manifestations. Similarly, Foucault did not embrace an identity politics that might in the name of homosexuality combat the regulatory effort to produce the symptomatic homosexual or to erase the homosexual from the domain of intelligible subjects. To take identity as a rallying point for liberation would be to subject oneself at the very moment that one calls for a release from subjection. For the point is not to claim, "yes, I am fully totalized by the category of homosexuality, just as you say, but only that the meaning of that totalization will be different from the one that you attribute to me." If identity imposes a fictive coherence and

---

certain kinds of improperly sexed beings from the very category of the human subject. The journals of Herculine Barbin, the hermaphrodite (ed. Michel Foucault, *Herculine Barbin, Being the Recently Discovered Memoirs of a Nineteenth-Century Hermaphrodite*, tr. Richard MacDougall [New York: Colophon, 1980], demonstrate the violence of the law that would legislate identity on a body that resists it. But Herculine is to some extent a *figure* for a sexual ambiguity or inconsistency that emerges at the site of bodies and that contests the category of subject and its univocal or self-identical "sex."

[10]This gives some clues to what a deconstructive critique of Foucault might look like.

consistency on the body or, better, if identity is a regulatory principle that produces bodies in conformity with that principle, then it is no more liberatory to embrace an unproblematized gay identity than it is to embrace the diagnostic category of homosexuality devised by medico-juridical regimes. The political challenge Foucault poses here is whether a resistance to the diagnostic category can be effected that does not reduplicate the very mechanism of that subjection, this time—painfully, paradoxically—under the sign of liberation. The task for Foucault is to refuse the totalizing category under either guise, which is why Foucault will not confess or "come out" in the *History of Sexuality* as a homosexual or privilege homosexuality as a site of heightened regulation. But perhaps Foucault remains significantly and politically linked to the problematic of homosexuality all the same.

Is Foucault's strategic *inversion* of identity perhaps a redeployment of the medicalized category of the invert? The diagnostic category "invert" presumes that someone with a given sex somehow acquired a set of sexual dispositions and desires that do not travel in the appropriate directions; sexual desire is "inverted" when it misses its aim and object and travels wrongheadedly to its opposite or when it takes itself as the object of its desire and then projects and recovers that "self" in a homosexual object. Clearly, Foucault gives us a way to laugh at this construction of the proper relation between "sex" and "sexuality," to appreciate its contingency, and to question the causal and expressive lines that are said to run from sex to sexuality. Ironically, or perhaps tactically, Foucault engages a certain activity of "inversion" here but reworks that term from a noun to a verb. His theoretical practice is, in a sense, marked by a series of inversions: in the shift to modern power, an inversion is performed; in the relation of sex and sexuality, another inversion is performed. And with respect to the category of the "invert," yet another inversion is performed, one that might be understood to stand as a strategy of refiguration according to which the various other inversions of the text can be read.[11]

---

[11] If sexuality takes sex as its instrument and object, then sexuality is by definition more diffuse and less uniform than the category of sex; through the category of sex, sexuality performs a kind of self-reduction. Sexuality will always exceed sex, even as sex sets itself up as a category that accounts for sexuality *in toto* by posturing as its primary cause. In order to claim that one is a given sex, a certain radical reduction must take place, for "sex" functions to describe not only certain relatively stable biological or anatomical traits but also an activity, what one does, and a state of mind or psychic disposition. The ambiguities of the term are temporarily overcome when "sex" is understood as the biological basis for

The traditional invert gets its name because the *aim* of its desire has run off the rails of heterosexuality. According to the construction of homosexuality as narcissism, the aim has turned back against itself or exchanged its position of identification for the position of the object desired, an exchange that constitutes a kind of psychic mistake. But to locate inversion as an exchange between psychic disposition and aim, or between an identification and an object, or as a return of an aim upon itself is still to operate within the heterosexualizing norm and its teleological explanations. Foucault calls this kind of explanation into question, however, through an explanatory inversion that establishes sexuality as a regulatory regime that dissimulates itself by setting up the category of "sex" as a quasi-naturalistic fictive unity. Exposed as a fiction, the body becomes a site for unregulated pleasures, sensations, practices, convergences, and refigurations of masculine and feminine such that the naturalizing status of those terms is called radically into question.

Hence the task for Foucault is not to claim the category of invert or of homosexual and to rework that term to signify something less pathological, mistaken, or deviant. The task is to call into question the explanatory gesture that requires a true identity and, hence, a mistaken one as well. If diagnostic discourse would make of Foucault an "invert," then he will

---

a psychic disposition, which then manifests itself in a set of acts. In this sense, the category of "sex" functions to establish a fictive causality among these dimensions of bodily existence, so that to be female is to be disposed sexually in a certain way, namely, heterosexually, and to be positioned within sexual exchange such that the biological and psychic dimensions of "sex" are consummated, integrated, and demonstrated. On the one hand, the category of "sex" works to blur the distinctions among biology, psychic reality, and sexual practice, for sex is all of these things, even as it proceeds through a certain force of teleology to relate each of these terms. But once the teleology is disrupted, shown to be disruptible, then the very discreteness of terms like biology and psyche becomes contestable. For if sex proves no longer to be as encompassing as it seems, then what in biology is "sex," and what contests the univocity of that term, and where, if at all, is sex to be found in the psyche, if sex can no longer be placed within that heterosexualizing teleology? These terms become disjoined and internally destabilized when a biological female is perhaps psychically disposed in nonheterosexual ways or is positioned in sexual exchanges in ways that the categories of heterosexuality cannot quite describe. Then what Foucault has called "the fictive unity of sex" is no longer secure. This disunity or disaggregation of "sex" suggests that the category only works to the extent that it describes a hyperbolic heterosexuality, a normative heterosexuality, one that, in its idealized coherence, is uninhabitable by practicing heterosexuals and as such is bound to oppress in its status as an impossible idealization. This is an idealization before which everyone is bound to fail and which of course is a failure, for clear political reasons, to be savored and safeguarded.

invert the very logic that makes something like "inversion" possible. And he will do this by inverting the relation between sex and sexuality. This is an intensification and redoubling of inversion, one that is perhaps mobilized by the diagnosis but that has as its effect the disruption of the very vocabulary of diagnosis and cure, true and mistaken identity. This is as if to say: "Yes, an invert, but I will show you what inversion can do; I can invert and subvert the categories of identity such that you will no longer be able to call me that and know what it is you mean."

The pathologization of homosexuality was to have a future that Foucault could not have foreseen in 1976. For if homosexuality is pathological from the start, then any disease that homosexuals may sometimes contract will be uneasily conflated with the disease that they already are. Foucault's effort to delineate a modern epoch and to claim a break between the era of epidemics and that of recent modernity must now become subject to an inversion, which he himself did not perform but which in a sense he taught us how to perform. For Foucault claims that the epidemic is over, and yet he may well have been one of its hosts at the time he made that claim, a silent carrier who could not know the historical future that arrived to defeat his claim. Death is the limit to power, he argued, but there is something that he missed here, namely, that in the maintenance of death and of the dying, power is still at work and that death is and has its own discursive industry.

When Foucault gives his grand narrative of epidemiology, he can only be mistaken, for to believe that technological advance forecloses the possibility of an age of epidemic, as Linda Singer has called the contemporary sexual regime,[12] is finally evidence of a phantasmatic projection and a vainly utopian faith. For it not only presumes that technology will ward off death, or already has, but that it will preserve life (a highly questionable presumption). And it fails to account for the way in which technology is differentially deployed to save some lives and to condemn others. When we consider which technology receives federal funding, and we note that recent AIDS appropriations bills have been drastically cut, it becomes clear that inasmuch as AIDS is understood to afflict marginalized communities and is itself taken as a further token of their marginalization, technology can be precisely what is withheld from a life-preserving deployment.

---

[12]See her "Bodies—Powers—Pleasures," *differences* 1 (1989): 45–66; see also her forthcoming book *Erotic Welfare: Sexual Theory and Politics in the Age of Epidemic* (Routledge).

On the Senate floor one hears quite specific references to AIDS as that which is somehow *caused* by gay sexual practices. Here homosexuality is itself made into a death-bearing practice, but this is hardly new. Jeff Nunokawa argues that a longstanding discursive tradition figures the male homosexual as always already dying, as one whose desire is a kind of incipient and protracted dying.[13] The discourse that attributes AIDS to homosexuality is an intensification and reconsolidation of that same tradition.

On Sunday, October 21, 1990, the *New York Times*[14] ran a memorial story on Leonard Bernstein who had recently died from lung disease. Although this appears not to be a death from AIDS or from AIDS-related complications, a journalistic effort is nevertheless made to link his death with his homosexuality and to figure his homosexuality as a death drive. The essay tacitly constructs the scene of his death as the logical consequence of a life that, even in the romantic music he liked, seemed to know that "death was always standing in the wings." It is usually friends, admirers, lovers who stand in the wings when a conductor performs, but here it is somehow death who is uneasily collapsed into the homosexual phantasm. Immediately following this statement comes another: "his compulsive smoking and other personal excesses certainly could be interpreted in classic death-wish terms. In the Romantically committed mind, for every plus there must be a minus, for every blessing of love, a compensating curse." Here death is understood as a necessary compen-

---

[13] Jeff Nunokawa, "*In Memoriam* and the Extinction of the Homosexual," *English Literary History*, forthcoming.

[14] Donal Henahan in section H, pp. 1, 25. Later Henahan remarks that "It struck some who knew him as contradictory that the conductor who struggled to reveal himself in every performance, faithful to the great romantic tradition, nevertheless kept his private life out of the public eye. His homosexuality, never a secret in musical circles, became more overt after the death of his wife, but, perhaps, out of his concern for his carefully cultivated image, he was not eager to disillusion the straight-arrow public that had adopted him as the all-American boy of music." Here the romantic tradition of self-disclosure would appear to demand that he disclose his homosexuality, which suggests that his homosexuality is at the heart of his romanticism and, hence, his commitment to being cursed by love. The use of "straight-arrow" for straight imports the sense of "straight as an arrow," a phrase used to connote honesty. The association here suggests that to be straight is to be honest, and to be gay is to be dishonest. This links back to the question of disclosure suggesting that the author takes Bernstein's insistence on privacy as an act of deceit and, at the same time, that homosexuality itself, that is, the content of what is concealed, is a kind of necessary deceitfulness. This culminates the moralistic circle of the story, which now constructs the homosexual as one who, by virtue of his essential deceitfulness, is cursed by his own love to death.

sation for homosexual desire, as the *telos* of male homosexuality, its genesis and its demise, the principle of its intelligibility.

In 1976 Foucault sought to disjoin the category of sex from the struggle against death; in this way he sought, it seems, to make of sex a life-affirming and perpetuating activity. Even as an effect of power, "sex" is precisely that which is said to reproduce itself, augment and intensify itself, and pervade mundane life. Foucault sought to separate sex from death by announcing the end of the era in which death reigns. But what kind of radical hopefulness would consign the constitutive power of death to an irrecoverable historical past? What promise did Foucault see in sex, and in sexuality, to overcome death, such that sex is precisely what marks the overcoming of death, the end to the struggling against it? He did not consider that the regulatory discourse on sex could itself produce death, pronounce death, even proliferate it, and that, insofar as "sex" as a category was supposed to secure reproduction and life, those instances of "sex" that are not directly reproductive might then take on the valence of death.

He warned us, wisely, that "we must not think that by saying yes to sex, one says no to power; on the contrary, one tracks along the course laid out by the general deployment of sexuality. It is the agency of sex that we must break away from."[15] And that is right, for sex does not cause AIDS. There are discursive and institutional regimes that regulate and punish sexuality, laying down tracks that will not save us, indeed, that may lead rather quickly to our demise.

One ought not to think that by saying yes to power, one says no to death, for death can be not the limit of power but its very aim.

Foucault clearly saw that death could become an aim of politics, for he argued that war itself had become sublimated into politics: "the force relationships that for a long time had found expression in war, in every form of warfare, gradually became invested in the order of political power."[16] He writes in *The History of Sexuality*: "One might say that the ancient right to *take* life or *let* live was replaced by a power to *foster* life or *disallow* it to the point of death."[17]

When he claims that "sex is worth dying for," he means that preserving the regime of "sex" is worth dying for and that political wars are waged so that populations and their reproduction can be secured. "Wars are no

[15]*History of Sexuality*, p. 157.
[16]Ibid., p. 102.
[17]Ibid., p. 138.

longer waged in the name of a sovereign who must be defended; they are waged on behalf of the existence of everyone; entire populations are mobilized for the purpose of wholesale slaughter in the name of life necessity: massacres have become vital."[18] He then adds:

> the principle underlying the tactics of battle—that one has to be capable of killing in order to go on living—has become the principle that defines the strategy of the states. But the existence in question is no longer the juridical existence of sovereignty; at stake is the biological existence of a population. If genocide is indeed the dream of modern powers, this is not because of a recent return of the ancient right to kill; it is because power is situated and exercised at the level of life, the species, the race, and the large-scale phenomena of population.[19]

It is not only that modern states have the capacity to destroy one another through nuclear arsenals but that "populations" have become the objects of war, and it is in the name of whole "populations" that ostensibly defensive wars are waged.

In a sense, Foucault knew full well that death had not ceased to be the goal of "modern" states but only that the aim of annihilation is achieved through more subtle means. In the political decisions that administer the scientific, technological, and social resources to respond to the epidemic of AIDS, the parameters of that crisis are insidiously circumscribed; the lives to be saved are insidiously demarcated from those who will be left to die; "innocent" victims are separated from those who "deserve it." But this demarcation is, of course, largely implicit, for modern power "administers" life in part through the silent withdrawal of its resources. In this way politics can achieve the goal of death, can target its own population, under the very sign of the administration of life. This "inversion" of power performs the work of death under the signs of life, scientific progress, technological advance, that is, under the signs that ostensibly promise the preservation of life. And because this kind of dissimulated killing takes place through the public, discursive production of a scientific community in competition to find a cure, working under difficult conditions, victims of economic scarcity, the question of how little is allocated and how

---

[18]Ibid., p. 137.
[19]Ibid.

poorly it is directed can hardly be heard. The technological aim to preserve life, then, becomes the silent sanction by which this dissimulated killing silently proceeds. We must not think that by saying yes to technology, we say no to death, for there is always the question of how and for what aim that technology is produced. The deeper offense is surely to be found in the claim that it is the failure neither of government nor of science but of "sex" itself that continues this unfathomable procession of death.

Part IV

THE UNIVERSITY AND ITS DISCIPLINES

EXTRALOGICAL EXCAVATIONS
Philosophy in the Age of Shovelry

Chuck Dyke

There is a bizarre irony involved in producing learned disquisitions on Foucault's "theory" of normalization. The irony deepens to patent absurdity when Foucault's light is turned on the intellectual disciplines themselves, for then the learned disquisition becomes its own object. At best, the grand disquisitor produces a case in point; at worst, a parody. Or maybe it's the other way round.

The philosophers have only interpreted Foucault in various ways; the point is to use him. And, indeed, there's really no other choice short of falling into a compromising and embarrassing posture, legs splayed to the sky. It is no tribute to a thinker to hermeneuter him to the threshold of dead boredom. For thinkers, the highest honors come when they are used without citation and, indeed, with insouciance. What follows here is intended to honor Foucault, and fails to do so only insofar as it refers to him, occasionally, directly.

Most Anglo-American philosophers are teachers of philosophy. This places them in a practice situated at the junction of a tradition thousands of years old and contemporary institutions of discipline and normalization. This junction is available for serious investigation—an investigation of ourselves. Such investigation will require the adoption of a suitable perspective, one that will allow us to emerge as objects. I suggest beginning with the perspective of our apprentices, those students who confront us and our introductory courses as (rather strange and unfamiliar) objects each semester. We want to find eyes to see what awaits our apprentices at the site of their philosophical initiation.

SPADEWORK

Extremely typical among the first artifacts young apprentices encounter is an apology. It was written long ago and, they are made to understand, it is a sacred text. The text narrates the story of an ancient Greek, Socrates by name, who is apparently (but only apparently) on trial for his life. Philosophy begins in deepest drama. It dons the armor of Galahad and deploys the test of purity as a legitimation strategy. It's traditional. Here in the first recorded use of this strategy Socrates (Plato's Kermit the Frog) defends himself against the charges of impiety and, in the last analysis, treason by deconstructing the common wisdom upon which Athenian democratic rule is based. This common wisdom is not rationally grounded. It lacks the authority to underwrite a sentence of death.

The apprentice is immediately confronted with a second artifact. For, like all sacred texts, this one has achieved a canonical reading,[1] an artifact in its own right. And, indeed, this second artifact is so dazzling that the first is nearly obscured. The canonical reading is that Socrates is a noble and courageous seeker after truth, and that the shame of the Athenian democracy was that it could not stand the shining light of Socrates, feared

---

[1] Graduate students faced with a set of preliminary examinations of potentially mystifying scope often plead for a list of sacred texts. This is a foolish plea. They could produce the list themselves. What they really need is an account of the canonical reading accorded the texts. And this is never straightforwardly available to them.

him, and put him to death. In his apology, his truth-seeking openmindedness is put forth to us as an exemplar: the form of the philosopher.[2]

We know, of course, that all the early "Socratic" dialogues are devoted to the conveyance of the same message. *In situ*, that is, in the Athens of the fourth century, at the point of final decay of the city-state system, the Kermitic message had an extremely high political charge—the grounds for the overthrow of the Athenian democracy. *In situ contemporaneo*, that is, within the four walls of the philosophy classroom, the message could well be the same, the defeat of common wisdom as the grounds for democratic participation. And the message may actually be read in that way more often than we seem to suspect. But by and large we are sufficiently abstracted from the political context, dancing, as we do, behind the seven veils of ignorance, so that the Kermitic message has a more local charge. It is the first therapy in the moral orthopedic reconstruction of the rational man. The chiropracticality of succeeding therapies depends on the success of this first one. Apprentices must be made to feel the superior nobility of Kermit. He must represent the only responsible intellectual stance. Forgive me, father, for I have erred—or at least it's always possible that I may have erred; and that's as great a sin, more awful in its totalizing modality.

But there are other bracing therapies to be employed, based on very similar artifacts. We can have the apprentices meditate to a Cartesian mantra. To the question "What is Descartes' starting point?" some wag once answered, "Well, let's look at the first sentence of the *Meditations* and find out." Novel enough to give it a try. The apprentices find that "Several years have now elapsed . . . ," and that they are at the beginning of an autobiographical narrative—a narrative they are asked to share, to retraverse, to adopt as their own. They are intrigued to find that it is once again the narrative of guilt and expiation of Kermit the Frog. Aided by the therapeutic ministrations of evil demons submitting them to temptations of pride, self-confidence, and common knowledge, they are asked to purify themselves in readiness for the reception of rational grace. Failing purification, they will fail to pass through the philosophical gates. They will be lost. Since we are their teachers, they confess their unworthiness to us. "I am lost," each says. Fables? Bowdlerized bits of the past?

---

[2]The reading of the *Apology* involved here is abetted by Moses Finley, *Democracy Ancient and Modern*, rev. edn. (New Brunswick: Rutgers University Press, 1985), and T. M. Robinson, *The Greek Legacy* (Toronto: CBC, 1979).

Not at all. This very week, as if predestined, I received a copy of a modest volume entitled *What Does It All Mean?*.³ It is written by a practitioner of the philosophical discourse possessing the highest credentials of legitimation. We assume that the volume is meant, at best, to supplement and explain the sacred texts and, at worst, to substitute for them in the service of efficiency. After a bracing invitational preamble, the first sentence addressed to the apprentices is: "If you think about it, you will realize that the only things you can be certain about are the contents of your own mind." This, then, is a work that celebrates the discovery of the starting place, which need never be groped for again. No evil demons here; no confessions of Kermitic ignorance. The primal therapy is assumed to have been completed; only the reconstructive surgery remains to be performed. What confidence! Is it justified? Well, we live in a very uncertain age. Adolescence too is a very uncertain age. By this time the retreat into the privacy of our own egos is constantly reinforced by a world of institutions and practices celebrating our private acquisitive egos. Our social identity as desiring egos is subject to constant nurture. So the confidence may well be justified.

I confess (it becomes a habit, a matter of style) that I never read the second sentence. There is a slight chance—a vanishingly small probability, as they say—that succeeding sentences subject the trope of the lonely, isolated, disembodied ego to deconstructive scrutiny. But I doubt it. I doubted it sufficiently to put the book aside forever. I don't believe that there are evil counterdemons powerful enough to tempt the author away from his origins.

THE PHASE SPACE OF PHILOSOPHY

How could the apprentices account for these artifacts? They are in a position very much like that of the archaeologist unearthing shards and trying to reconstruct the cultural whole within which those shards had a life and a sense.

As Davide Lajolo put it, we must *Vender l'erba dalla parte delle radici*—examine the grass from the point of view of the roots. To do so we will

---

³Thomas Nagel, *What Does It All Mean?: A Very Short Introduction to Philosophy* (New York: Oxford University Press, 1987). The quotation is from page 8.

need a shovel. At the outset we can let the progress of the digging take its course, subject only to the contingencies of the excavation site: a boulder here that can't be moved; a tree there whose roots are too big and strong to be cut through by the shovel. But at least initially there's so much to find that giving ourselves over to contingency should be no impediment to fruitful shovelry. We will, however, have to be careful of the rhetoric of shovelry. There must be no pretence that shovelric inscription is any less contingent than the activity of inscription it inscribes. In particular, the voice of pure reason does not speak through the shovel. Rather, the contingent recovery of artifacts allows the provisional reconstruction of the system of contingencies in terms of which the artifacts are to be understood. Some preliminary reconstruction can be done in the field, but most will have to be done in the laboratory, where the unearthed artifacts will be hermeneutered more thoroughly.

As we take shovel in hand, our familiarity with the turf will help turn up the artifacts. On the other hand, our very familiarity with the turf is itself one of the controlling contingencies. We are no doubt predisposed to exhibit certain artifacts and ignore others.

All this unearthed detritus, contingent and problematic on the one hand, emblematic on the other, may not indicate any coherent underlying culture. But in the spirit of narrative lust common to archaelogists we should at least try to put together a story that "fits." Underdetermination and overdetermination being what they are, we can make no definitive claim to the uniqueness of our story. Perhaps the entertainment value of the story can be its excuse.

There is no reason, though, why we can't make the story an organized one. The pattern of organization is equally a story of contingency, but, then, what isn't? It will serve in the way all models serve: namely, it will make things very familiar to us sufficiently unfamiliar that we'll be able to see them.

The unearthed artifacts can be organized in a phase space with four axes. Each of the axes is a segment of a historical trajectory. Our ability to construct these four axes is a contingent benefit of our vantage point. Each axis is a synchronic "Poincaré section" of a complex diachronic process. The first is called "theology." The second is called "science." The plane they define is called by some "truth," and by others "legitimacy," where "legitimacy" refers to the authority of the sayer of sooth.

The third axis is called "discipline." The fourth is called "education." The plane these two axes define is called "curriculum." Similarly, the plane defined by "theology" and "education" is called "ethos"; that defined by "theology" and "discipline" is called "ontology"; that defined by "science" and "discipline" is called "credentialization"; and that defined by "science" and "education" is called "political economy" somewhat to the surprise of science educaters. "Liberalism" and "Humanism" are (frequently conjoined) constraints on the phase space.

LOW QUACKS

Many artifacts wander about this four-dimensional phase space, which is correspondingly very large. As an approximative simplification we will begin by exploring only a part of that space as potential locations for our unearthed artifacts, namely, that part that can roughly be identified as "twentieth-century Anglo-American philosophy," insofar as it can be simultaneously identified as "analytic philosophy." This will produce certain distortions we will need to straighten out. Those who think of themselves as analytic philosophers think of themselves with pride, hence will be pleased to be singled out for special attention.[4]

Twentieth-century Anglo-American philosophy seems to have embarrassing problems with its origins. These origins are in the sacred texts offered for unearthment by the apprentice. When we date those texts, we find that some derive from the early Enlightenment and some derive from earlier periods. On the other hand, the canonical readings of the sacred texts all date from the early Enlightenment. The early Enlightenment is the period when the balance of intellectual power shifted from religious to secular culture. Now this transition (never fully completed, of course) involved two valorizations: that of *homo oeconomicus*; and that of science as

---

[4]The phase space defined here is adequate to situate phenomena such as analytic philosophy that are rooted in the Enlightenment. Phenomena rooted in the nineteenth century fit badly or not at all in this space. That is, recent Hegelianisms, Marxisms or Marxianisms, and post-Nietzscheanisms must be thoroughly bowdlerized to be made available here. Interestingly, serious pragmatisms such as Dewey's fit badly in this space, but recent appropriaters of the epithet "pragmatism" in the age of Rorty fit well. Similarly, the early Frankfurt School doesn't fit, but the later neo-Kantian hand-waving of Habermas fits well—hence its availability for "reapproachment" with the "analytic tradition." Finally, "structuralism" is a very mixed bag, but the key figure, Lévi-Strauss, again an explicit neo-Kantian, fits well. In this sense, "post-structuralists" can be thought of as dismantling the phase space constructed here.

the locus of legitimated and legitimating discourse. This double valorization set the truth trajectory for the "secular" wing of Anglo-American philosophy for the succeeding three hundred years. The issue, briefly put, is to replace the god-legitimater of truth by a secular (quasi-secular, pseudo-secular) equivalent, that is, to accept the canon of legitimation from the older theological tradition, but to reject the traditional executor of the canon in favor of a scientific or quasi-scientific executive power effecting a pseudo-secularization of a sacred function.

It is in pursuit of this transition that in this century analytic philosophers elected themselves nightwatchmen on nonsense patrol and have tried to police intellectual discourse against potential invaders of secular culture. This police function has proceeded largely through coalition with scientific discourse, logical empiricism being the most obvious example of this coalition. But there are two interpenetrating reasons why the philosophy/science coalition is unstable. These exhibit themselves as stresses at interplanar junctions.

The first stress is that the *conception of the philosophical task* adopted by the nightwatchmen *looks* as if it comes from the same roots as do canons of scientific responsibility. But this is an illusion. The role of the nightwatchman derives from the role of the *propaganda fides*, the defense of the faith against heterodoxy and heresy. While there are obscuring factors at play, we can still manage to distinguish the role of intradiscursive criticism in the hands of certified and competent scientists from the role of the nightwatchman. The main mark of distinction is that the nightwatchmen are *not* credentialized.[5]

This brings us to the second reason for the instability of the science/philosophy coalition. The role of the nightwatchman must constitute a distinct niche in the intellectual division of labor. If it does not, then philosophy disappears as an autonomous discipline or field and is dissolved into the other disciplines as part of a normal critical activity. For philosophy as an institution, with boundaries, autonomy, and self-credentialization, requires that the domain of its activity be disjunct from that of the other disciplines. The desperate attempt of Anglo-American philosophy to maintain this domain creates extraordinary stress. One of the most illuminating examples of the stress is the following.

---

[5]This fact ought to be considered in the light of the credentialization of some of the eminent forebears of the tradition, Russell, Whitehead, and Frege, who were all serious mathematicians. It ought also to be considered in light of the changing curricular patterns of not only the American universities but also Oxford and Cambridge.

The classical Cartesian treaty between religious and secular intellectual life was enabled by the convenient soul/body dualism available within Christianity. The dualism allowed thinkers of the classical period to hammer out a division of labor that has remained more or less stable to this day: body is the province of science; soul (and eventually mind) the province of theology or its surrogates. It has to be noticed, of course, that the stability of the division of labor is challenged from the right, center, and left. From the right (and almost exclusively in America) there are those who want the treaty annulled. The creationists are the best example of such an attitude. From the left, Marxian theory, properly understood, rejects the terms of the treaty by rejecting the dualism it rests on.

These two challenges to the division of labor are obvious and expectable. The third challenge, from the center, is also inevitable. Scientific materialism sought to *reduce* the entire field of cognizable objects to those of science, asserting its totalized hegemony over the ontological plane. The eventually canonical version of this view, twentieth-century logical positivism, continued by asserting an internal reductionism, so that "body" is eventually to be understood in terms of whatever ontological reduction base physicists have unearthed at a particular time.

Now the analytic philosophers could easily reject both challenges to the dualistic division of labor from the extremes. Neither the reassertion of religious totalization nor the Marxian alternative is given credence (because they are outside the phase space). But the challenge from the center had to be dealt with, for it is well within the phase space, and, if it succeeded, autonomous philosophy would disappear, to be replaced by the constituted first-order sciences as the only legitimated intellectual activities. Indeed, some near-positivists such as Quine seem almost willing to have philosophy disappear. Yet we can't fail to notice the space left by the radical distinction between logical and empirical truths, recreating a dualism internal to the "scientific" enterprise, hence a quasi-autonomy for philosophers-as-logicians.

However, for those desiring a higher degree of autonomy, and not willing to reduce philosophy to formal logic, especially in its extensionalist form, some version of the old division of labor, somehow expressed, is the only live option—hence the disconcerting re-emergence of "Cartesianisms." Now these "Cartesianisms" never show up in the classic form anymore. They are more likely to show up as assertions that intensionality is ineradicable (thus blocking the move to philosophy as the domain of extensional logic), and that all cognition is linguistically mediated. This latter assertion insures a radical discontinuity between the linguistically competent and the rest of "nature." Culture is conceived of as the realm of language. Mind is linguistic and irreducible to the nonlinguistic. (*Homo Loquax* is irreducibly autonomous.) This strategic combination undeniably has its force in polemic with positivism. The reductionism essential for the success of the positivist program was never plausibly completed in any case, and it isn't very difficult to conduct successful border skirmishes against its pretensions. A side benefit of the strategy is that philosophical *activity* at the borders is interminable. As long as there are positivists and anti-positivists (in whatever guise happens to be current) vying against one another in the field, the game goes on.

Peculiar difficulties arise within this polemic, however. For the path of legitimation of both polemical combatants leads back to the old alliance between science and philosophy, which now turns out to be a two-edged sword. If the options are confined to reductive positivism and its quasi-dualistic rejection, then only the positivists have access to any advances the sciences may make with respect, say, to an understanding of the biological roots of linguistic competence. Such advances must be *delegitimated* by philosophers as a source of answers to questions about linguistic competence as those questions arise in a philosophical discourse asserted to be autonomous. Thus neurophysiology, for example, has to be either treated as a reduction base for linguistic phenomena normally articulated in the philosophical discourse (perhaps rebaptized as "folk psychology") or else rejected as irrelevant. But if the latter option is chosen, where has the science/philosophy alliance gone? What is the source of legitimation for the autonomous discourse? Science moves on; philosophy marches in place, prevented by its aspirations for autonomous credentialization from availing itself of its legitimation base.

Well, there are two possible moves. The first is to search beyond the boundaries of analytic philosophy for new sources of legitimation, perhaps phenomenology. But in its foundationalist versions phenomenology is all too subject to criticism, and in its nonfoundationalist forms all too weak. The second alternative is to pick and choose among the bits of science and bits of phenomenology to be deployed. This is the strategy of the analytic philosophers of the "ordinary language" persuasion. Arguments put forward by this tribe tend to wind back to linguistic intuitions as their quasi-phenomenological fundament. We (in the halcyon days of the theory) were continually enjoined to decide what one would say in such and such circumstances—or, in the quasi-secularized version, what "we" would say. We must be sure to remember that this move had to be performed in the context of an autonomous philosophical discourse, so the questions "Who are we?" and "Why would we say that?" had perforce to be rejected as illegitimate.

This strategy has an honored founding father. We can imagine apprentice archaeologists of an earlier age unearthing some truly amazing artifacts. At some gestative stage of the modern philosophical fashion G. E. Moore, the Prince Myshkin of philosophy, dramatically raised his hand in front of his face (and presumably that of his students) and solemnly proclaimed its reality. Among the immortal words he uttered on that or a similar occasion were these:

> I think, therefore, that in the case of all kinds of "things," which are such that if there is a pair of things, both of which are of one of these kinds, or a pair of things one of which is of one of them and one of them of another, then it will follow at once that there are some things to be met with in space, it is true also that if I can prove that there are a pair of things, one of which is one of these kinds and another of another, or a pair both of which are of one of them, that I shall have proved *ipso facto* that there are at least two "things outside of us." That is to say, if I can prove that there exist now both a sheet of paper and a human hand, I shall have proved that there are now "things outside of us," etc.; and similarly I shall have proved it, if I can prove that there exist now two sheets of paper, or two human hands, or two shoes, or two socks, etc. Obviously, then, there are thousands of different things such that, if, at any time, I can prove any one of them, I shall have proved the existence of things outside of us. Cannot I prove any of these things?[6]

Additional text has been unearthed within which we can follow these lucubrations for hundreds of pages. Laying aside the infantile parolysis, when Moore waved his hand in front of his nose he provided a transcendental (though not transcendent) argument to the effect that, if he could prove both his hand and his ass to exist, then he could commodiously scratch his ass.

[6]"Proof of an External World," in *Philosophical Papers* (New York: Collier, 1962), pp. 143–144.

The strangest feature of Moore's "proof" is that it was introduced into the one and only discursive practice where it could fail—the practice of pure philosophizing in the omnipresence of skepticism. *Outside* such a philosophical practice, Moore's manual gesticulations have quite another impact. A vast range of fundamental practices rests on the reality of our hands. A defense of common sense is, above all, the legitimation and celebration of such practices and can be defeated only by discrediting the practical activities of those who use their hands. Outside Moore's own discursive practice, his wave of the hand would have to be taken as the lamentable sign of the onset of senility. But inside his practice the wave is a gesture of futile impotence. Inside his practice the skeptic always has the last move. So the answer to Moore's plaintive concluding question is, within his discourse, no. Or, to be precise, given its tortured formulation, yes.

This suggests that the key question in situating a view in the phase space is "Where do arguments terminate?" And this has to be taken as a question of beginnings, not a question of origins. For we can *unearth* the sought-for termination points independently of the mythology of rational origins. It is *characteristic* of the Cartesian discourse that arguments end in the assertion of authority for intuitions of one sort or another. Concomitantly, a methodology of analysis is constructed or presupposed. Analysis then consists in the rearrangement of cognitive space so that it can be seen as exhausted by an array of intuitions (of whatever sort have been put into play on the local field). Analytic philosophy began in hot pursuit of the "logical atoms" or the "sense data," "qualia," etc., that were to be both the results of rigorous analysis (hence the appellation "analytic philosophy") and the legitimated foundational intuitions. No candidate emerging within the practice fared very well. Largely in consequence of this failure, the practice took a linguistic turn. In the age of the linguistic turn, intuitions are characteristically couched in appeals to "what *we* would say," or, more rarely, what *we* do say. Thus, for example, *we* were told (in a classic instance) that persons are those entities to whom *we* ascribe P-predicates.

It took surprisingly long for someone to point out the obvious. This answer begs to be questioned. Who are *we*? Under what conditions do *we* do this ascribing? Why do *we* do it? How did *we* learn to do it? Are madmen included among the *we*? But these questions are all outside the canonical discourse and barred by the closure rules governing the discourse.

We (for example, the *we* who ascribe P-predicates) are not historically imbedded *we*'s, genetically constituted in a life of learning and sensuous experience. *We* are the *we* of Cartesian abstraction, cognitive minimalists scrupulously confining ourselves to the certain foundations upon which the rational reconstruction must rest. Unfortunately, as we *all* know, this "*we*" is perpetually threatened with truncation to the Cartesian "I". The language of the rational reconstruction is everywhere and always locked inside the always potentially solipsistic ego. In contrast, the language of the historical constitution of *we* explains us, insofar as we currently understand ourselves as practical sojourners in a difficult but negotiable world. It does so in a way that allows that nominative and the accusative to replace one another freely as grammar dictates. It is a language utterly unsuitable for the rational reconstruction of *we*.

The pseudo-foundational status of our linguistic intuitions—except perhaps with respect to moral judgment—was inherently unstable, even arbitrary. There are those who retain their unshaken faith in such termination points for philosophical reflection, but there is an air of arrested development about them these days, even in the nostrils of sympathizers. More frequently, nowadays, the magic of natural selection is invoked as the generative background of philosophical truth.[7] That is, our linguistic intuitions have been forged in the crucible of (natural and social) survival and have their legitimacy in their sheer presence. Call our talk of minds and culture "folk psychology" if you will, but this folk psychology is and has been the successful mediater of interpersonal existence for a long time.

So the lot is cast with Darwin. This seems a safe enough strategy. No commitment has to be made to the particulars of a Darwinian, or neo-Darwinian, program. Only the shining promise of the soundness of adaptationism need be invoked. By now there is an air of commonsensicality about the adaptationist picture, if it isn't pursued too rigorously. And of course a philosopher would never do that. To the apprentices it can be made to sound like the reaffirmation of the coalition with science; but no commitment ever need be made to any serious science.

Now our only task here is to provide a story that will account for the artifacts encountered by the apprentice archaeologists. So we could leave this segment of the saga right here without worrying about its eventual outcome. But it's worth noticing how unstable the adaptationist story is as

---

[7]Hence the emergence of an "evolutionary epistemology" industry in the last few years.

an account of the reliability of our linguistic intuitions when these have such an important role to play in holding together all the dimensions of the philosophical phase space. First of all, of course, there is the misfortune that totalized adaptationism is itself under attack within biology. So the philosopher wanting to avail himself of the theory is stuck either with betting that the outcome of the current debate within biology will fall out his way (and perhaps lending whatever discursive powers he has to the side of the adaptationists) or with lapsing into the old-style rationalism that still attracts him so and trying to provide an *a priori* defense of adaptationism. Neither strategy is very comfortable. Moreover, the game is probably not worth the candle, for the only version of adaptationism that will validate the intuitions at the root of epistemology or ethics is an *optimizing* one underwriting the *necessity* for the survival of *just* those intuitions the philosopher discerns in himself. Anything less will result in no more than the claim that the intuitions in question, held at the time they are held, are *at least not inconsistent, at least so far*, with survival. And not very much follows from that.

The flirtation with Darwinism does, however, epitomize analytic philosophy's uncomfortable situation within, or beside, the legitimated discourses of science. If the epistemological lucubrations of philosophy are to have their old authority as foundations of science, then they must have foundational legitimacy; and this necessarily locates the philosophical discourse outside science, yet close enough to it so that science can protect it from a relapse into an alliance with theology.[8] For a while, the hope of eventual success for a canonical rationalism or empiricism buoyed the hopes of those who desired a "first among equals" relationship with the sciences. With the disappearance of these hopes, philosophy has wavered insecurely between the old theological agenda and subsidence into the sciences themselves. Nietzsche saw the emergence of this uncomfortable stance perfectly well and availed himself of its instability to attack the old theologies and rationalism simultaneously, with the same arguments. Philosophy has also proved to be extremely vulnerable to twentieth-century versions of the Nietzschean attack, most recently pursued by Derrida and Foucault.

For both Nietzschean reasons and reasons generated internally as the

---

[8]Here the narrowness of our field of exploration becomes particularly obvious, for we cannot fail to be aware of the present philosophical "scene" in which every presupposition of the preceding sentence is challenged.

analytic philosophers play king-of-the-hill with one another, the foundationalist pretentions have been laid aside. But the more scrupulous practitioners have noticed that as the foundationalist pretentions go, so do *necessity, a priorism*, and the *autonomous discourse of philosophy*. Intuitions as starting points become contingent. People begin to talk of relativism—perhaps even of *robust* relativism. This move requires a specification of that to which relativisitic knowledge is relativized and a robust account of robustness. Where are these specifications and accounts to be found? If they are to be found *within* the scientific discourses, then the freedom of the philosopher to pick and choose the bits of science to accept must be forsworn. The autonomy of philosophy is dissipated and dispersed throughout the scientific community upon which the philosophers find themselves dependent.

Alternatively, the specifications and accounts necessary for the grounding of relativism and robustness may be looked for *outside* the sciences. And where, in this day and age, might that be? Philosophers willing to think of themselves as theologians of a sort can avail themselves of the power of long-honored tradition. Analytic philosophers have no option but to create tradition out of a canonical reading of sacred texts—those of Locke, Berkeley, Hume, and Kant in particular. For the short period during which the analytic philosophers were hegemonic in their academic fastnesses, this strategy succeeded. But success was temporary. Examination of the canonical texts by readers not already committed to the canonical reading shows that in every case legitimacy is claimed on the basis of continuity with science, theology, or both.

In the end, the analytic philosopher has no *legitimate* ground to stand on as he tries to drive the apprentices away from their accumulated common knowledge to another more foundational program. Apologies and Meditations reveal themselves as the disciplinary instruments of an elite trying to recruit acolytes. Yet this is one of the most fundamental reasons for their reliable availability to apprentices. For it can now be urged that the omnipotentiality of skepticism puts all cognitive activity in the same boat. Everyone is equally at sea with the philosophers. In classrooms where they study other disciplines, a different story is being told the apprentices. How do philosophers imagine apprentices adjudicate the discrepancies?

DISCIPLINE AND PUBLISH

We are here in a position to see yet another way in which the Cartesian discipline is articulated, how the autonomy of philosophy is defended. We are told that there are philosophical questions and there are empirical questions. We are cautioned never to confuse the two. Philosophical questions aim at providing a rational reconstruction. Empirical questions are directed to matters of genesis. This desperate bid for philosophical autonomy occurs at the crashing intersection of all six planes of the philosophical phase space, and the waves it creates oscillate across all six planes. We can watch the waves if we experimentally insert a particular formulation of the autonomy claim into the system and set it to work. The formulation we insert is "Philosophy deals with conceptual problems." These conceptual problems are to be distinguished, of course, from the "empirical" or "first-order" problems dealt with by the constituted sciences. The waves generated by the acceptance of the implied distinction are as follows:

A. *Legitimacy*. If there are distinct conceptual and empirical problems, then it must be decided which has priority. If empirical problems (and their solutions) are prior, then philosophy is parasitic on the constituted sciences, and furthermore it is far from clear why any conceptual issues are not better entrusted to the practitioners of the sciences within which they arise. But if conceptual problems are prior, then some way must be found to evaluate solutions to them, and this evaluation must not rest on any "empirical" findings. Are we now thrown back on the odyssey of linguistic intuitions? Should we seek out extraspelunkian epiphanies?

B. *Ontology*. If philosophy has conceptual problems as its province, and if disciplines must establish the reality of their objects of study, then concepts must be real. If conceptual investigations are to be contrasted sharply with empirical investigations, then concepts cannot be the object of empirical investigation. A first guess would be that analytic philosophy is consequently obliged to adopt some sort of Platonic realism, or some sort of conceptualism parasitic on private access to conceptual contents of minds. The latter accounts for the countless hours spent by analytic philosophers in a search for some canonical reading of the sacred texts of Locke, Berkeley, and Hume on just this issue. Indeed, Platonisms and conceptualisms drift into and through the practice of analytic philosophy;

but they are constantly threatened by practitioners of more spartan ontological intuitions. The consequence is a standing wave, a sinusoidal still-life oscillating year in and year out in the canonical journal literature.

C. *Credentialization*. Eventually, young apprentices in a discipline seek to become masters. Their credentialization must be based upon an objective assessment of their attainments with respect to the subject matter of the discipline. Otherwise the discipline will have no credibility. In the nature of the case, credentialization in philosophy has two parts. The first part has the prospective master pledge allegiance to the canonical reading of the sacred texts and exhibit mastery of that reading. Beyond that is the preparation of the masterpiece. This must fulfill two basic requirements, both of them designed to insure the reproduction of the practice. First, the masterpiece must exhibit conformity with current practice (canvass the relevant journal literature). Second, it must pay homage to the distinction between conceptual and empirical problems and confine itself to the former. All examining credentializers must be allowed the challenge "That isn't philosophy!" and their challenges must be met. In particular, no main contention in the masterpiece may rest on inscriptions established in a scientific discourse (competence in philosophy entails incompetence in everything else). For, if the major contentions of the masterpiece were to rest on empirical findings, then the objective judgment on their merit would rest with a discipline other than philosophy, and autonomy would be surrendered. The waves involved here manifest themselves as turbulence at the boundaries of the container. Departments that have let their vigilance slip enough to be faced with masterpieces at or outside the boundaries of the purely conceptual are extremely unhappy ones.

D. *Ethos*. If concepts are suitably distinct from the empirical, then they must be timeless. Any apparent historical conceptual fluctuations must be thought of in terms of successive approximations to clear conceptualization. Ethoi are historical, the consequence of education and upbringing on the basis of theological truth. Such ethoi must be rejected in favor of a purified, timeless system of conceptualization of ourselves, others, and interpersonal relations. These, not some ethos, form the rational matrix of our lives. Kant, the genius of the philosophical phase space, is never out of earshot. In the end, as a recent theorist has argued, we can be moral only if we don't know who we are.

E. *Curriculum*. There isn't much to add here that can be made to look much different from what we have already seen. No books can be written that do not allow of a reading independent of empirical truth. This means that the core of the philosophy curriculum must always be organized around the traditional interminable debates. "Philosophies" of this or that are grudgingly tolerated but must remain marginalized in the hands of practitioners whose purity is suspect. For example, a philosophy of science course is legitimately part of the curriculum to the degree that it avoids science in favor of "conceptual issues," that is, issues of standard metaphysics and epistemology. Philosophy of science was in better odor under the positivists. For in their hands, at least, attention to science itself honored their allegiances, and philosophy of science courses gave them a place to hide their metaphysics.

Similar remarks can be made about philosophy of the social sciences. Recent developments have created serious waves. Positivism went into eclipse partly because of internal criticism to the effect that "conceptual" and "empirical" issues could not be clearly demarcated. This has spawned a generation of philosophers of science who insist on doing their philosophy of science *within* the boundaries of one or another of the sciences. Analytic philosophers are extremely uncomfortable about this situation and are finding it increasingly difficult to discipline their students to the purity of ignorance required by conceptual analysis. Fortunately for the analytic philosophers, learning science is hard work, and they can find acolytes among the lazy. Yet, increasingly, every new wave of entering students is harder to keep under control than the last. The oscillations at the boundaries of the philosophical curriculum are among the most destabilizing forces currently perturbing the system.

F. *Political Economy.* This plane, defined by science and education, has received little direct attention in this essay so far. It contains two major attracters for events primarily located on the curriculum plane: technology and commodification. These can be informally amalgamated as the requirements for provision of marketable skills. First, the newer technologies of education press toward the quantitative evaluation of "the attainment of skills," and the technocrats can't see why some suitable quantitative criteria can't be applied to philosophical training. But success with respect to conceptual problems is not readily susceptible to quantitative evaluation. Nonetheless, the attempt must be made. So, drawn to this attracter by its desire for collegial respect, philosophy is led first to valorize "the ability to reason." Since this ability is "objectively" evaluable only in terms of the frequency of avoiding mistakes, philosophy is led to prioritize logic—formal and informal—in its curriculum, especially its service curriculum. Indeed, many departments in public universities have found a place in the political economy by administering "critical thinking" requirements and, in some cases, virtually spawning a semi-autonomous subfaculty for this purpose within their department walls.

The second attempted insertion of philosophy into the political economy is, of course, "applied ethics," currently the most thriving of all the philosophical industries. Operating as it does under the constraints of liberal humanism (of which more below), philosophy must maneuver very cleverly to preserve its conceptual purity while applying itself. The *concept* of rights, for example, must be applied to the *concept* of business in order to clarify the junction of the two *concepts*. You wouldn't think that activities of this sort would be acceptable commodities in the society that spawns them, but that couldn't be more wrong. There are enormous benefits to be gained from a circulating discourse of rights skipping without closure from business to law to the environment to medicine. The illusion of reflective criticism, so important to liberalism, can be maintained without fear of a penetration of this critical discourse into the world of business, medicine, environmental movements, etc. Analytic philosophy is a prime ideological defender of the end of ideology. Its self-conception admirably suits it for such a role.

WITHIN THESE HOLLOWED HOLES

The fate of analytic philosophy lies entirely within the academic division of labor. Thus this context must be examined more closely. To be founded as a discipline, an investigative activity must be able to identify a reasonably well delimited group of objects, events, and phenomena with which it will be concerned exclusively. It must also adopt an array of research strategies well enough circumscribed to allow at least provisional decisions about what counts as activity within the discipline and what doesn't. Finally, the normal discipline (as normalized) must contain critical norms that allow investigative activity to be judged successful or unsuccessful.

The current importance of the alliance of a discipline with the established sciences cannot be overestimated. An early excavation in the peat bog of curriculum provides illustrative artifacts. A faculty curriculum committee is found confronted with the following scenario. A liberal arts college has devised a "distribution" system of the usual sort, categories of courses are defined, and students are required to take a sampling of courses from each of the categories in order to qualify for the degree. Not surprisingly, one of the categories devised is "Natural Science" and another is "Social Science." The boundaries between them are established by an initial decision to adhere to departmental lines and, in the university in question, to *divisional* lines, where the three divisions are Natural Science, Social Science, and Humanities. Nearly immediately petition is made to readjust the boundaries. In particular, requests are made by the Geography Department to have physical geography included in the Natural Science category and by the Anthropology Department to have physical anthropology included in the Natural Science category.

Hearings are held. Reasons are offered for the proposed inclusions. Reasons are offered against. Data are marshalled. The professor of physical geography introduces grade sheets demonstrating a distribution of grades more characteristic of the natural sciences than the social sciences. He offers depositions from his students to the effect that they have worked as hard in the physical geography course as they normally do in a natural science course (and, *sotto voce*, much harder than they normally do in a social science—let alone humanities—course). The anthropologists exhibit the pundit squares and other mathematical objects that figure in the physical anthropology course. Rigor is avowed. Essential continuity with recognized natural science is emphasized. Interdisciplinary connections with recognized sciences are exhibited. Decisions in other universities are unearthed and offered as precedent and (given the prestige of these other universities) authorization.

Is the curriculum committee being asked to *discover* the true nature of the academic division of labor? Is it being asked to define "science"? Is the act of defining an act of discovery? A sovereign decree? What are the unmistakable signs of a science? Of *any* "discipline"?

These questions are especially acute as philosophy departments attempt to succeed in the normal academic terms. The terms of success are, in the end, reputation and growth. Here we will deal primarily with growth. This will skew our discussion toward the philosophy department in its role within the undergraduate program. Reputation is relevant only at the "higher" levels of graduate student recruitment and the pursuit of "glory by association" in faculty recruitment. There are, however, two ways in which reputation affects growth. First, a department's resources may be skewed toward its best undergraduate majors, who will be sent on to graduate schools as ambassadors of reputation. This will affect course offerings, hence workload. Second, workload is also sensitive to reputation. Philosophers who successfully sport a wide reputation can cut down the number of students they need to see in a semester, as well, of course, as the number of sections they have to teach.

Keeping in mind the potential adjustments implied by the preceding remarks, it can be said that growth within the academic marketplace is managed in a rather straightforward way. Increased numbers of students argue for increased faculty. Now there is a crucial distinction to be made between colleges and universities that have a substantial philosophy requirement and those that don't. Further, in those places where a substantial philosophy requirement exists, it is important to know how stable the presence of the requirement is. An assessment of these stability conditions is quite complex. Some examples: Does the college think of itself as offering "a strong liberal arts education"? If so, the presence of philosophy requirements is probably stable, and the philosophers will probably have virtually complete control over curriculum. In contrast, if the liberal arts part of an average student's education is only a half-hearted nod to breadth, then the philosophy department will have to work to maintain its place among the liberal arts requirements. A certain sign of erosion is the clumping of philosophy with a number of other options, for example, in "a humanities elective." In such a case a philosophy department really has little autonomy with respect to curriculum and will find itself skewing its curriculum in the direction of courses where its disciplinary distinction is least: the "service" courses, the "philosophies of . . . ," the "applied ethics" and "critical thinking" courses.

From what social strata do the students come? What are their typical aspirations? What are their likely trajectories independent of aspiration? Analytic philosophy survives with purity in high prestige institutions catering to a social elite. Philosophy is and ever has been the province of an intellectual elite with the time to spare from day-to-day affairs. This intellectual elite is best served in the maintenance of its distinction, not by useful knowledge, but precisely by useless knowledge, dialectically made useful as a mark of elite distinction. The apprentices from the social elite don't mind being Kermitically deconstructed at the outset of their philosophical careers. Indeed, having the leisure to be so deconstructed is another mark of distinction for them. In addition, of course, the promise of ultimate arrival at intellectual superiority is one that reinforces their already exalted self-conceptions. So the colleges and universities of the upper crust offer just the space analytic philosophy needs to reproduce its system of autonomy. Philosophy in these settings is well buffered from challenges in every dimension of the phase space. In particular, of course, the attracters in the political economic plane attract weakly or not at all in such a setting.

In contrast, in universities and colleges with a student body that is learning to damp its aspirations and to settle into the middle of the middle class, every source of instability will perturb the place of philosophy in the curriculum. In such places growth will occur, if at all, at the margin.

Where is the power among the faculty? Does it reside in the sciences and social sciences? These are embattled days for the humanities, and virtually everywhere philosophy is lumped into this division. If the humanities are weak in faculty circles, then traditional arguments about educational breadth and the values of liberal education will not be strong enough to support the growth of philosophy departments. In such circumstances, there is a temptation to court the favor of the sciences and social sciences by acceding to their claims to superior seriousness and legitimacy. This, however, is a dangerous strategy, for it puts into play all the ambiguities of legitimacy we have already seen. Philosophy may persuade a faculty of its scientific superiority to the literature folks, but it may equally well fall short and be subject to the charge of pretending to what it cannot attain. Given the philosophical phase space, there is no reliable way this charge can be rebutted.

Furthermore, it must be realized that the attainment of respect from colleagues in another discipline has two dimensions that must be managed carefully. The first dimension is safe and preferable: the compilation of a long bibliography. It obviously doesn't matter whether the published work is of high quality. Indeed, given the chronic lack of closure in philosophy, it is virtually impossible to make reliable judgments of quality in any case. It may, however, matter *where* the work is published. At any moment there is always a rough aura of respectability surrounding the "leading journals in the field," and this aura lingers independent of what these journals have been publishing in their recent past. If colleagues in other disciplines somehow come to have a sense, of whatever sort, of the "leading journals," then the philosophers are bound by that sense irrespective of its grounds.

Often, for example, when college or university evaluations of departments take place, "outside" experts are called in. All departments know that the careful selection of the outside expert is essential for control over the evaluation process. The department wants its own conception of its place in the university and discipline to be ratified. This outcome normally can be managed.

This circulation of outside examiners is going on all the time, driven by the credentializing bureaucracies. It has effects on all six planes of the phase space. Its primary effect is the stabilization of orthodoxy. For the outside experts are useless unless they are credible. Their credibility depends either on their affiliation with an elite institution or on their visible established reputation in the core of the field. Affiliation and reputation are a function of orthdoxy. This system has allowed relatively orthodox analytic philosophy to maintain a decently stable existence in colleges and universities where all the other conditions for its stability (some of which are sketched above) are lacking. Thus the standard range of artifacts is distributed to a wider range of apprentices than would otherwise be possible.

In addition, during earlier waves of immigration, universities (like the old CCNY) were able to teach philosophy within the scope of the Ellis Island model of higher education. The immigrants brought cultural sensitivities from the old country and social aspirations that they connected with the necessity of becoming fluent in the high culture of their new world. Those days have ended. The current Ellis Island equivalents bring us immigrants who have judged American culture more accurately than their predecessors did. They know that high culture is a useless veneer and aim precisely at the technical and business skills they know to be the real key to success. A philosophy course, for them, is an annoying interruption of their march to affluence.

LIBERAL HUMANISM

We must now examine the constraints on the phase space, for this will allow us to understand a last unearthed artifact. Philosophical apprentices encounter long pages and long hours of ethical discourse—talk of rights, duties, utility, maxims, egos, and intuitions. In these days ethical discourse is very likely to circulate in the context of medical concerns (patients' rights, doctors' duties, etc.) or in the context of the world of business. We have seen that these contexts have been created precisely to attract apprentices to the philosophical site.

Apprentices approach the artifact of ethical discourse with some trepidation, of course. Are these folks really going to change their lives? The way they think? The way they maneuver through the jungles of job, marriage, family, and (a recent fave) death? Are they going to be shaken from their laissez-faire narcissism? So they pick up and handle the artifact "moral discourse" very gingerly. What are they going to have to make believe in order to write the term paper or pass the final? But they need not fear. Trepidation soon turns to relief. The artifact in the apprentices' hands is an anthological supermarket of silly ideas. Kant said this; Plato said that; Butler held that so and so; Hume believed whatever; Mill maintained that such and such; Rawls urged us to assume such and such a position (at least initially).

Each savant has definitive answers to all the others. Each knows why each of the others is wrong. As the shelves of the supermarket scroll by, even narcissistic laissez faire has its place (in the junk food section, but that's no problem). To pass the final, apprentices need only catalogue the contents of the shelves and, perhaps, remember some of what was on the labels. *Hedonism may be bad for your health; trees have rights; be careful, you never know who you may be tomorrow; eat, drink, and be merry, but leave enough so your grandchildren can eat, drink, and be merry.*

It is from their dominant culture that apprentices have learned to walk into the classroom bearing some version of narcissistic laissez faire as their solemn tribute to the life of the market and the rhetoric of democratic equality.[9] The apprentices have learned not to be "judgmental," not to hold others to whatever standards of behavior they may have (mysteriously) come up with for themselves. Toleration raised to the level of institutionalized indifference is the pride of the American adolescent newly come to sophisticated maturity. This constitution of the apprentices is the condition for the appearance of artifacts to them.

The rules of the pedagogical game "moral discourse," rules imposed by liberal humanism, are kind to the acquired attitudes of the apprentices. The humanist contribution is to rule out an appeal to a theological ground

---

[9] A range of laissez-faire narcissisms is explored in Robert Bellah et al., *Habits of the Heart* (Berkeley: University of California Press, 1985), where the range is lamented and various feckless alternatives bravely offered.

for moral principles. This is essential. Atheists can't be closed out, for they tend to be numerous in the environs of modern intellectual life. Furthermore, modern western democracies grudgingly allow atheists free run of social space. This tolerance is not absolutely stable. The atheists have to offer their trust in god every time they pay for something in dollars. But atheists get good at ignoring this condition of their involvement in economic life. Moreover, a theological grounding for moral principles would require a decision between theologies, a decision that modern pluralist societies cannot afford to make. An attempt has to be made to burrow beneath the particulars of particular theologies for the "human commonalities" shared by us all and available as shared "premises" of the moral life. We have no ethos, so our ethics has to try and get along without one. We do have a species. So we try to work with humanism. Theologians, pet lovers, and defenders of the rights of trees will have to struggle at the margin of this humanism. Small price to pay.

Now we fold liberalism, contributor of canons of toleration, individualism, and economism, into the humanist synthesis. Here we have the main source of the interminability of moral discourse. For liberalism enjoins us to respect all reasonable participants in the moral debate and to respect all opinions in the name of free inquiry. It forbids closure on moral discourse short of the establishment and demonstration of a pathology of either participants or opinions. (Only the rational need apply.) It then questions the criteria of pathology. (The irrational share our humanity.) It focuses on "rights" as the fundamental moral category and bars closure on potential bearers of rights and the rights they can bear. Pets and trees find their way back in. (They share our life). Liberalism opens spaces humanism seemed to have closed.[10]

In this, its traditional project of liberation, liberalism liberates us from all stable moral judgment and (as McIntyre and others have pointed out) from any stable moral practices. As a consequence it ecumenically empowers every conceivable subcategory of being to compete in the political supermarket for the assignment of special rights. It doles out special treatment on an infinite moral bankroll, incidentally empowering its critics to perpetuate their repressive agenda by managing the bankroll. It is no trick, these days, for the critics of liberalism to demonstrate the

---

[10]Thoughts of this kind about orthodox analytic ethics are not unique to me. See, for example, "On Transforming the Teaching of Moral Philosophy" by Kai Nielsen, *APA Newsletter on Teaching Philosophy*, November 1987.

absurdities of the infinite moral bankroll. Liberalism is helpless to reply. It cannot even make an appeal to history, for history disappears for the liberal in favor of a free-standing blueprint—utilitarian or deontological by turns—but in either case ungrounded. Meanwhile, we may recall, the apprentices are struggling to discern how this differs from their own laissez-faire narcissism.

Liberalism cannot avoid these consequences in the pedagogical and political arenas. Closure on moral discourse entails foreclosure on liberalism itself. Closure on moral discourse is an appeal to moral truth of some kind or other, and liberalism vows to put all such truths into question, that is, to withdraw closure from the debate about their truth. If closure begins to appear with respect to some such truths, then the debate must shift to an examination of the closure conditions, and closure on their acceptance must be withdrawn. As we have seen before, the skepticism must be affirmed to be omnipossible, and here we have the ethico-political roots of this requirement. Just as an autonomous legitimated discourse of philosophical truth must try to squeeze in between theology and science, so must moral discourse float freely between the two.

As this system spins its way endlessly through the circle of moral debate, another coalition is dialectically fulfilled. For, if moral debate were ever to be settled, the philosopher's job would be over. Religions normally secure the employment of their functionaries by insisting upon an ever renewed religious commitment or ever renewed relationship with the godhead. Philosophy can secure the continued employment of its functionaries only by holding moral truth just a tiny bit out of reach. The existence of autonomous philosophy within liberal humanist constraints is inextricably linked to the rejection of ethos. To the ancient question "Can morality be taught?" analytic philosophy must answer "Morality *must not* be taught." Again the analytic philosophers must try to pretend that theology is not an axis of their phase space. Yet the legitimacy of their ethical activity requires that this be the major axis of moral space. Meanwhile, the apprentices can walk out of the final with laissez-faire narcissism intact. Life can go on as before. Nothing has changed. Everything is as normal.

ACKNOWLEDGMENTS

The editors, the editorial board of Penn State Press, and the others responsible for the publication of this essay have been gracious enough to include the surrounding essays as data for further archaeological investigation. These essays, with one or two exceptions, are not dealt with directly in my text, but are provided as exercises for the spade of the reader.

In addition, honesty forces the admission that many of the artifacts upon which this paper are based have been suppressed. These artifacts were collected at meetings of the Greater Philadelphia Philosophy Consortium. A perhaps misplaced delicacy accounts for the suppressions. Genuine gratitude for free Chinese food, graciously offered, also stays my hand.

PANOPTICISM AND POSTMODERN PEDAGOGY

Mary Schmelzer

Panopticon, the Benthamite prison machine, an "architecture transparent to the administration of power, made it possible to substitute for force or other violent constraints the gentle efficiency of total surveillance. . . ."[1] Observation became an efficient means of control by authorities. From a central vantage point, inspection of prisoners was continuous, general, and facile. The panopticon allowed relatively few officials to control large numbers of prisoners by foregrounding both hierarchy and visibility. The panopticism I address here foregrounds neither; it does, however, enable meticulous control over the network of power relations that produce and sustain the truth claims of an institution by means of an economical surveillance. It multiplies and mystifies the visible and centered gaze of

---

[1] Michel Foucault, "Complete and Austere Institutions," in *The Foucault Reader*, ed. Paul Rabinow (New York: Pantheon, 1984), p. 217.

the machine into the countless instances of observation of a mechanism. Its operation is distributed to every body in a system of power relations that constitute an institution. It works pervasively and invisibly. Every *I* in that system becomes an eye that sees what the institution asks it to see, in a request so naturalized that it is often little more than subliminal echo. Panopticism blinds to other ways of seeing and controls gazes and gazers. It most blinds a body to its own objectification, to its having become a site and a sight line. Moreover, panopticism seems to work most efficiently when bodies are set in opposition.

To particularize this discourse I speak of a copy machine and the English seminar room. Both problematize my relationship with my department's administrative assistant in ways that confirm the coercive fix of the surveillant gaze from multiple positions in the web of power relations that constitute the university. But in practice the situation seems simpler. I like this administrative assistant. She brings me coffee when I have been seeing students for uninterrupted hours (a gesture that at the moment it occurs I appreciate, but abhor on principle). She works too many hours meeting too many other people's deadlines for much too little money. The institution is not unwise in asking such a person whose daily needs can only be met by fiscal conservation to ride herd over people who use too many paper clips and file folders. As for the copy machine, I need to use it more frequently than my colleagues. In fact, few classes in my critical theory seminars pass without my offering students something else to read. This, of course, as I am regularly reminded, costs the university money. By spending more than anyone, perhaps everyone else together, I fail to serve the best interests of the university. I am a statistical aberration that the well-intentioned but literal-minded assistant cannot comprehend. A sense of a fiscal norm and the excessive contours her thinking fully; she sees herself an acolyte at the altar of an economy that posits all needs as being equal. What we do in classrooms is a thing called teaching, a self-evident term. To attempt to explain that most of what I ask my students to think about has not yet written itself into anything so coherent as a textbook, or that I cannot always know in December what Stephen Greenblatt will write in January that might be germane to a topic we consider in April, is an exercise in futility. She serves the university well as she husbands its purse and reminds me that I might ask my students to pay for the copies. For my part, I cannot sanction their paying (more than they have already) for what should be a free exchange of ideas. She will not be dismissed, but I must not capitulate and I write a check. My scandalous profligacy has cost me lunch for three days.

The administrative assistant informs me that the English seminar room is to be locked at all times, thus ensuring that the books therein never get into the hands of students who might read them and, perhaps, not return them to their proper places on the shelves. Moreover, the notion that such a space might encourage students to sit around after class and continue a discussion of, say, temporality in *To the Lighthouse* is violative of her agenda. They might leave coffee cups and candy wrappers scattered on the table. Her gaze fixes on order as well as economy. I cannot lock the door, and I receive regular reminders of my transgression. I am cheerful and profess myself hopelessly scatterbrained, a professorial category she can accept as normal. But I never lock the door.

In both of these instances this assistant protects the university from my excesses and impinges on my pedagogy. In small but smarting ways her diligence distances us from each other. While our sometimes frustrating game comes to little, I welcome the constant reminder that this surveillance "is that of a network of relations from top to bottom, but also to a certain extent from bottom to top and laterally; this network 'holds' the whole together and traverses it in its entirety with effects of power that derive from one another: supervisors perpetually supervised. . . ."[2] We—for I am as implicated as she is—meet different needs of the system, see things from different positions: optical elements of panopticism, not blinded, perhaps, but tunnel-visioned eyes. The power network seems to function best when labor and laborers are divided, when each is assigned a site where her gaze is privileged and imperative.

Surveillance monitors and determines pedagogic norms in countless obvious and subtle tactics that delimit classroom activity in profound ways. The uniform length of all semesters and of class hours per credit per semester implies that all intellectual work (can we name for certain what constitutes intellectual work?) is equally accomplished in similar time frames. The shockingly truncated fall semester that ends in mid-December in order for the institution to conserve energy leaves little time for sustained intellectual work from students who must take fifteen credit hours to stay on schedule and avoid the financial burdens of summer sessions or an extra semester. (Notice how here again a norm implies that students learn at the same rate: aberrance is punitively costly.) Professors

---

[2] Foucault, "The Means of Correct Training," ibid., p. 192.

assign research when there is time for none, encouraging cheating and misprision of the scholarly project. Grades must be distributed on a grid that primarily serves the bookkeeping contingencies of the institution. These instances uncover institutional economic exigency as they reflect the lateral gaze of the keepers of the exchequer whose narrow observations enmesh themselves in the tightly knit grid of material coercions and oppositions that panopticism engenders.

Opposition intensifies when one worker comprehends little of the agenda of another. Cheating: "You are only cheating yourself," common lore repeats, but never says of what. Why are students at universities? Don't many of us, on our best or worst days, allow that it might be a happier place without them? Students expect a variety of things from the academy, but mainly they want degrees. And that seems to be what the institution wants for them also. It has developed programs, curricula, requirements that must be met in order that a degree might be earned. But the reasons for the shape of that protocol are only vaguely explained. As hurdles to be leaped over, in many students' minds, any means will do. Ironically, a student who cheats and does not get caught serves the institution as well as one who does his own work—each meets the institutional objective, each can be granted a degree. In the panoptic network, institutional objectives override particular concerns. When there is no heat on the first floor, the man in the boiler room tells me the "system doesn't work that way." The particular need of one person who keeps an extra sweater in her office for students who shiver through conferences matters little in the larger institutional picture. In fact, her need is invisible because the average temperature of the building is 68 degrees. Orchids could grow in the third-floor classrooms. This is not an important issue, but if a biological study requires more time or money than is available, the system does not work that way either.

While architecture proves itself in many ways the enemy of good academic work generally, it is particularly pernicious in a decentered pedagogy. I am certain I am not the only one who has seen desks nailed to the floor in rigid rows, an efficiency move with the janitorial staff in mind who, when the desks are movable and moved, encourage you—with serious notices, material marks of vested power to oversee and judge—to restore order, to normalize the space, to efface the transgression. Nor am I alone in having faced curved tiered rows that form perspective lines to the center of power like those that confirmed James I's sovereignty at Whitehall. The sovereign sees all and all see the sovereign.

It must not go unnoticed that this professorial sovereignty remains a sustaining myth in the academy. At the same time, the equally mythic hypothesis of absolute truth goes largely unchallenged in a network of power relations that control the unwieldy slipperiness of untethered intellectual discourse. This configuration positions the professor at a precarious fulcrum in the network, at once the most seeing and the most seen. She is the paradigmatic guardian of the flame and the individual whose avowed autonomy metonomically signifies the double purpose of the institution—to preserve an embedded knowledge system and to encourage individual intellectual productivity.

What makes this contradictory position possible is the normalizing function of panopticism through which bodies of individuals are distributed along a determined norm. Authority derives from the a priori notions institutionalized power relations create and cede to it. The individual is a carefully monitored creation of these relations. That is to say, networks of power form an endlessly tangled mobius strip that defines, confirms, supports, and polices the truth claims of an institution. As such, they are replete with places that seem specific but are actually endlessly repeated within a closed and covert system. Individuality is rewarded only within the limits of this norm. Tellingly, normative work can be quirky and eccentric. Think of the academic types who frequently are nominated for, or win, teaching awards: slightly edgy, often young, casually dressed, charismatic, ingenious, inventive—all qualities that, on the surface, challenge the norm but, on closer observation, are fully determined by it. In the humanistic university the autonomous subject needs to be preserved, at least on the surface. Teachers are most usually rewarded for method and style. The most successful have found new ways to do old things. Their very particularity announces pedagogic freedom that remains unchallenged only if what they do participates in the economy of the system, only if it preserves its truth claims.

What individuates this individual? The panoptic gaze objectifies the subject, making it a text, an unwieldy collection of file folders united under the aegis of a name. Reports from positions: from students, who note that she graded fairly, knew her material, presented it in a lively and coherent fashion so that students rarely fell asleep, respected their opinions, encouraged discussion, was always prepared and punctual, spoke clearly, and dressed neatly; from colleagues, who value her contributions to faculty discussion, her willingness to cover classes for them, her congeniality and wit; from her department chair, who points to the clarity of her course outlines, the appropriateness of her testing methods, the acuity of her choice of texts, her willingness to serve on committees and oversee undergraduate activities, the punctuality with which she answers memos, fills out book orders, and reports grades; from her dean, who reads all this testimony and knows besides that she has served on the curriculum committee and kept her files up to date.

Every one of these judgments made about the individual is relational and normative and thoroughly inside expectations. Frequently students will take notice of my clothes, the pictures on my office wall, or the books on my shelf. They are either "not at all" or "exactly" what they expected of a professor. These are judgments based on expectations and, as such, only look to see how the individual relates to the norm. They do not scrutinize the unexamined status of those expectations. It has not occurred to them that things are not as self-evident as they seem. But they are not alone in that obliviousness.

By keeping her own file up to the minute, the professor turns her surveillance skills on herself, generating the literal submissions that figure forth her subjection as she anticipates the expectations of the institution. To be singled out for exemplary individuality requires that the subject objectify herself and contour her performance to encourage the accolades of those who fix their gaze on her. She must meet their expectations and confirm the power relations that create a body of knowledge. Foucault explains:

> For a long time ordinary individuality—the everyday individuality of everybody—remained below the threshold of description. To be looked at, to be observed, described in detail, followed from day to day by uninterrupted writing, was a privilege. The chronicle of a man, the account of his life, his historiography, written as he lived out his life, formed part of the rituals of his power. The disciplinary methods reversed this relation, lowered the threshold of describable individuality, and made of this description a means of control and a method of domination. It is no longer a monument for future memory, but a document for possible use.[3]

The vestiges of monument inhabit the concept of individual history enough to keep it an object of desire. The panoptic gaze is, after all, most

---

[3]Foucault, ibid., p. 203.

effective when it is more congratulatory than punitive, most able to produce positive object lessons or objects as lessons. It is, however, continuous and ongoing, serving functions wider than the valorizing of momentous objects. No pedagogic move escapes its scrutiny or observation.

Singling out an individual teacher serves the institution in a number of ways. It mystifies institutional control of product and production, it sustains the myth of professorial sovereignty, and it encourages teachers to work towards the institution's goals. These rewards may satisfy, but tenure, promotion, and merit compensation are the staff of life. So far as they depend on what a person does in a classroom, her careful self-situation in the nexus of power relations is crucial to her survival. She must be seen to be doing what she needs to do in order to garner the nods she needs from every observer. It is here that a postmodern professor (an oxymoronic epithet) whose theoretical bias disowns the truth claims that the institution's power relations make visible is in most peril.

Panoptic gazes underscore her marginality. She cannot profess certainty, so students judge her ill-prepared or incompetent. When she covers for a colleague, she might muddy the waters with inappropriate questions. Her book lists are often noncanonical and possibly not long enough if she, as I am, is asking her students to read less and see their work as other than closing off and summarizing. She confounds the curriculum committee with her insights. She cannot ring a bell-shaped curve. She is not certain about what or how to test, and she frequently asks students for journal accounts of their reading and other responses that seem, from the institution's perspective, impressionistic, intellectually flaccid work that is neither analytic nor definitive. She values collaborative learning that fails to foreground individual accomplishment and generally disturbs the pedagogical underpinnings of the academy's power network. She makes a singularly unappealing text, neither a well-seen nor a productive seer.

Surveillance and examination presuppose the temporal priority of theory over practice, while the performative pedagogy of the postmodern resists this separation. This moment shapes the dilemma. The deviation is not standard. The postmodern theorist exceeds eccentricity and trangresses the norm by questioning the truth claims the system privileges. How can someone, the *I* of this text, for instance, negotiate these troubled waters?

In "Intellectuals and Power" Foucault suggests that the specific intellectual (one who labors in a discrete discursive circumstance in opposition to the traditional universal intellectual whose object is transcendent knowledge) can "sap power in an activity conducted along side those who struggle for power."[4] This strategy allows the intellectual to engage in a struggle to reveal and undermine what is most invisible and insidious in prevailing practices while seeming to use those practices. What he encourages is local resistance to an essentialist agenda, accomplished by continuous critique, showing that things must be reconfigured in uncentered, unclosed, uncomfortable discourses that "show that things are not as self-evident as one believed, to see that that which is accepted as self-evident will no longer be accepted as such. Practicing criticism is a matter of making facile gestures difficult."[5]

But the question remains, how can I resist and survive? How can I use old ways to do new things, move desks and minds around? Uncovering the enabling assumptions of the institution while continuing to work in it demands the chicanery and intellectual rigor of the Derridian double gesture. Developing strategies that can be read in multiple ways from multiple surveillance positions might be a beginning. My gradebooks are full of marks and checks and numbers that confirm that I am scrutinizing my students, but they do not show that my quizzes ask what they noticed as they read, why they think that their attention was drawn to those issues, and what they might have overlooked by pressing forward with a particular agenda. Nor is it obvious that these exercises were performed collaboratively and that they became the topics for discussion in the remainder of the class. Beating the system at its own game changes the game.

Asking students questions that call their expectations into question changes students. Who told them that they should be comfortable? What is it to be comfortable? Why is the meaning of a text more significant than any other of its attributes? How can what an author meant when she wrote something be available to a reader? What constitutes meaning? Does the author always know what he means? Can anyone say what he means? If nothing is taken for granted, everything is open to speculation. When students take these kinds of questions seriously, they begin to

---

[4]Foucault, "Intellectuals and Power: A Conversation Between Michel Foucault and Gilles DeLeuze," in *Language, Counter-Memory, Practice*, ed. Donald Bouchard, tr. Donald Bouchard and Sherry Simon (Ithaca: Cornell University Press, 1977), p. 208.

[5]Foucault, "Practicing Criticism," in *Politics, Philosophy, Culture: Interviews and Other Writings, 1977–1984*, ed. Lawrence D. Kritzman, tr. Alan Sheridan et al. (New York: Routledge, 1988), p. 155.

reshape their world and their panoptic position. They are less able to tick off answers on an evaluation sheet when they see how inside a set of unexamined assumptions the expectations of the questioners are; they take their questioning to other classrooms (thus introducing a virus into the network). Once this happens, such students no longer see only from the position that the system reserves for them; they can focus, instead, on the system itself and disrupt the circulation of power.

Because people in literary studies have been squabbling longer, louder, and more publicly than most other disciplines (the annual MLA meeting has become a media event and a scandal), we now seem to be reaching for ways out of our difficulties in order that we can get on with our work. In the guerrilla warfare of the late seventies and early eighties the halls of English departments were strewn with wounded warriors. Wresting power from the formalist hegemony initially united the postmoderns (who, by the way, would not have used that locution). When a space was carved out for a new agenda, the offensive coalition dissolved into opposing camps. Feminists confronted Marxists, who sought to shoulder out New Historicists. Splinter groups separated in odd ways so that one might find an MLA session considering the radical Maoist feminism of late Victorian novels. The territorializing of the discipline was replicating the surveillance and conformity paradigms of the panoptic agenda.

In December of 1990 I attended a seminar at the Folger Library during which Stanley Fish, chair of the English department at Duke University, addressed the disjunction in literary studies. In what seems an eminently sensible insight, Fish urged a redirection of the way that we see each other that is at once simple, subtle, and radical. He encouraged us to pay attention to the rigor of intellectual work as a value in itself rather than to the ways such work might move one's agenda forward in the shifting power relations of the academy. He asked that our surveillant gazes be redirected in ways that, as Foucault posits, detach "the power of truth from the forms of hegemony . . . within which it operates at the present time."[6] Instead of insisting that any paradigm—Feminist, Marxist, or New Historicist—control the discipline, becoming the coercive norm, Fish asks that we learn to see the erudition and value in Feminist, Marxist, or New Historicist *work*. Such a move confirms that our collegial relationship need not be adversarial, and that the value of any work inheres in its generating scholarship rather than in the support it lends to the truth statements of

---

[6]Foucault, "Truth and Power," in *The Foucault Reader*, p. 75.

power networks. The surveillant gaze is not erased, but it no longer maintains the truth claims of the institution. Fish's focusing on scholarly activity as opposed to a scholar's conclusions suggests a productive new way to expand the definition of normal inside the panoptic practices that must, at the same time, be resisted.

This seems to me, finally, the move that postmodern pedagogy as well as research must make to continue resistance at productive margins. Even this separation of teaching and research can be seen as an opposition enabled by systemic relations. This essay, for instance, by its status as an entry in a scholarly text, announces a conviction that writing seriously and rigorously about teaching is productive activity. At the same time, the scholarship inherent in developing a thoughtful course is only infrequently considered research. On a curriculum vitae that work is invisible. I am not certain how this invisibility can be illuminated, and I offer it to you as a parting gift. For if resistant critique is to effect changes in the power operations of the network we inhabit, each of us must find ways to continue to work despite the monitoring, measuring, and the subtle power relations that constrain serious rethinking of what it means to teach or to learn.

FOUCAULT AND THE NATURAL SCIENCES

Joseph Rouse

INTRODUCTION

The philosopher who would look to Michael Foucault's investigations of the prison and sexuality for insight into the natural sciences confronts several initial obstacles. Foucault's own concerns were explicitly focused upon what he once called the "dubious disciplines," psychology, sociology, and other fields whose status as sciences has been fiercely contested; he aimed to produce "a genealogy of the modern soul."[1] When explicitly asked whether his studies of power/knowledge might extend beyond the human sciences, Foucault was guarded. In a 1977 interview, for example, he said, "if, concerning a science like theoretical physics or organic

---

[1] Michel Foucault, *Discipline and Punish: The Birth of the Prison*, tr. Alan Sheridan (New York: Pantheon, 1977), p. 29.

chemistry, one poses the problem of its relations with the political and economic structures of society, isn't one posing an excessively complicated question? Doesn't one set the threshold of possible explanations impossibly high?"[2] Later he seemed to draw a distinction between power, which characterizes actions upon the actions of others, and "capacities," which denote knowledge and control of things.[3] This suggests that Foucault accepted that there are important differences between the natural and the human sciences as more or less unified epistemic and political practices. Gary Gutting has recently argued quite persuasively that, "with regard to the well-established natural sciences, Foucault seems content to accept the approach of Bachelard and Canguilhem,"[4] an approach that does not problematize the practices that organize disciplined investigation, in the way that Foucault's own studies do.

Apart for his own intentions, Foucault's theoretical position poses further obstacles to extending his analyses much beyond the specific epistemic regimes he targeted. He claims not to offer a *theory* of power, such that the domain of the theory might be expanded by appropriate arguments. Nor does he provide any general account of knowledge, whose scope might include knowledge of things along with self-knowledge and knowledge of others. Foucault self-consciously presented what he called an "analytics" of power/knowledge, which "treats questions of scientific rationality in 'regional' terms, eschewing grandly global theories for specific studies of particular disciplinary and chronological domains."[5] Foucault was highly suspicious, for both political and epistemic reasons, of theorizing that tries to escape the bounds of particular historical configurations.

Despite these initial obstacles, however, I remain convinced that Foucault's discussions of knowledge and power offer important suggestions for how to approach the natural sciences philosophically. Before we give in too readily to the contrary considerations I have just mentioned, it is worth remembering that Foucault's genealogies also problematize any

---

[2]Michel Foucault, *Power/Knowledge: Selected Interviews and Other Writings, 1972–1977*, ed. Colin Gordon, tr. Colin Gordon et al. (New York: Pantheon, 1980), p. 109.

[3]Michel Foucault, "The Subject and Power," in Hubert Dreyfus and Paul Rabinow, *Michel Foucault: Beyond Structuralism and Hermeneutics*, 2d edn. (Chicago: University of Chicago Press, 1983), pp. 217–219, and "What Is Enlightenment?" in *The Foucault Reader*, ed. Paul Rabinow (New York: Pantheon, 1984), pp. 47–49.

[4]Gary Gutting, *Michel Foucault's Archaeology of Scientific Reason* (Cambridge: Cambridge University Press, 1989), p. 255.

[5]Ibid., p. 53.

conception of the "human" or of the "subject" of representation and action, such as might ground a principled distinction between the natural and human sciences. Foucault's own studies frequently cross over into aspects of the life sciences that confound any attempt to distinguish sharply human from natural science: anatomy and physiology, taxonomy, and clinical medicine. In any case, a strong epistemic or political distinction between nature and society would clearly be subject to the central motivating question of Foucault's work: "in what is given to us as universal, necessary, obligatory, what place is occupied by whatever is singular, contingent, and the product of arbitrary constraints?"[6]

But clearly the most important question to be asked is what we would gain by adapting Foucault's discussions of strategies of power and knowledge to try to understand the modern sciences of nature. If such adaptation provides no illumination, the question of its possibility is of little interest; while if it does advance our understanding, objections in principle may be plausibly brushed aside. I have already argued in some detail elsewhere[7] that Foucault's genealogies of power/knowledge can be effectively mobilized to disclose specific features of the practices of the natural sciences and their political engagement. In this essay I will raise two further considerations that were at best implicit in my earlier discussion. First, I will claim that Foucault's critique of the problematic of sovereignty in political theory has an important parallel in epistemology and philosophy of science. Second, I will argue that Foucault points philosophy of science more effectively toward a *dynamic* understanding of knowledge. Together these two themes promise a significant reconceptualization of knowledge.

KNOWLEDGE AND POWER REVISITED

To see the point of this reconceptualization, I first need to recapitulate and extend some of the argument from *Knowledge and Power*. Although "modern" science has its canonical origins in the Copernican Revolution and its Newtonian consolidation, I looked to the "Baconian sciences" of chemistry, electricity, heat, life, and earth, which came of age in the

---

[6]"What Is Enlightenment?" in *The Foucault Reader*, p. 45.
[7]Joseph Rouse, *Knowledge and Power* (Ithaca: Cornell University Press, 1987), Ch. 7.

eighteenth and nineteenth centuries, for a crucial transformation that paralleled Foucault's discussions of more dubious sciences.[8] Foucault had emphasized the interdependence of the discursive practices of criminology, psychiatry, pedagogy, and the like with the nondiscursive disciplinary practices that made their objects of study newly available for investigation. I argued that the discursive and theoretical practices of these new sciences were inconceivable without the manifold phenomena made available through the construction or isolation of controlled "microworlds" is laboratories, clinics, and field sites.[9] The subsequent advances of science in almost all fields involved the novel construction or refinement of phenomena as much as the theoretical modelling that more typically engages philosophers of science; indeed, I insisted upon the mutual reinforcement of theoretical and experimental practices.

The parallels were close between the intertwining of discursive and nondiscursive practices in the natural sciences and that occurring in the disciplines that were the focus of Foucault's studies. In both cases, a change in scale was crucial, as objects and events were opened to far more detailed scrutiny in their behavior and microstructure. Such detailed understanding was the consequence of new forms of surveillance and tracking of things, coupled with the careful documentation and retrieval that made *knowledge* accessible and control relentless. Typically these surveillance practices were applied to things enclosed, partitioned, separated, and purified to manifest new forms of behavior or old forms more strikingly. Their classification and theoretical articulation were in accord with these various dividing practices, which produced standardized or normalized objects with patterns of deviance and distortion. The objects of investigation do not remain docile and silent, whether in the disciplines studied by Foucault or in the natural sciences. They are constrained to produce signs, which are to be validated in authoritative interpretations. The Catholic and psychoanalytic confessionals were Foucault's classic cases of forced signification, but the natural sciences have also produced myriad ways in which things are forced to "speak." In the book I suggested

---

[8]Although I disagree on important issues with their more philosophical conclusions, Steven Shapin and Simon Shaffer in *Leviathan and the Air-Pump* (Princeton: Princeton University Press, 1985) give an excellent historical account of Robert Boyle's work on the air-pump as one of the earliest significant such "Baconian" developments.

[9]I use "phenomena" in the special sense suggested by Ian Hacking in *Representing and Intervening* (Cambridge: Cambridge University Press, 1983), in which phenomena are clear, discernable, and reliable manifestations in the public world, whether found or made.

the examples of radioactive labeling, cloud and bubble chambers, x-ray crystallography, and the various forms of chromatography, spectroscopy, microscopy, and telescopy, but the inventiveness of scientific work has proliferated such techniques well beyond these classic cases. On the one hand, such practices enable things to reveal themselves; on the other hand, these disclosures only count as genuine within the authoritative interpretive constraints that distinguish data from artifacts or noise.

In my argument, laboratories and field sites thus joined prisons, asylums, hospitals, barracks, factories, and schools as disciplinary "blocks" from which new forms of knowledge and constraint emerged together. But the emergence of these practices from their relative isolation within such blocks is an important part of their constitution as bearers of knowledge. How do the capabilities and phenomena disclosed in laboratory manipulations come to count as knowledge of things that circulate (often in quite different guise) in other contexts? I argued, in effect, that the extension (in the semantic sense) of scientific concepts and theories is predicated upon the achieved or promised extension (in the spatiotemporal sense) of experimental capabilities beyond the laboratory.[10]

To understand my point, it is useful to see its connection to a more familiar view about the content of scientific theories. Thomas Kuhn, Nancy Cartwright, and Ronald Giere have all argued that the content of theories cannot be adequately expressed propositionally, but is instead located in models (Kuhn's "exemplars") that explicate the theory by showing what it says about various kinds of situation. Understanding the theory is knowing how to extend the canonical models in an indefinitely open way; the range of possible extension of the models is the extension of the theory.[11] What I add to this view is the claim that the elements of the theoretical models are only attached to real objects through laboratory disclosures and the ability to extend or project them into the world. This semantic achievement is often overlooked, but it is crucial to the intelligibility and epistemic success of science, and is often problematic,

[10] In Chapter 5 of *Knowledge and Power* I argued that the resulting view of semantics and ontology is not antirealist, but rather undercuts the presuppositions shared by scientific realism and the standard instrumentalist and constructivist antirealisms. This argument is too long and complex to recapitulate here.
[11] See Thomas Kuhn, *The Structure of Scientific Revolutions*, 2d edn. (Chicago: University of Chicago Press, 1970); Nancy Cartwright, *How the Laws of Physics Lie* (Oxford: Oxford University Press, 1983); and Ronald Giere, *Explaining Science* (Chicago: University of Chicago Press, 1988).

as several influential studies have shown. Thus, for example, Ludwik Fleck documented the complex achievement through which a condition of the blood made manifest in the Wasserman reaction came to count as knowledge of *syphilis*, and Bruno Latour traced some of the struggles required for Pasteur's cultures of bacilli to represent *anthrax*.[12]

There is a further parallel here between natural scientific knowledge and Foucault's study of power/knowledge in the prison that I failed to recognize in *Knowledge and Power*. Foucault noted that "prison 'reform' is virtually contemporary with the prison itself: it constitutes, as it were, its programme."[13] The systems of knowledge and constraint that constitute and control delinquency have always fallen far short of their goals; and the prescription for reform, Foucault notes, has always been more of the same. Failures represent the inadequate extension or improper use of the normalizing practices that govern incarceration and constitute delinquency as an object of knowledge; more complete knowledge and more detailed normalization will supposedly rectify its shortcomings. Now there may seem initially to be a sharp contrast in this respect between natural scientific knowledge and the disciplines that make up the field of criminology. The history of natural sciences and laboratories is comparatively one of success, such that the standardization of scientific phenomena is not typically marred by any kind of "recidivism." But once we recognize that even natural scientific knowledge is constituted by a promissory extension of its laboratory-based capabilities to any objects or events within its projected domain, the analogy reappears. For the projected solution to any failures is always more research and more stringent application of the procedures through which things are made scientifically accountable. The adaptation of the laboratory and the re-formation of the world to become more thoroughly knowable scientifically are as intrinsic to the natural sciences as social and institutional reforms have been to the prison.

When we recognize the semantic and epistemic significance of this extension of disclosive capabilities outside of various disciplinary blocks, laboratories included (what Foucault once called the "swarming" of the

---

[12]See Ludwik Fleck, *Genesis and Development of a Scientific Fact*, tr. Fred Bradley and Thaddeus J. Trenn (Chicago: University of Chicago Press, 1979); and Bruno Latour, *The Pasteurization of France*, tr. John Law (Cambridge: Harvard University Press, 1988).

[13]*Discipline and Punish*, p. 234.

disciplines[14]), we can see how the interweaving of knowledge and power runs through the natural sciences as well as the dubious disciplines. Extending knowledge outside the context of the laboratory typically requires also extending the materials and practices that made possible the disclosure and tracking of laboratory phenomena. The world we inhabit is riven with enclosures, partitions, and purifications, marked by measurements, counts, and timings, and tracked by new forms of visibility, documentation, and accounting, all in order to make scientific knowledge possible. The things within it have become analyzable and interchangeable stocks of resources, and our dealings with them have become more tightly coupled and interactively complex.[15] Both the configuration of our political life and many of the conflicts that arise within our politics are shaped by these practices that are part of the growth and reaffirmation of natural scientific knowledge. Or so I argued in *Knowledge and Power*. Of course, as Foucault himself would have insisted, these are not just constraints; they are productive of such things as wealth, mobility, health, or military force, as well as knowledge.

But it might still be objected, as perhaps Foucault himself might have objected, that there is a basic difference between expanding capabilities over things and expanding power. However, even if one insists on limiting power to the shaping of human action or the possibilities for intelligible action, this does not effectively remove the connection between power and natural scientific knowledge. Recall the forms of visibility and surveillance that were proposed in Bentham's model of the Panopticon. Not only the prisoners were to be subjects of the panoptical gaze, which also reflects back upon the occupant of the central tower. A visitor can tell at a glance whether the observer has been vigilant, by seeing whether all is in order with the prisoners. The same is true of the new forms of visibility and constraint developed in laboratories and fieldwork and extended indefinitely outside the microworlds they embody. People must conform to the disciplines of the laboratory in order for the knowledge and capabilities developed there to be sustained and extended. And the extent of their, our, conformity is readily visible in the functioning of those capabilities themselves.

[14]Ibid., pp. 211–212.
[15]For a detailed discussion of the meaning and significance of interactive complexity and tight coupling, see Rouse, *Knowledge and Power*, pp. 230–231, or Charles Perrow, *Normal Accidents* (New York: Basic Books, 1984).

EPISTEMIC SOVEREIGNTY

What I have said so far is basically recapitulation and commentary upon my use of Foucault's work in *Knowledge and Power*. In that book, however, I did not thematize some of the most radical implications of my arguments for philosophical accounts of knowledge, implications that also deepen the uses I would like to make of Foucault's discussions of power/knowledge. The place to begin is with what I shall call the problematic of "epistemic sovereignty."

At several points in his writings Foucault situates his own reflections within the tradition of political theory in terms of a challenge to the tradition's orientation toward the problem of sovereign power: "At bottom, despite the differences in epochs and objectives, the representation of power has remained under the spell of monarchy. In political thought and analysis, we still have not cut off the head of the king."[16] Foucault notes that, in order to understand sovereignty as a political problematic, one must look to the origins of monarchy. Although modern political theory posits the question of legitimating a sovereign political power as the "original" political problem, Foucault reminds us that the actual role of the modern state, initially located in the person of the sovereign, presupposed a complex prior network of power relations. It is worth quoting this passage at some length, for we shall have occasion to refer back to it.

> The great institutions of power that developed in the Middle Ages—monarchy, the state with its apparatus—rose up on the basis of a multiplicity of prior powers, and to a certain extent in opposition to them: dense, entangled, conflicting powers, powers tied to the direct or indirect dominion over the land, to the possession of arms, to serfdom, to bonds of suzerainty and vassalage. If these institutions were able to implant themselves, if, by profiting from a whole series of tactical alliances, they were able to gain acceptance, this was because they presented themselves as agencies of regulation, arbitration, and demarcation, as a way of introducing order in the midst of these powers, of establishing a principle that would temper them and distribute

---

[16]Michel Foucault, *The History of Sexuality, Volume I: An Introduction* (hereafter cited as *HS*), tr. Robert Hurley (New York: Pantheon, 1978), pp. 88–89.

them according to boundaries and a fixed hierarchy. Faced with a myriad of clashing forces, these great forms of power functioned as a principle of right that transcended all the heterogeneous claims, manifesting the triple distinction of forming a unitary regime, of identifying its will with the law, and of acting through mechanisms of interdiction and sanction.[17]

The sovereign was a unifying agent, standing above the various conflicting powers as impartial referee, and guarantor and protector of legitimacy in the form of law, to be enforced against those subordinate powers that overstepped its bounds. Of course, as Foucault suggests, this was a promise that no actual monarch could fulfill, since the monarchy was itself a player in the power struggles that it supposedly stood above as neutral arbiter. Hence the subsequent critique of monarchy in political theory deployed this conception of the sovereign's role against its nominal occupant.

> Criticism of the eighteenth-century monarchic institution in France was not directed against the juridico-monarchic sphere as such, but was made on behalf of a pure and rigorous juridical system to which all the mechanisms of power could conform, with no excesses or irregularities, as opposed to a monarchy which, notwithstanding its own assertions, continuously overstepped its legal framework and set itself above the laws.[18]

In the end, sovereignty came to represent not a real position within actual political struggles, but an analytic construct with respect to which those struggles were to be assessed. Even the tactics employed by actual sovereigns to secure popular recognition of their legitimacy were themselves to be assessed for their own conformity to principles of right, from the disembodied standpoint of sovereignty.

Foucault does not argue that sovereignty ceased to be at issue through the political transformations that he claimed to discover in the eighteenth and nineteenth centuries. Rather, he argues that the political forms and practices of sovereign power remained in place, but that they were gradually invested by and ultimately sustained on the basis of power

[17] Ibid., pp. 86–87.
[18] Ibid., p. 88.

relations that functioned on a different scale. A crucial feature of sovereign power is that, while there are no limits to its proclaimed scope (all actions, persons, and goods are in principle subject to the sovereign), in practice its capacity to exercise power is discontinuous and solely constraining. The sovereign can prohibit actions, kill or imprison persons, and tax or confiscate goods, but its productive abilities are quite limited. Increasingly, he argues, the sovereign apparatus came to be dependent upon what he called the "capillary" power relations through which various "goods"—knowledge, health, wealth, and the like—were actually constructed or enhanced: "the ancient right to *take* life or *let* live was replaced by a power to *foster* life or *disallow* it to the point of death."[19] Thus, in political theory, he argues that theories of sovereignty overlooked the many ways in which power was deployed outside the framework of the state apparatus or class domination; he also claims that the theory of sovereignty failed in its own terms, since it could not adequately grasp the ways in which sovereignty itself came to be constituted and exercised through tactics on a different scale that were not at the sovereign's disposal.

Yet virtually all of the dominant political theories worked within the framework of sovereignty, differing only in where sovereignty was to be located: in the people and their representatives, in the ownership of the means of production, in social elites, or in patriarchy. As Foucault notes, even more radical critics of law and sovereign power did not escape the problematic of sovereignty (today, we might think of Critical Legal Studies in this role):

> A much more radical criticism was concerned to show not only that real power escaped the rules of jurisprudence, but that the legal system itself was merely a way of exerting violence, of appropriating that violence for the benefit of the few, and of exploiting the dissymmetries and injustices of domination under cover of general law. But this critique of law is still carried out on the assumption that, ideally and by nature, power must be exercised in accordance with a fundamental lawfulness.[20]

I shall soon return to the question of how Foucault proposed to break outside the political problematic of sovereignty, as well as why he thought

[19] Ibid., p. 138.
[20] Ibid., p. 88.

the modern exercise of power could not be adequately understood unless such a break were made. But I must first explain the significance of this detour through political theory in the course of a discussion of natural scientific knowledge.

Although Foucault insisted that knowledge is always intertwined and mutually reinforcing with relations of power, his discussions of power/knowledge never explicitly included an analytics of knowledge comparable to the general reflections upon power to be found in Part Four of *History of Sexuality, Volume I*, Part One of *Discipline and Punish*, and elaborated upon in various interviews and lectures. Yet I want to suggest that it is possible to construct a parallel discussion of sovereignty as an epistemological problematic, whose critique is also undertaken in Foucault's work. I will also argue that this implicit challenge to epistemic sovereignty is important for understanding the practices and achievements of the natural sciences.

All of the central issues of political sovereignty are reproduced in epistemology: the constitution of a unitary regime, based upon legitimacy through law, established from an impartial standpoint above particular conflicts, and enforced through discontinuous interventions that aim to suppress illegitimacy. The problematic of epistemic sovereignty is fundamentally located in the standard contrast between knowledge and belief or assertion. Knowledge arises from a confusing multiplicity of conflicting assertions that circulate through a wide range of communicative interactions. Knowledge is a unified (or consistently unifiable) network of statements that can be extracted from the welter of confused and conflicting contenders and legitimated in accord with rules of rational method, the epistemic surrogate for law. Here is where the figure of the epistemic sovereign is theoretically important. Sovereignty need not be located in any actual sovereign knower, any more than political sovereignty requires a monarch. But just as the sovereign power must be one that *could* consistently be embodied in a single will, sovereign knowledge must be consistently representable in a single coherent propositional system.

Like the political sovereign as arbiter among competing powers, epistemic sovereignty is projected as an impartial referee among conflicting claims. The establishment and especially the deployment of the rational methods of evaluation that distinguish sovereign knowledge from subordinate assertions must in principle be impartial among particular substantive statements.[21] Assertions are rationally justifiable only so long as they can be *independently* shown to accord with the law.

The binary categories invoked by the sovereign power in the name of law also have clear epistemic counterparts. From the standpoint of rational legitimation, statements are true or false, warranted or unwarranted, rationally permissable or forbidden. And although the question of the rational legitimation of statements is in principle appropriate at all times and places, its application is episodic. The cumbersome procedures of impartial rational evaluation are not deployed to produce assertions, but only to assess them in retrospect, and then only in very limited circumstances. There has always been a close theoretical parallel between the court of reason and the court of law, and in both institutions the vast majority of possible cases are either never arraigned or else plea bargained. Few criminal cases are tried, and perhaps even fewer statements and their justifications are rationally reconstructed before the tribunal of reason.

Epistemology as a discipline constituted by the problematic of sovereignty has been organized around four basic issues. First and foremost is the question of where epistemic sovereignty is to be located. For the dominant liberal tradition, any rational person may represent the sovereign. The law, in the form of rational method, can be applied by anyone who can place his or her self in the impartial, rational standpoint. Marxism offers an alternative placement of epistemic sovereignty: there is an epistemically privileged class, whose standpoint alone enables the rational critique of ideology. Post-Kuhnian philosophy and sociology of science have revived communitarian conceptions of sovereignty, which situate the rational evaluation of belief within a shared form of life. Even the various forms of relativism are tenaciously located within the problematic of sovereignty, which enable them to recognize or confer equal epistemic "rights" upon individual or cultural worldviews.

There is a second, distinct question concerning the level at which epistemic sovereignty is to be deployed: can statements be rationally assessed one by one, or must method intervene only at the level of the

---

[21]The typical philosophical response to claims that method and adjudicating evidence are theory-laden has not been to abandon the standpoint of sovereignty, but to reconstitute it at a different level. Hence one finds accounts of rationality at the level of the research program or scientific domain (as in the work of Imré Lakatos, Larry Laudan, and Dudley Shapere) or at the level of metatheoretical explanation of theory-dependent instrumental success (scientific realism).

theory or research program? A third question concerns the final form of the unification of knowledge. Does the systematic, sovereign unification of knowledge require reduction to a single vocabulary, or does it permit autonomous regions of knowledge at irreducibly different levels of description?

Of course, the fourth and final question is ultimately the crucial one. What constitutes legitimate exercise of sovereign epistemic judgment? What methods of epistemic adjudication could legitimately claim the force of law? And here, as with the political theory of sovereignty, the question must be kept rigorously distinct from considerations of how judgments are actually made or enforced. For just as the sovereign power and its legislation are always in principle subordinate to the law, the reigning practices of adjudicating knowledge claims must themselves be subjected to rational scrutiny.

BEYOND THE PROBLEMATIC OF SOVEREIGNTY: THE DYNAMICS OF KNOWLEDGE

As I noted above, Foucault's principal arguments for rejecting the problematic of sovereignty within political theory were that many politically important phenomena could not be adequately understood in its terms, and indeed that those phenomena were in the end constitutive of the modern institutions and practices of sovereignty themselves. I want to suggest a similar line of argument against the way epistemological reflection has been shaped by the notion of sovereign knowledge. The practices of natural scientific research cannot be adequately understood in terms of the legitimation of a unified regime of knowledge, and indeed the actual certification of knowledge is shaped by those practices that transgress the analysis of epistemic sovereignty. But the parallel goes deeper than just the basic structure of the argument. I want to suggest that many of the fundamental themes of Foucault's analytics of power will have analogues in a more adequate reflection upon scientific knowledge.

Foucault's analytics of power was supposed to transgress the limits of the categories of political sovereignty by restricting inquiry to how power is exercised. Power was to be understood not as a thing possessed, but as a dynamic network of relations. My introduction of the notion of epistemic sovereignty was intended to suggest that we might take very seriously Foucault's insistence on the intertwining of knowledge with relations of power and consider in similar ways how to transgress the categorial limits of sovereign knowledge. What could it mean to ask about the 'how' of knowledge in lieu of what knowledge is or why it is legitimately knowledge? What, in short, must be done in epistemology in order to cut off the head of the king? And why would such an epistemological regicide be important for understanding the natural sciences?

My account will focus initially upon some of Foucault's more general remarks about power, as indications of what it would mean to bypass the issue of political sovereignty. However, I will not attempt an exposition of Foucault on power; instead, I will try to show how some of his central themes can be adapted to understand scientific knowledge. I shall consider six points:

1) Power is dynamic. It is not a commodity, an institution, a structure, or any other sort of *thing* (hence it is also not something possessed by agents, classes, or institutions), and it only exists through its exercise. If there is stability over time in power relations, it is because these relations are reenacted and reproduced: "[power] is the name that one attributes to a complex strategical situation in a particular society."[22]

2) Power is disseminated throughout the body politic. Power relations are material and locally situated; hence, as Foucault once put it, power is omnipresent "not because it has the privilege of consolidating everything under its invincible unity, but rather because it is produced from one moment to the next, at every point, or rather in every relation from one point to another. . . . It comes from everywhere."[23]

3) These disseminated power relations become linked or opposed to one another tactically and strategically: "these relations find support in one another, thus forming a chain or a system, or on the contrary, disjunctions and contradictions which isolate them from one another."[24]

4) Power is always contested: "the existence of power relations depends upon a multiplicity of points of resistance [which] play the role of adversary, target, support, or handle, [and which] are present everywhere in the power network."[25]

[22]*HS*, p. 93.
[23]Ibid.
[24]Ibid., p. 92.
[25]Ibid., p. 95.

5) Power needs an "analytics" instead of a theory. It does not constitute a self-contained domain, but is better understood as one way of looking at the same phenomena that could also be seen in other terms. Hence "relations of power are not in a position of exteriority with respect to other types of relationships (economic processes, knowledge relationships, sexual relations), but are immanent in the latter."[26]

6) Power is productive. It does not merely tax, prohibit, or abolish various social goods, but helps produce or constitute them.

Stated so briefly, this list is undoubtedly oracular and cryptic, and it could be dismissed as a repetition of one of the most infuriating aspects of Foucault's written style. I trust, however, that this litany will seem less obscure once we have considered how we might understand *knowledge* as likewise dynamic, disseminated, strategically linked, contested, analytical, and productive.

A dynamic understanding of knowledge may seem initially strange. Whatever one wants to say about power, surely knowledge *is* something possessed by a knower and transmitted or exchanged through communicative interaction. Indeed, the content of knowledge (both the propositions known and the evidence and reasoning that warrant them as knowledge) may seem to be independent of particular embodiments in texts, utterances, or thoughts and of the specific history through which those propositions came to be known.

To understand scientific knowledge in this way, however, as an ideal, ahistorical content that a knower grasps or possesses is to overlook the complex practical achievements through which scientific domains become accessible. Only within such a complex practical field, shaped by the availability of functional and reliable equipment and a variety of subtle technical and theoretical skills, do electrons, viruses, tectonic plates, or quasars become possible objects of knowledge or discourse. Thus the propositions in which sovereign knowledge is supposedly expressed get their sense from a complex and heterogeneous field of practices and capabilities.

Foucault had discussed extensively how the body, the individual soul, and the population are constituted as possible objects of knowledge, and how sexuality and delinquency are organized as fields of knowledge. Individuals become knowable only through detailed practices of classification and documentation. Populations require different practices, most

---

[26] Ibid., p. 94.

notably the tangled interconnection between categorization, counting, and statistics. Sexuality and delinquency have different kinds of history, shaped by patterns of association and strategies of intervention. Recall, for example, Foucault's claim that sexuality as a field of possible knowledge emerged from the nineteenth-century identification and association of "four privileged objects of knowledge, which were also targets and anchorage points for the ventures of knowledge: the hysterical woman, the masturbating child, the Malthusian couple, and the perverse adult. Each of them corresponded to [a] strategy."[27]

The natural sciences have their own histories of disclosure, through which domains of possible inquiry are also shaped by heterogeneous skills, practices, and equipment. The "gene," for example, becomes *available* for discussion in quite different ways, and hence as a different object of *knowledge*, through successively the hybridization studies of Mendel and his contemporaries,[28] the chromosome mappings initiated by Morgan and his colleagues, its molecular identification by Avery and Watson and Crick, and the sequencing and manipulation of genetic elements in recent molecular biology. We are all too familiar with the retrospective reconstructions through which we have come to understand Mendel, de Vries, Morgan, McClintock, Avery, Crick, Berg, and Genentech to be talking about the same thing. There is of course a sense in which this reconstruction is not incorrect. But it required the excision or transformation of many of the forms of practice and knowhow that at various points helped constitute knowledge of the gene.

I spoke in *Knowledge and Power* of the importance of *local* knowledges in this respect. "Genes" emerge as the objects of possible discourses through often arduous accumulations of capabilities and insights in specific contexts (for example, specific laboratories with their own projects, protocols, and materials, but also specific experimental systems such as drosophila, maize, and bacteriophage). This knowledge cannot be extended to other locations, or related objects, without complex and subtle mutual adaptations. Laboratory practices and equipment themselves, and the knowledge they embody, must be standardized, simplified, and adapted to new purposes, while the working environment (both material

---

[27]Ibid., p. 105.
[28]For an account of Mendel that emphasizes the *continuity* of his researches with those of contemporary plant breeders, in terms of both his research practices and his skills, see Robert Olby, "Mendel no Mendelian?" in *History of Science* 17 (1979): 53–72.

and conceptual) to which they are extended must also be modified to accommodate them. I think it is useful to understand these gradual transformations, reproductions, extensions, and mutual alignments of local knowledges as strategic. Out of a confusing array of interacting projects, practices, and capabilities, there gradually emerges an overall pattern or direction (or, rather, a plurality of them). Not, however, because this pattern was what was intended, however dimly, all along, but because some practices turn out to reinforce and strengthen one another and are taken up, extended, and reproduced in various new contexts, while others remain isolated from or in conflict with these emergent strategies and gradually become forgotten or isolated curiosities. Yet, I argued, these outcomes have little to do with any intrinsic faults of the discarded practices.

An epistemological dynamics takes these strategic alignments to be constitutive of knowledge. Thus knowledge is not a status that attaches to a statement, a skill, or a model in isolation or instantaneously. Rather, their epistemic standing depends upon their relations to many other practices and capabilities and especially upon the ways these relations are reproduced, transformed, and extended. Knowledge is temporally diffused or deferred: to take something as knowledge is to project its being taken up as a resource for various kinds of ongoing activity (whether in further research or in various "applications" of knowledge). In this sense, the word "application" is somewhat misleading, since in the broadest sense we do not first gain knowledge, then apply it; something only counts as knowledge through the ways it is interpreted in use.

Knowledge in this sense *circulates*, and even the various points at which it is articulated, or even collected and assessed, are caught up in its circulation. What is proposed as possible new knowledge, whether in informal discussion or in initial publication, has an element of tentativeness about it. What is gathered together in retrospective judgment is always oriented toward a further advance and shaped by that projection.[29] What I would now conclude from my argument in *Knowledge and Power* and a subsequent paper is thus that there is no place where epistemic sovereignty is actually located. The scientific literature itself is always continually reorganizing what is known as a resource for further investi-

---

[29] I argue in more detail for the temporal situatedness and dispersion of all articulations of scientific knowledge in *Knowledge and Power*, Ch. 4 (esp. pp. 120–25), and in "The Narrative Reconstruction of Science," *Inquiry* 33 (1990): 179–196.

gation; it is also always contested. Yet philosophical attempts to stand outside or above the contested recycling of knowledge always verge upon irrelevance. As I have argued elsewhere,[30] if a judgment from a philosophical standpoint of supposed epistemic sovereignty were to conflict with the ways knowledge claims are taken up and deployed in the course of research, they could only be vindicated within the contested strategic field in which knowledge claims are transformed, reproduced, or left behind.

I need to say more about this claim that scientific knowledge is always contested, the parallel to Foucault's insistence that power always confronts resistance.[31] Once it is recognized that knowledge only exists through its reproduction and circulation, the importance of conflict becomes evident: conflict focuses and directs that circulation. Knowledge is developed in an agonistic field and will typically be contested in very specific respects. And it is precisely in those respects that knowledge will be developed and articulated most extensively and precisely. Where there is (possible) resistance, new and more powerful techniques will be sought, more precise and careful measurement will be provided, and theoretical models will be refined to eliminate or bypass possible sources of inaccuracy or unrealistic assumption. These various refinements are themselves new knowledges and often in turn provide further new directions or problems for research. Hence, around the specific points where knowledge is resisted, there emerges a whole cluster of new local capabilities and their extension into new contexts. But the contrary is also true: where

---

[30]"The Narrative Reconstruction of Science."

[31]I am using the term "resistance" in a broader sense than might be expected. Obviously, there is resistance to a knowledge claim when there are people who refuse to accept it and attempt to counter it by producing counterevidence or other arguments or even by trying to bypass it or studiously ignore it. But there is also resistance to a claim when the purported objects of that claim do not behave in accordance with it. It is important not to separate these two aspects of resistance to knowledge too sharply, because of the ways they reinforce and even constitute one another. What *counts* as successful accord between knowledge and its objects is often itself contested, and the outcome of such conflicts is typically the result of successful negotiations (both negotiating with those who oppose the claim about the standards of success and renegotiating the practices and procedures through which the objects of knowledge make themselves manifest). The concept of "resistance" one needs to understand the dynamics of scientific knowledge is one that does not respect any sharp distinction between actions by people and behavior by things. Detailed arguments for such a conception of "resistance" are provided by Bruno Latour in *Science in Action* (Cambridge: Harvard University Press, 1987) and by Andrew Pickering in "Living in the Material World," in David Gooding et al., *The Uses of Experiment* (Cambridge: Cambridge University Press, 1989), pp. 275–297.

knowledge goes unchallenged, where a claim "goes without saying," there is little or no articulation or development. And where previous resistance vanishes, knowledge also ceases to proliferate.

The forms taken by resistance to knowledge cannot be easily reduced to traditional epistemic categories. Obviously, knowledge can be resisted because there are gaps in the data, dubious assumptions in the theoretical models, or countervailing evidence. But it can also be resisted because the procedures and capabilities for its articulation and development are too expensive, environmentally unsound, cruel to animals, politically sensitive, of too little or too much interest to the military, unprofitable, and so forth. Philosophers have often tried to separate considerations internal to knowledge from those which impinge upon it from the outside. The distinction is almost always bound up with a conception of epistemic sovereignty: only those issues that are codified in terms of method, the sovereign law in the realm of knowledge, count as "internal."

Yet the discovery of the local knowledges and their dynamics through which epistemic sovereignty is exercised undercuts any attempt to make such a distinction. The sense of a claim and the ways in which it is articulated and deployed in further research and development depend upon considerations that transgress the boundaries that would constitute sovereignty in the realm of knowledge. All of the small local decisions about research materials, equipment, procedures, funding, personnel, skill development, and the like shape the actual development of the knowledges that invest and underwrite the sorts of knowledge claims that philosophers typically investigate. The actual justifications offered for these decisions typically interchange and balance supposedly internal and external considerations. Thus a physicist may argue for a particular experimental strategy against its competitors by claiming that it is cheaper, provides a less diffuse particle beam, takes best advantage of the skills of available personnel, might interest new funding sources in the military, is more reliably established in the literature, would be adaptable to a variety of experiments, and would leak less radiation and thus counter the recently vocal objections by local environmental groups. These heterogeneous concerns and reasons function together in the shaping of knowledge.

This heterogeneity of knowledge and resistance to it thus points to the inadequacy of that aspect of epistemic sovereignty that presents knowledge as a distinct domain of investigation, which would be the object of a theory. Foucault's analytics of power was a recognition that power is not a more or less enclosed domain of objects, but a collection of strategies for codifying and intervening in things that could also be organized in overlapping and countervailing ways under other headings (economic, epistemic, sexual,[32] etc.). Knowledge should be similarly thought of as a strategic intervention rather than an isolable domain.[33] Understanding knowledge dynamically takes us into considerations that would "properly" belong to other domains if the world presented itself in such discrete bundles. But an adequate understanding of knowledge (even scientific knowledge) in all its local proliferation and heterogeneity regularly transgresses the boundaries of epistemic propriety. One could add, of course, that the same is true of other kinds of interventions. An investigation of economics or sexuality would have much to say about science and could not be confined to considerations "external" even to knowledge narrowly construed. There is, after all, much to be said about the value and the pleasures of methodological rigor.

In concluding this introductory survey of a Foucauldian epistemological dynamics, I trust I do not need to say a great deal about the senses in which knowledge is productive. The ongoing practices in which knowledge is embodied are also increasingly the site of the production of health, wealth, military force, etc. I use the word "production" advisedly. From within the circulation of knowledge (re-)production, there emerge new ways to be healthy (low cholesterol and high fiber, adequate T-cell count), new forms of wealth (most obviously in the form of access to and control of information), and new projections of destructive force. There also emerge, not accidentally, a proliferation of new knowledges. For the extension of Foucault's analytics of power to an epistemological dynamics

---

[32]Anyone who doubts that a useful approach to understanding science could not plausibly be organized under the heading of sex should look closely and imagine extrapolating the discussion of the sexuality of particle accelerators and detectors in Sharon Traweek, *Beamtimes and Lifetimes* (Cambridge: Harvard University Press, 1988).

[33]Steve Fuller in *Social Epistemology* (Bloomington: Indiana University Press, 1988) has made a similar point, in objecting to what he calls the "textbook fallacy": the family, the economy, cognition (or "science"), education, etc., may be naively introduced to students as if they were discrete domains, when in fact they are overlapping categorizations. Thus he points out (on page 16) that, even in the context of textbook naiveté, "it is unlikely that a discussion of the family will be restricted to the formation and maintenance of *gemeinshaftlich* bonds. In addition, the reader is likely to find an analysis of the family as an economic unit, as a vehicle for transmitting political ideology, and the like." One should add that, in the end, such analyses of the family cannot be confined to discrete subsections either. And of course Fuller shares my principal point that it would be an error to think that knowledge can be isolated as a sovereign realm any more than can the family.

shows more clearly how the continual *expansion* of scientific knowledge and its associated controls and constraints is not merely incidental, but is integral to the ways in which knowledges circulate and are validated. Indeed, this is the parallel to the complicity between the prison and its reform that Foucault observes to be integral to modern practices of confinement. One might say that the laboratory also embodies a dream of a "complete and austere institution."

LEGITIMATION AND THE SPECTER OF RELATIVISM

I want to conclude with a brief reflection upon a likely source of resistance to a dynamic, nonsovereign epistemology. Foucault has often been chastised as an arch-relativist, who denies any grounding to the legitimation or critique of power or knowledge.[34] My attempt to bypass or overcome the problematic of epistemic sovereignty may seem to suffer from the same, possibly self-defeating incapacity. A postsovereign epistemology would presumably offer no standpoint, outside the contested domain in which conflicting and heterogeneous knowledge claims circulate, from which to assess what one *ought* to believe, including whether one ought to believe the assertions of postsovereign epistemology.

There is, however, a slippery inference underlying this fear that the actions of tyrants and the beliefs of fools can no longer be effectively countered. This is the inference from there being *no* epistemic sovereignty, no privileged standpoint for legitimating knowledge, to *all* knowledge claims being equally valid, however wacky or offensive they may be. But the latter sort of relativism is not only not entailed by the denial of epistemic sovereignty, they are mutually inconsistent. Relativism is an assertion of epistemic sovereignty that proclaims the epistemic "rights" of all knowers or knowledges. The most fashionable forms of epistemic relativism today, which are also those frequently and mistakenly associated with Foucault, are those that dismiss all claims to objectivity or

[34] Such criticisms have been articulated most influentially by Charles Taylor, "Foucault on Freedom and Truth," in *Foucault: A Critical Reader*, ed. David Hoy (Oxford: Basil Blackwell, 1986), by Jürgen Habermas, "Taking Aim at the Heart of the Present," ibid., and by Nancy Fraser, *Unruly Practices* (Minneapolis: University of Minnesota Press, 1989). They are sufficiently widespread almost to go without saying in many contexts—see, e.g., Hilary Putnam, *Reason, Truth, and History* (Cambridge: Cambridge University Press, 1981).

truth as merely masks for power. But such claims are the exact epistemological parallel to the radical critique of law as itself a form of violence, which Foucault insisted always "assumes that power must be exercised in accordance with a fundamental lawfulness."[35] To make this assumption, whether about power or knowledge, is to remain committed to a conception of sovereignty, from which such fundamental lawfulness can be rightly assessed.

What, then, does a postsovereign epistemology have to say about the legitimation of knowledge? The crucial point is not that there is no legitimacy, but rather that questions about legitimation are on the same "level" as any other epistemic conflict and are part of a struggle for truth.[36] In the circulation of contested, heterogeneous knowledges, disputes about legitimacy and the criteria for legitimacy are part and parcel of the dynamics of that circulation. Understanding knowledge as "a strategical situation" rather than as a definitive outcome places epistemological reflection in the midst of ongoing struggles to legitimate (and delegitimate) various skills, practices, and assertions. Recognizing that the boundaries of science (or of knowledge) are what is being contested, epistemology is within those contested boundaries.

An example will clarify my point. What does it mean to say, about a recently prominent family of biological claims, that creationism has now been shown to be false? The standard epistemological interpretation of this claim is that it promises to stand above the myriad claims for and against creationism and assess which actually belong to the unitary regime of knowledge. A postsovereign epistemology would take this sentence to be a *commitment* to marshal available evidence sufficient to demonstrate to anyone audacious enough to challenge this claim that their challenge fails. Now the sovereign epistemologist will immediately ask about the standards of success and failure in any such ensuing contest. The challenger cites scripture, the defender responds with data from fossils and breeding experiments. And the worry is that, without a sovereign standpoint to determine which appeals and standards are relevant and legitimate, scripture is just as good as data.

[35]*HS*, p. 88.
[36]A closely connected view about the "level" of analysis can be found in some versions of "disquotational" accounts on truth, for which "*p* is true" is materially equivalent to "*p*"; see Paul Horwich, *Truth* (Oxford: Basil Blackwell, 1990); Arthur Fine, *The Shaky Game: Einstein, Realism, and the Quantum Theory* (Chicago: University of Chicago Press, 1986), Chs. 7–8; and Rouse, *Knowledge and Power*, Ch. 5.

But this conflict among competing standards will appear irresolvable only when one removes the conflict from any real setting, in which there are interested parties and something at stake. In any real conflict there is a burden of proof,[37] which is sustained by a strategical alignment of people and things that can be relied upon to support and enforce that burden.[38] Epistemic conflict is always shaped by the goods, practices, and projects whose allocation and pursuit are at issue, and by the institutions and social networks that are organized around those pursuits. In such real contexts there are constraints upon which arguments and evidence will count as relevant and persuasive, based upon the need for support from others and for reliability from things. It matters what will count as persuasive to others who occupy strategic points in the circulation of knowledge and argument, and it also matters how things will manifest themselves in the contexts in which their behavior is recognized to be relevant.

It is crucial to recognize, however, that the alignment that determines the burden of proof and the standards that must be met is subject to challenge. Not long ago creationism was readily dismissable as irrational, crackpot science, by appeal to standards that were recognized as relevant and decisive by a powerful social network that controlled access to the educational system and to the other social goods to which adequate (or at least certified) knowledge of biology provided access. But this appeal was not "merely" a recourse to power; implicated in it was the history of the discovery and interpretation of fossils and other geological data, of political practices and goods surrounding religious life, of the institutional organization and placement of science, and so forth. This complexity and its dynamics are evident in the ways in which the proponents of creationism tried, with some success, to alter the epistemic and political alignment that denied their views any serious recognition.

---

[37] Steve Fuller, in Chapter 4 of *Social Epistemology*, offers an illuminating discussion of the role of the burden of proof in scientific and philosophical argument and of the ways in which the burden of proof can be shifted.

[38] I take this notion of an "alignment" to be a commentary upon Foucault's discussion of networks or chains of power/knowledge and their strategic and tactical interaction, but the term itself is taken from Thomas Wartenburg, *The Forms of Power* (Philadelphia: Temple University Press, 1990), whose account of the dynamic and heterogeneous character of social power has interesting parallels with the epistemological dynamics I have been developing here. Wartenburg's own view, while elaborated in original and insightful ways to which I am indebted, is closer to Foucault's position than his own interpretation of Foucault would suggest.

Indeed, the recent prominence of this example testifies to the partial effectiveness of their resistance to the dominant alignment. For the new creationists did not meekly accept their allotted place and vainly reassert the superiority of religious belief to science. They tried to claim the epistemic and political resources of science on multiple fronts: challenging the connection between fossil data and dominant interpretations of evolutionary theory, citing philosophical disputes about the demarcation of science, transforming their own views to resist attacks upon their "unscientific" character, and turning against their opponents their objections to using political power to enforce scientific belief. Of course, they also mobilized a religiously committed political base and chose a sympathetic venue (legislatures and courts in states with strong ties to Christian fundamentalism and relatively weak ties to scientific and education establishments). Their strategies were an interesting mix of trying to subvert or coopt elements of the dominant epistemic alignment that established and enforced the rationality of belief in Darwinian theory and trying to create alternative alignments (Christian schools, creationist research and textbooks, etc.) that would enable them to bypass it.

Their initial successes in this strategy compelled defenders of mainstream biology to confront arguments and respond to strategies whose dismissal previously went virtually without saying. This response in the end was largely successful, as there were effective counters to many of the new creationist strategies and arguments. As a result, one still need not consider scripture in most contexts in order to assess or advance biological knowledge. But new arguments, new knowledges (about the epistemic gaps in the Darwinian orthodoxy, about the creationist resistance, about religion, science, and politics), and new alignments were created in the course of these responses; resistance partially refocuses the organization of knowledge even when it substantially fails to overturn its target.

It is useful to compare this example with that of recent feminist challenges to sexist orthodoxies in many disciplines. Like creationism, feminist critiques could once be dismissed in most contexts without having to be taken seriously. When articulated, the dismissal rejected not just their specific contributions to knowledge, but the very possibility of such contributions, which could only represent the illegitimate intrusion of religion or politics into knowledge. Like creationists, the feminists combined a new program of research with resourceful appropriation and redirection of elements of orthodoxy and the creation of alternative alignments that reduced their dependence upon unregenerate opponents (feminist presses and journals, professional associations and graduate programs, but also a variety of more straightforwardly political alliances).[39] The feminists have been rather more successful than have creationists, despite considerable remaining opposition. But this success must be understood in simultaneously epistemic and political terms. Their arguments were more persuasive. Sexism and gender have shown themselves to be more resilient and readily manifest objects of inquiry than is biblical creation. And the new feminist alignments made it more difficult to ignore or dismiss their arguments, avoid their vocabulary, or refuse to certify their achievements.

Were the feminists more rational, or more warranted in their claims, than were the creationists? Yes. But that judgment does not stand above the fray as an assessment of the unsituated rationality of each set of arguments and conclusions. That judgment is itself a move in ongoing epistemic struggles, which both draws upon and reinforces the successes and failures of each view. My own arguments, and allusions to arguments, were responses to the burden and standards of proof that I take to be effective in the context in which this is written; in their small way, they also aim to reinforce or transform the standards to which they appeal.

The moral for epistemology is, I hope, clear. The turn to a nonsovereign epistemological dynamics does not replace argument or a concern for truth with power and domination, even while insisting that argument and claims to knowledge are never politically innocent. The contested circulation of opposing knowledges, which cannot be consistently combined into a unitary framework of propositions, is a struggle for truth. Truth matters. Precisely because it matters, truth is often fiercely contested. And if we cannot stand outside that contest to assess it from a neutral standpoint, this does not mean that all claims to truth can be put forward on an equal basis. Knowledge claims are historically, socially, and materially situated in contexts that govern what can be intelligibly and seriously asserted and how much or what kind of argument is necessary to support it. But such epistemic contexts are always in flux; their boundaries and configuration are continually challenged and partially reconstructed, as epistemic alignments shift. And these alignments are always inter-

---

[39]Wartenburg, ibid., offers a very informative account of such feminist strategies as part of a discussion of new social movements, in order to exemplify the insights offered by his dynamic account of power.

twined with alignments of power and political resistance. To recognize this interconnection is not to devalue knowledge or science for political purposes, but to take seriously the stakes in struggles for knowledge and truth and to place epistemology and philosophy of science squarely in their midst.

Part V

THE WORKPLACE

LAW, NORMATIVITY, AND THE LEVEL PLAYING FIELD
The Production of Rights in American Labor Law

Robert Moore, Jr.

Throughout his writings, but especially in *Discipline and Punish* and *The History of Sexuality*, Michel Foucault focused on the disciplinary aspects associated with institutional settings such as prisons and hospitals and human sciences such as criminology and psychiatry.[1] In many ways his work in these areas was influenced by and had implications for several areas of law, yet Foucault attempted little or no analysis of specific statutes or the relatively discrete bodies of law that grew out of them. Indeed, Foucault's writings on power/knowledge are in large measure oriented toward challenging the idea that law and legal systems constitute some kind of privileged institutional structure through which power is exercised. By focusing attention on the human body as it is affected by the

---

[1]*Discipline and Punish: The Birth of the Prison*, tr. Alan Sheridan (New York: Pantheon, 1977), and *The History of Sexuality, Volume 1: An Introduction*, tr. Robert Hurley (New York: Pantheon, 1978).

"microphysics" of power, Foucault forced theorists of power to rethink traditional approaches and to shift the object of study away from large-scale institutional structures such as law and economy.

Without disputing the importance of this shift, this essay attempts to utilize the Foucaultian perspective in an effort to understand contemporary American labor law and collective bargaining as a system of discipline and social control. The essence of the argument is that the legal structure informing U.S. collective bargaining law constitutes its own version of "truth," much like the systems underlying biology, psychiatry, or criminology. Within this structure, labor-management conflict is constituted as an object of scientific knowledge, and collective bargaining law is situated at the core of a larger discourse that mandates certain forms of therapeutic intervention.

Labor disputes constitute an object of scientific knowledge insofar as their examination is informed by the "sciences" of society (sociology, political science, economics) whose dominant paradigms proclaim harmony, stability, equilibrium, gradualism, and reformism as "normal" and conflict (class or otherwise) as "pathological." The legitimacy of therapeutic intervention is found in the institutional creation of a legal framework for collective bargaining law. When labor-management relations are disrupted, creating a "pathological" state, this framework prescribes that expert arbitrators intervene in order to restore harmony and a "level playing field." Within this system, employees and employers are viewed as equal beneficiaries of the procedural rights that constitute the foundation of collective bargaining law.

In recent years discussions in the sociology of law have frequently been framed by a debate between Marxists and functionalists.[2] At one extreme, the "vulgar" Marxist view portrays law as a thinly veiled means of enforcing capitalist social relations of production. Labor law, with its focus on the central problematic in Marxist theory, offers adherents of such a perspective a classic case study on economic domination of the state. At the other extreme, the simplistic functionalist formulation views law as the formalized codification of widely held cultural norms and beliefs. According to this view, rather than representing the embodiment of class conflict, labor law signals the negotiated end to such turmoil. In spite of the vast and many differences between these two models, both must ultimately explore the ways in which legal rules and cultural values

---

[2]For a general overview of dominant theoretical perspectives in sociology, see George Ritzer, *Sociological Theory* (New York: Alfred Knopf, 1983).

are internalized through socialization. For the Marxists, this process often results in false consciousness; for the functionalists, socialization represents the means by which legitimate cultural values come to be embraced by the population.

Although he does not present his work in such terms, Foucault also examines the central role of socialization in constituting the human subject. Indeed, his approach is very much concerned with the specific avenues whereby the dominant norms, values, and beliefs of society are internalized. This is particularly true where these norms, values, and beliefs embrace and constitute systems of expertise that directly and indirectly administer and shape the behavior of populations.

The following analysis of American labor law combines Foucaultian and Marxian views of law and socialization in a critique of the mainstream functionalist/formalist model. While differing in significant ways, the Marxian and Foucaultian models share one premise that distinguishes them from their mainstream counterpart: social relations created by law are neither entirely consensual nor neutral in their effects.

THEORETICAL ISSUES AND HISTORICAL BACKGROUND

The dominant form of traditional legal reasoning, known as formalism, "explains legal outcomes in terms of deduction from or 'reasoned elaboration' of rules" and relies on "analysis of legislative intent, application of 'policy considerations,' and so on."[3] Critics of this traditional approach in legal scholarship argue that it defines issues too narrowly, often bracketing out the most relevant questions. The result is a preoccupation with strictly defined "black letter law" in the form of legal rulings or legislative pronouncements and a dismissal of the political nature of the decision itself, the assumptions underlying its logic, or its social impact. A more critical approach to legal scholarship challenges this orientation by examining black letter law within its political and economic context.

This paper expands upon this critical approach by incorporating Foucaultian analysis. I will argue that the legal structure that grew out of

---

[3]See Karl Klare, "Traditional Labor Law Scholarship and the Crisis of Collective Bargaining Law: A Reply to Professor Finkin," *Maryland Law Review* 44:3 (1985): 748.

the National Labor Relations Act (NLRA) facilitates bureaucratic control and disciplinary structures within the workplace, encourages the proliferation of bureaucratic structures in unions, and ultimately ensures within American labor law the contemporary status of the arbitrator as "expert," authorized to order therapeutic intervention when the harmony of the system is disrupted.

The NLRA (or Wagner Act) was signed into law by Franklin Roosevelt on July 5, 1935, with its stated purpose being to "diminish the cause of labor disputes burdening or obstructing interstate and foreign commerce [and] to create a National Labor Relations Board."[4] The Act's statement of Findings and Policy contained the following language:

> SEC. 1. The denial by employers of the right of employees to organize and the refusal by employers to accept the procedure of collective bargaining lead to strikes and other forms of industrial strife or unrest, which have the intent or the necessary effect of burdening or obstructing commerce. . . .
>
> *The inequality of bargaining power between employees who do not possess full freedom of association or actual liberty of contract and employers who are organized in the corporate or other forms of ownership association substantially burdens and affects the flow of commerce.* . . .
>
> Experience has proved that protection by law of *the right of employees to organize and bargain collectively safeguards commerce from injury, impairment, or interruption, and promotes the flow of commerce by removing certain recognized sources of industrial strife and unrest,* by encouraging practices fundamental to the friendly adjustment of industrial disputes arising out of differences as to wages, hours, or other working conditions, *and by restoring equality of bargaining power between employers and employees.*[5]

I have emphasized the passages that explicitly acknowledge the inequality of bargaining power between employees and employers. Behind the drafting of such language was the view that large business entities had attained a level of monopoly power enabling them to disrupt what had

---

[4]See Robert F. Koretz, *Statutory History of the United States: Labor Organization* (New York: McGraw-Hill, 1970), p. 267.

[5]For a general overview of these cases, see Christopher L. Tomlins, *The State and the Unions: Law and the Organized Labor Movement in America, 1880–1960* (Cambridge: Cambridge University Press, 1985), Ch. 3.

previously been a system based on free contract. Under the free contract system, employees and employers were considered equal parties to a mutually beneficial employment relationship; the company was free to terminate the relationship at any time, as was the employee. Numerous U.S. Supreme Court cases affirmed the solemnity of freedom of contract by denying the constitutionality of efforts to introduce wage and hour standards or any other form of "government interference."[6]

The Great Depression of the 1930s soon made it clear that employee and employer no longer stood on equal ground. With hundreds of thousands of people unemployed, it became necessary for government to act if it was to maintain legitimacy and avert class conflict. Drafters of the Wagner Act pursued the goal of reducing industrial strife by restoring equality of bargaining power through what has often been referred to as the establishment of a "level playing field." Wagner Act jurisprudence was concerned with the process of institutionalizing class conflict within the peaceful operation of collective bargaining and the grievance system.[7] This system operated under the "industrial pluralist" assumption that the collective bargaining structure would provide the equality of opportunity required for fair treatment and representation of the interest groups involved. "Industrial pluralism" assumed that the Wagner Act provided both employers and employees with the framework necessary to engage in their own form of self-contained "industrial self-governance."[8] Like the more generalized view of political pluralism found in the writings of Robert Dahl,[9] "industrial pluralism" postulated that elected (union and company) officials would represent their respective interest groups in a neutral (collective bargaining) arena and that the party representing the most meritorious view would emerge victorious.

As Katherine Stone has argued, the Wagner Act and its subsequent adjudication established industrial pluralism as the implied yet dominant paradigm governing the collective bargaining process in the United

---

[6] E.g., *Coppage v. Kansas*, 236 U.S. 1 (1915) and *Adair v. United States*, 208 U.S. 161 (1908); see generally Elizabeth Mensch, "The History of Mainstream Legal Thought," in David Kairys, ed., *The Politics of Law*, rev. edn. (New York: Pantheon, 1990), pp. 13–37.
[7] Karl Klare, "Judicial Deradicalization of the Wagner Act and the Origins of Modern Legal Consciousness, 1937–1941," *Minnesota Law Review* 62 (1977–78): 265–339.
[8] Katherine Stone, "The Post-War Paradigm in American Labor Law," *Yale Law Journal* 90 (1981): 1509.
[9] E.g., *Who Governs?* (New Haven: Yale University Press, 1961).

States. This can be viewed as a basis for production of truth, from a Foucaultian perspective, insofar as "advances" in the social sciences regarding, for example, the "logic of industrialism"[10] are comparable with positive progress in the behavioral and cognitive sciences. In both cases, scientific advancement of knowledge leads to the ability to know certain truths: in psychiatry it is the ability to know the truth of madness; in criminology it is the capacity to know the truth of deviance. The industrial pluralist model proclaimed its ultimate capacity for producing "truth" by asserting the ability of social science to understand and administer a system of labor relations that could restore the system to its "neutral" state when faced with potential conflict and threats to harmony.

While this development may have ideological implications,[11] it need not be reduced wholly to ideology as some form of negative mystification, a view usually attributed to Marxism. So-called vulgar Marxian analyses have portrayed ideology as a kind of shroud that conceals an underlying truth; if one can pierce the "ideological veil," then one can discover the real meaning of social relationships. This view implies that ideology is some form of propaganda that induces a false consciousness, and once the misleading nature of the propaganda is revealed, it is possible to know the real "truth." Perhaps Herbert Marcuse, in *One-Dimensional Man*, best illustrates the shift in Marxian thinking towards a model whereby ideology no longer is viewed as something that *obscures* the truth; rather, ideology is something that *produces* truth. No longer are humans able to awaken from their propaganda-induced, dreamlike state—because they are actually living the dream.[12]

The same argument can be applied to this discussion of the framework created by industrial pluralism, labor relations, and collective bargaining law. To the extent that actual social relations are governed by its terms, the model is not simply a form of ideological mystification. Indeed, the model positively produces its own truth when combined with other legal rational claims regarding the validity of expert knowledge and the ability of social science to understand social reality and to counsel intervention when normal behavior is disrupted. It is at the intersection of discourses

---

[10]See Clark Kerr et al., *Industrialism and Industrial Man* (Cambridge: Harvard University Press, 1960).

[11]See Karl Klare, "Labor Law as Ideology: Toward a New Historiography of Collective Bargaining Law," *Industrial Relations Law Journal* 4 (1981): 450.

[12]*One-Dimensional Man: Studies in the Ideology of Advanced Industrial Society* (Boston: Beacon Press, 1964).

in functionalist sociology, liberal political theory, and neoclassical economics that collective bargaining law finds its legitimation. Grounded in positivist notions of the ability of social science to understand the world, a joint program is outlined according to the norms of applied science. This is most clearly revealed in the increasingly important role that arbitration and the arbitrator play in the maintenance of the "normal" operation of industrial relations. The next section explores the historical development of this model.

NORMALIZATION OF WORKPLACE RULES AND THE RISE OF ARBITRATION IN AMERICAN LABOR LAW

The National Labor Relations Board (NLRB), established by the Wagner Act, had been in existence only a few years when its operation was suspended with the advent of World War II, and labor policy in the United States came under the administration of the National War Labor Board (NWLB). Immensely influential in setting a national postwar pattern, the NWLB came "to regard an appropriate grievance procedure, with its terminal point in an *impartial umpire*, as indispensable to the establishment of justice within the industrial community. So universal became the adoption of this system that its deployment seemed a *natural and inevitable evolution of a mature system of industrial relations.*"[13] As discussed below, this inevitability was assumed by the postwar Supreme Court as well, and it forms the basis for the so-called quid pro quo doctrine, whereby the right to strike during the term of a contract is presumed to be canceled by the existence of an arbitration clause. The "impartial umpire" would use expert knowledge to "balance" the interests of both parties. As the Supreme Court wrote in 1960:

> The labor arbitrator performs functions which are not normal to the courts; the considerations which help him fashion judgements may indeed be foreign to the competence of courts. . . . The parties expect that his judgement of a particular grievance will reflect not only what the contract says but, insofar as the

[13]Nelson Lichtenstein, "Industrial Democracy, Contract Unionism, and the National War Labor Board," *Labor Law Journal* 33 (August 1982): 528 (italics added).

collective bargaining agreement permits, such factors as the effect upon productivity of a particular result, its consequence to the morale of the shop, his judgement whether tensions will be heightened or diminished. For the parties' objective in using the arbitration process is primarily to further their common goal of uninterrupted production under the agreement, to make the agreement serve their specialized needs. The ablest judge cannot be expected to bring the same experience and competence to bear upon the determination of a grievance, because he cannot be similarly informed.[14]

Thus the arbitrator is both expert and judge, called upon to "balance" the competing claims of labor and management in a neutral arena, relying on social scientific claims as well as authority that flows from the contract. The general result of this "balancing" procedure is often the narrow interpretation of the statutory and procedural rights of workers and the broad interpretation of contractual rights implicitly or explicitly reserved to management.

As much as any other single rule in contemporary American labor law, the quid pro quo doctrine that grew out of the arbitration system encouraged during World War II has had the effect of channeling most forms of shopfloor conflict into the bureaucratic machinery of the grievance procedure. For example, prior to the implied collective bargaining agreement clause requiring that disputes be submitted to a "neutral umpire," workers may have simply elected to stop production, occupy the plant, and not leave until the dispute was settled. Or, as illustrated in the *Boy's Market* case discussed below, workers may have decided to strike instead of arbitrate.[15] The quid pro quo doctrine effectively precluded such actions and required that all grievances be pursued exclusively through the arbitration process. Failure to work within the framework of the arbitration system meant a clear-cut violation of the terms of the contract, and the courts moved quickly to punish those not abiding by contractual provisions.

The law is obviously a very significant instrument of social control. Law ultimately relies upon the coercive power of the state for enforcement, and to the extent that individual persons violate specific rulings there are

[14]*United Steelworkers* v. *Warrior & Gulf Navigation Co.*, 363 U.S. 574 (1960).
[15]*Boy's Market, Inc.* v. *Retail Clerks Local* 770, 398 U.S. 235 (1970).

direct coercive consequences. Yet a focus on this instrumental application of force diverts attention from the more subtle and perhaps more important ways in which law shapes human behavior. In this regard, the following analysis explores U.S. collective bargaining law by focusing on its interaction with bureaucratic and technical structures of work, as well as the hierarchical social structure that tends to govern labor unions in the United States. In Foucaultian terms, this approach enables a better understanding of the multiple points where power is felt by the social body.

The following discussion traces the connections between labor law and its penchant for arbitration, on the one hand, and hierarchical labor union structures and bureaucratic forms of work organization, on the other. Arbitration presumes a neutral, nonpolitical organizational structure oriented toward efficiency and continuity of production.[16] This is true for the organization of the particular workplace as well as for the organization of the body that represents the workers. These presumptions are implicitly embedded in collective bargaining agreements where each component clause represents a social understanding corresponding to a given point in the process of physical production.

For example, if an individual worker's responsibility is to place the spare tire into the trunk of an automobile, there is a job description in the collective bargaining agreement that outlines in specific detail how this job is to be performed. This description not only prescribes the physical acts to be performed by the worker; it also circumscribes the organizational context in which the worker acts and reveals the cultural understandings about his or her role in the overall production process. The worker does not have a choice in how to perform the specific operation, nor a choice in whether to perform the task at all. Indeed, if the worker is instructed by a supervisor to perform the task in a manner differing from the job description in the collective bargaining agreement, the worker does not have a choice regarding the appropriate manner of resistance. He or she must "work now and grieve later," for the collective bargaining agreement specifies that the worker must maintain production and then follow appropriate procedure in filing a grievance with the person duly authorized to act upon it.

---

[16]See generally Frank Elkouri and Edna Asper Elkouri, *How Arbitration Works*, 4th edn. (Washington D.C.: Bureau of National Affairs, 1985).

Thus the job description goes far beyond the physical act and encompasses a whole range of social and cultural concerns. It is at the numerous points where the physical production process intersects with the labor contract and its surrounding assumptions that we can locate the web of power relationships governing the collective bargaining process in particular and establishing normativity with regard to labor relations in general. The contemporary labor contract contributed to normalization of the working population by specifying an entire range of appropriate (and inappropriate) behavior. Yet, in spite of the degree of specificity found in the labor contract, much of the worker's behavior was still governed by "extra-legal" penalties. As Foucault observed in *Discipline and Punish*:

> The workshop . . . [was] subject to a whole micro-penalty of time (lateness, absences, interruptions of tasks), of activity (inattention, negligence, lack of zeal), of behaviour (impoliteness, disobedience), of speech (idle chatter, insolence), of the body ("incorrect" attitudes, irregular gestures). . . . [17]

What is interesting and significant about these sorts of activities is that they are not explicitly proscribed in collective bargaining agreements, yet they have found their way into what arbitrators have referred to as the "common law" of the workplace. James Atleson has done a particularly interesting study on the use of profanity directed by workers to their supervisors. Although there are no rules in the collective bargaining agreement prohibiting the use of such language, workers are routinely disciplined by management for doing so and the disciplinary measures are affirmed by arbitrators.[18] In the aftermath of numerous such rulings, workers increasingly learn to discipline themselves as the normalizing power permeates the social structure and culture of the workplace.

Normalization of the work process was closely linked to the rationalization of the collective bargaining process, the latter being largely shaped by the no-strike pledge during World War II and the concurrent emphasis on arbitration as a means of dispute resolution. These combined forces had immediate consequences for union leaders who had pledged to

---
[17]*Discipline and Punish*, p. 178.
[18]James B. Atleson, *Values and Assumptions in American Labor Law* (Amherst: University of Massachusetts Press, 1983).

cooperate with the NWLB. Acceptance of arbitration by these leaders required a rejection of the various forms of direct action that had previously won them the most support from their members. The most obvious example of this is found in "sit-down" strikes, whereby workers ceased production but still occupied the plant. This strategy was tremendously effective for the United Auto Workers in 1936 when they successfully organized workers at the General Motors plant in Flint, Michigan. Under almost all collective bargaining agreements since that time, such activities are contractually forbidden and unions are held liable for breach of contract if workers engage in such unauthorized activity. By agreeing contractually to claims about management's rights over private property, unions are then obligated to serve as the enforcer of management claims.

Likewise, automatic payroll deductions for "maintenance of membership" and "dues checkoff" resulted in a situation where it was easier for union leaders to distance themselves from the demands of the rank and file, since members could no longer quit or withhold their dues in protest of union policy. Unions became increasingly bureaucratized as union leaders and staff assumed responsibility for administering the terms of the contract, and the contract itself became increasingly detailed and complex.

Although several factors account for the proliferation of work rules and job categories found in collective bargaining agreements during this period, it is central to this analysis that the corollary to efficient contract administration is an increasingly detailed set of work rules to measure the proper compliance of workers in an increasingly detailed subdivision of labor. These work rules and their administration thus parallel the increasingly bureaucratic nature of the organization of work itself with its self-evident rational character.[19]

This bureaucratic form of workplace control and discipline has a structural as well as a normative component. Stephen Hill has offered the following definition of these two dimensions of workplace control:

> *Structural Dimension*: the way a firm is organized to ensure the co-ordination of activities and direction of employees.

---

[19]See generally Dan Clawson, *Bureaucracy and the Labor Process: The Transformation of U.S. Industry, 1860–1920* (New York: Monthly Review Press, 1980), and Richard Edwards *Contested Terrain: The Transformation of the Workplace in the Twentieth Century* (New York: Basic Books, 1979).

Normative Dimension: this includes the elements of the organizational value system which regulates the conduct and performance of the members.[20]

Hill's formulation points to the symbiotic relationship between the structural and the normative dimensions of workplace control and indicates the ways in which the two must necessarily combine for ultimate effectiveness as a disciplinary system. This is a central requirement of advanced forms of bureaucratic control: a given structural form necessitates normative content that establishes its legitimacy and elicits compliance from the population administered within it. Thus the hierarchical, rationalized structure of workplace production and union organizations finds its necessary counterpart in a set of beliefs and values that accord legitimacy to such structures.

For example, the assembly line represents a form of work organization premised on achieving maximum productivity through hierarchy and specialization. Collective bargaining agreements that designate job descriptions based upon this system implicitly acknowledge that maximum productivity and efficiency, as opposed to maximum human creativity and fulfillment, are the normative goals that guide conduct in the workplace. Precisely because normative and structural dimensions appear to require one another, their inevitability seems beyond question; they both seem inevitable in a way that neither by itself would. Thus bureaucratic control of the workplace is embedded in both structural and normative dimensions.

Integral to the development of this type of control is a general theory that can explain the inevitability of hierarchy, the superiority of rationalized forms of organization, the basis for expert knowledge, and the positive role that parliamentary, reformist procedures can play in restoring balance and equilibrium to a system threatened by dysfunctional forces. Such a theory is implicitly embedded in the assumptions that have historically formed the basis of industrial psychology and sociology, as well as most political science. These various discourses intersect and constitute the ideological framework that informs the general contours of contemporary American collective bargaining law.

From a Foucaultian perspective, this framework ultimately leads to

---

[20]*Competition and Control at Work: The New Industrial Sociology* (Cambridge: MIT Press, 1981), p. 91.

discipline of individual workers and others operating in or around most workplaces. Like the Panopticon, the social and physical structure of the workplace is oriented toward regulation of workers and production by the workers themselves. By denying the existence of structured inequality in society, this framework proclaims that the structure of work and society itself is neutral and based on meritocratic principles. Under this model, problems stem from the inability of individuals or groups to be fully integrated into this self-regulating system, resulting in disruptions to production and behavior that threatens the stability of the system. Accordingly, organizations are viewed as entities that have objective properties, and the role of the theorist is to discover these properties empirically and to develop applied methods that will ensure the general balance and equilibrium that characterize such systems. The central question for collective bargaining law and the arbitrator is how to better integrate the individual into the system, consequently disciplining the particular worker and normalizing the behavior of working populations in general. Organizational theory thus validates bureaucratic control of the workplace and finds its counterpart in legal reasoning related to arbitration as the preferred form of dispute resolution.

ARBITRATION AND THE CONTAINMENT OF CONFLICT

American collective bargaining law in the 1950s and 1960s was developing into an increasingly procedural system, where substantive rights or goals were either hidden or excluded in favor of concerns about due process. In the "social contract" that developed between labor and management in the postwar period, combining elements of collective bargaining law as well as bureaucratic control, the emphasis was almost entirely on the *procedural* rights that would accrue to workers by submitting their demands to the arbitration process.

Since *Textile Workers* v. *Lincoln Mills* it has been the general policy of the federal courts to order arbitration in cases where disputes over arbitrability present at least a colorable claim that the question *may* be subject to arbitration under the collective bargaining agreement.[21] In developing the opinion, Justice Douglas reviewed the legislative history of the Act and

---

[21]*Textile Workers Union* v. *Lincoln Mills*, 353 U.S. 448 (1957).

concluded that there was a clear preference for arbitration over industrial strife.

Although his conclusion has been subject to much debate, Justice Douglas stated in *Lincoln Mills* that "the agreement to arbitrate grievance disputes is the quid pro quo for an agreement not to strike." Regardless of its alleged lack of statutory authority or empirical grounding (even within the standards of its own formalist tradition), this assertion has formed the fundamental assumption underlying practically all subsequent law relating to issues of arbitrability.

Douglas's concern with promoting arbitrability and discouraging strikes was made even more apparent in the cases that have come to be known as the "Steelworker's Trilogy." Justice Douglas wrote at length in the majority opinions about the limited role of the Court in ordering arbitration, as well as the "therapeutic" effects of arbitration in general. Regarding the role of the Court in ordering arbitration, Douglas wrote in *United Steelworkers v. American Manufacturing Co.* that the Court "is confined to ascertaining whether the party seeking arbitration is making a claim which on its face is governed by the contract."[22] Thus there is a presumption in favor of arbitration and the courts should not look too deeply into the substantive merits in order to determine arbitrability. Indeed, it has been argued that any challenge to arbitration on the merits will lose as will any challenge based on a contractual term because it also entails an examination of the merits. The language in these cases generally presumes that arbitration will be pursued, almost in spite of the intention of the parties.

In *United Steelworkers v. Warrior & Gulf Navigation Co.* Douglas reviewed the various factors that the Court could examine in determining whether or not a particular dispute should go to arbitration.[23] Specifically, Douglas mentioned the following:

> . . . apart from matters which the parties specifically exclude, all of the questions on which the parties disagree must therefore come within the scope of the grievance and arbitration provisions of the collective agreement. . . .
>
> . . . an order to arbitrate the particular grievance should not be denied unless it may be said with positive assurance that the

---

[22]*United Steelworkers v. American Manufacturing Co.*, 363 U.S. 564 (1960).
[23]*United Steelworkers v. Warrior & Gulf Navigation Co.*, 363 U.S. 574 (1960).

arbitration clause is not susceptible to an interpretation which covers the asserted dispute. Doubts should be resolved in favor of coverage.

. . . In the absence of an express provision excluding a particular grievance from arbitration, we think only the most forceful evidence of a purpose to exclude the claim from arbitration can prevail, particularly where, as here, the exclusion clause is vague and the arbitration clause quite broad.

Douglas's sweeping pronouncements create a general presumption in favor of arbitration and do not limit the arbitrator to the expressed terms of the contract. According to Douglas, "the industrial common law—the practices of the industry and the shop—is equally a part of the collective bargaining agreement although not expressed in it." This is clearly an interpretation that favors normative principles over legal ones as such. From a Foucaultian perspective, this represents an interesting development and calls into question the power of law by itself to mandate behavior within human populations. Contrary to the traditional view that law establishes behavioral standards to be transmitted in a top-down fashion, Douglas's language tends to support a more decentralized model embraced by Foucault. To the extent that individual workers embrace these normative assumptions, they are guided less by the threat of the exercise of coercive power and more by a normalized vision of "appropriate" worker performance. As Foucault has argued: "He who is subjected to a field of visibility, and who knows it, assumes responsibility for the constraints of power; he makes them play spontaneously upon himself; he inscribes in himself the power relations in which he simultaneously plays both roles; he becomes the principle of his own subjection."[24]

In the Steelworkers Trilogy, the Supreme Court performed two related functions. On the one hand, it reinforced notions of liberal political theory by preserving the sanctity of the private labor contract. This preservation can be claimed to have ideological value insofar as it portrayed labor relations as the product of an agreement freely entered into by rational agents. At the same time, the operation of the labor relations process became less a result of the rule of law and more a function of normative assumptions about labor and the organization of work in general. The dilemmas that flow from this approach are

---

[24]*Discipline and Punish*, pp. 202–203.

exemplified in cases relating to employer unfair labor practices. In each case where employees are confronted with employer abuses, they must determine—before engaging in any form of response—whether the abuse constitutes a contractual violation or an unfair labor practice.

From a strictly legal standpoint, whether an employer action is viewed as an unfair labor practice or as a contractual violation makes a crucial difference to whether the strike action of employees is protected or unprotected under the Act. If the strike is in response to an unfair labor practice, then the strike is protected and the employees are entitled to a legal remedy. If, on the other hand, the employer action is viewed as simply a *contractual violation* and not an unfair labor practice as defined by the Act, then an employee strike would not be considered protected activity. This means that the only way for workers to respond safely to an employer's unfair labor practice is to proceed *within the limited context of a bureaucratized grievance system*, with its delays and necessary abstraction from shopfloor reality. In other words, workers have forfeited their statutory right to strike by agreeing to a contractual obligation to arbitrate. If the workers use any form of protest other than grievance and arbitration, and it is determined at a later time that the employer's action was not an unfair labor practice, then the workers themselves could be penalized for engaging in a strike unprotected by the NLRA.

This is precisely what happened in the case of *Boy's Market*, where workers pursued nonarbitral means of resolving a labor dispute and were subsequently penalized. The facts of the case are fairly clear. Unionized employees observed management officials stocking shelves that, according to the collective bargaining agreement, were to be stocked only by unionized employees. When union workers objected to management and argued that the shelves should be emptied and restocked by unionized employees, management refused. In response, unionized employees were faced with the choice of pursuing arbitration or finding other means of resolving the dispute. They chose to strike. In so doing, the Supreme Court eventually determined, they had violated an implied term of their collective bargaining agreement prohibiting them from striking when an arbitration clause was in effect.

As Atleson has discussed, the rationale for *Boy's Market* does not flow automatically from the text of statutes or common law, but rather can be traced to certain core values and assumptions that underlie conceptions of labor relations. Atleson has identified five general values and assumptions underlying American labor law:

... continuity of production must be maintained, tempered only when statutory language clearly protects employee interference.

... employees, unless controlled, will act irresponsibly.

... [employees have a] limited status in the management of the industry.

... the "common enterprise" is primarily under management's control.

... employees cannot be full partners in the enterprise because such an arrangement would interfere with inherent and exclusive managerial rights of employers.[25]

Atleson argues that each of these assumptions is in tension with the statutory rights granted to employees under the National Labor Relations Act. Thus, when the statutory rights of workers come into conflict with closely held values and assumptions, judges pursue a line of reasoning that attempts to reconcile the two, often resulting in severe limitations on the protected activities of workers and the reduction of potentially beneficial substantive rights into hollow procedural formalities.

This governance of labor relations from a normative rather than a strictly legal basis lends support to the disciplinary model of power proposed by Foucault. The role of the arbitrator as expert is now mandated by law, yet its ascendency had less to do with instrumental manipulation of law and the legal process by powerful interests than with the general effect of normative assumptions on judicial interpretations. Rather than operating in a top-down fashion, power is more diffused and decentralized, relying less on force and manipulation than on widely held assumptions about the legitimacy of neutral decisionmaking frameworks and the authority of experts. Aspects of normalization and rationalization combine to produce a disciplinary system in the workplace comparable to that found in the prison.

Central to this disciplinary framework is the development of a normalized value system that embraces claims to the system's neutrality and objectivity. The notion of a "level playing field," policed by the arbitrator as neutral "umpire," is in essence the end product of this process. The next section explores the application of the "level playing field"

[25]*Values and Assumptions*, pp. 7–10.

concept as it is found in legal discourse related to strikes, lockouts, and the issue of replacement workers.

DISCIPLINING LABOR

The topic of lockouts and replacement workers has become increasingly important in recent years and provides an interesting case study for analyzing the disciplinary role that normative evaluations play in the collective bargaining process. Most pronounced in this discussion is the analogy of the "level playing field" and the presumably equal application of procedural rights produced from American labor law.

Although employer lockouts have traditionally been a defensive weapon associated with strikes, it is no longer true that management resorts to the lockout only when a strike is imminent. Following the 1986 NLRB ruling in *Harter Equipment*,[26] it is now acceptable for an employer to use the lockout as an offensive tool to discharge its union employees and hire temporary replacements, even when the employees desire to continue working under an extended contract or wish to pursue further negotiations.

The main conclusion of *Harter* is that the "employer did not violate [the] LMRA when it hired temporary replacements after lawfully locking out permanent employees for [the] sole purpose of bringing economic pressure to bear in support of [a] legitimate bargaining position."[27] The facts of the case were never disputed. The company (Respondent) and the Union had been engaged in successful collective bargaining from 1973 through 1981. Two months before the 1981 contract was going to expire, the Respondent informed the Union that it was experiencing serious financial difficulties and would need concessions from the Union. The Union opposed the concessions but offered to extend the contract for six months to provide additional bargaining time. The company refused to extend the contract and on December 3, 1981—two days after the contract expired—the company "locked out its employees in order to put pressure on the Union to agree to terms favorable to the [company]."[28]

[26]*Harter Equipment*, 280 NLRB 71 (1986).
[27]Ibid., p. 1219.
[28]Ibid., p. 1220.

The Board went on to state:

> In mid-January 1982, the Respondent commenced hiring temporary employees so that it could resume operations and meet fixed expenses. Negotiations continued through March, but at the time of the hearing the lockout continued and the temporary replacements were still employed. There is no evidence that Respondent was motivated by specific anti-union animus.[29]

The LMRA essentially guarantees three rights to workers:

1. The right to bargain collectively. [Sec. 8(a)(5)]
2. The right to strike. [Sec. 7]
3. The right to engage in union activities. [Sec. 8(a)(3)]

Thus, in order for the Board to locate an unfair labor practice in any given case, it must find interference with one of these three rights. As discussed above, the Board concluded that the actions of Harter Equipment violated none of these rights.

In developing its opinion, the Court relied primarily on two cases to support its position. The first case—*American Shipbuilding*[30]—presented facts similar to those in *Harter*, except the issue of hiring temporary replacements was not addressed. In declaring that the employer lockout did not violate the terms of the Act, the Court argued that such an "employer weapon" was justified for business reasons and that the impact of the lockout on the rights of the employees was comparatively slight as opposed to "inherently destructive," a determination that would automatically make it an unfair labor practice regardless of the intent of the employer.

The Court then went on to examine each of the three rights listed above to justify its conclusion that no unfair labor practice had been committed. Concerning the right to bargain collectively, the Court stated:

> The lockout may well dissuade employees from adhering to the position which they initially adopted in the bargaining, but the

---

[29] Ibid.
[30] *American Shipbuilding Co. v. NLRB*, 380 U.S. 300 (1965).

> right to bargain collectively does not entail any "right" to insist on one's position free from economic disadvantage.[31]

The Court was similarly abrupt concerning the effect of the lockout on the right to strike:

> . . . there is nothing in the statute which would imply that the right to strike "carries with it" the right exclusively to determine the timing and duration of all work stoppages.[32]

Lastly, in support of its conclusion that the lockout did not violate the employees' right to engage in union activity, the Court said:

> . . . the existence of an arguable possibility that someone may feel himself discouraged in his union membership or discriminated against by reason of that membership cannot suffice to label them violations of Section 8(a)(3) absent some lawful intention.[33]

There is a tone underlying the message of the Court that denigrates the cause of the workers. It is as if these employees thought the Act was going to "give them something for nothing" and the Court is warning them that they should cease complaining.

Underlying this message, however, is the Court's assumption that all of the parties engaged in collective bargaining are of equal standing. This relates to Stone's "industrial pluralism" model, which has framed the dominant discourse in collective bargaining in the postwar era. As discussed above, the industrial pluralist model, like its counterpart in the discipline of political science, is based on the view that roughly equal "interest groups" come together in a relatively neutral arena to challenge one another on particular issues. Since the institutional structure is presumed to guarantee equal opportunity, there is no reason why each "interest group" should not bring to the arena all of the resources at its disposal. From this vantage point, it makes perfect sense that if the employees have the right to strike, then the employer should have the right to lock out employees; after all, the Court seems to reason, it is only fair.

[31] Ibid., p. 309.
[32] Ibid., p. 310.
[33] Ibid., pp. 312–313.

Yet the Court went one step further in *Brown Food Store*,[34] the second case the Board relied on in *Harter*. In addition to locking out its employees—legally, according to the Court's analysis in *American Shipbuilding*—the employer in *Brown Food Store* also hired temporary replacements to staff its business during the lockout. In determining that the hiring of temporary replacements did not violate the Act, the Court stated:

> In the circumstances of this case, we do not see how the continued operations of respondents and their use of temporary replacements imply hostile motivation any more than the lockout itself; nor do we see how they are inherently more destructive of employee rights.[35]

In echoing the sentiments of the Court in *Brown Food Store*, the Board in *Harter* argued that there would be no tendency to discourage union membership because upon resolution of the bargaining dispute, even if on less favorable terms proposed by the employers, union members could return to their jobs and the temporary replacements would depart.[36]

It is difficult to reconcile the favorable solution for the employer in this scenario with the Court's conclusion in *American Shipbuilding* that "the right to bargain collectively does not entail any 'right' to insist on one's position free from economic disadvantage."[37] Yet, given this ruling, the employer is free to continue operating with temporary replacements after it has unilaterally forbidden its permanent employees from working. In fact, since it is almost certain that the temporary employees are being paid less than the former permanent employees, it could be argued that the employer receives an economic advantage when it locks its employees out.

Neither the Supreme Court nor the Board accepts this reasoning. In its opinion in *Harter* the Board again reflects the "industrial pluralist" assumption that the parties are in positions of equal bargaining power. Concerning the issue of employers continuing business operations with temporary employees after locking permanent employees out, the Board stated:

---

[34] *NLRB v. Brown Food Store*, 380 U.S. 278 (1965).
[35] Ibid., p. 284.
[36] *Harter Equipment*, p. 1221.
[37] *American Shipbuilding*, p. 309.

> There can be no more fundamental employer interest than the continuation of business operation. *Exercising the right to lockout in a bargaining dispute does not necessitate foregoing the option to secure business earning any more than exercising the right to strike requires employees to forego attempts to secure income by temporary alternative employment, strike benefits, or unemployment compensation (where permitted by state law).*[38]

The outgrowth of *Harter* is that employers can freely lock out their employees and continue business operations with temporary replacements. Further, the Board will not find an unfair labor practice unless the employer has displayed—in a manner that is blatantly obvious—behavior that is 'inherently destructive' of the rights of employees. With reference to the required 'substantial business standard' (developed in *Great Dane*[39]) that a company must have in order to justify a lockout, the current Board in *Harter* has defined it as meaning anything more than 'nonfrivolous.' In short, if a company can claim any 'nonfrivolous' business reason for locking out its employees, the Board will not look further to find an unfair labor practice.

The issue of *permanent* replacements during *strikes* has also received considerable attention in recent years, particularly since President Reagan permanently replaced striking air traffic controllers in 1982. Bills before the U.S. Congress that would outlaw such a practice were defeated under threat of presidential veto in the early 1990s. In the debate about the fairness of such a managerial option, numerous references have been made alluding to the notion of the 'level playing field' and the equal rights available to both management and labor. Secretary of Labor Lynn Martin argued the following before the House Labor-Management Subcommittee:

> Mr. Chairman, we are concerned that if the right to permanently replace economic strikers were prohibited, there would be little incentive for unions to moderate the use of the strike weapon. . . . Assessment of the risks of a strike would be skewed in favor of a strike, even where gains would be minimal. The balance as it exists today has proven to be well placed and in the public interest.[40]

[38]*Harter Equipment*, p. 1222 (italics added).
[39]*NLRB* v. *Great Dane Trailers*, 388 U.S. 26, 65 LRRM 2465 (1967).
[40]Peter Kilborn, "Ban on Replacing Strikers Faces Veto Vote," *New York Times*, March 6, 1991, p. A-1.

Secretary Martin's statements are clearly in line with the "level playing field" analogy that permeates discourse on American labor law. For Foucault, the question would focus on the extent to which this analogy has also permeated the consciousness of workers. As part of a larger system of normalized power relations, the disciplinary role of the "level playing field" analogy is achieved to the extent that it precludes workers from imagining forms of resistance transcending the "field" itself. As an empirical question, the relative decline in authorized strikes and the near absence of significant wildcat strikes in recent years provide some indication of the difficulty workers have experienced in developing effective forms of resistance.

CONCLUSION

I have attempted to use this case study of American labor and collective bargaining law to explore the relevance of Foucaultian insights for understanding disciplinary systems that affect work, workplaces, and workers. In performing this analysis, I have drawn upon the essential components of power/knowledge discussed by Foucault and have situated labor law and its surrounding social scientific framework within the larger themes of discipline and normalization found primarily in *Discipline and Punish* and *The History of Sexuality*. By way of analogy, I have argued that just as the human sciences embrace the disease model concerning the individual organism, so do the social sciences embrace the disease model concerning the social organism. In much the same way as human sciences constitute "truth" concerning madness and sexuality, so do the social sciences and law constitute "truth" regarding proper labor-management relations. Just as counselors and psychiatrists prescribe certain forms of therapeutic intervention based on expert knowledge, so does the arbitrator counsel treatments that will discipline individuals and restore the system to equilibrium and harmony.

Foucault's approach can be situated within more traditional approaches insofar as it utilizes elements of both radical and conservative frameworks in the sociology of law while undermining both of their essential claims. By focusing on the multiple points where power touches the social body, Foucault underscores some basic Durkheimian notions about collective consciousness and the internalization of law as societal norms. At the same time, he is arguing against Durkheim that internalization of these norms is not necessarily consensual nor is it without implications for power relations. In this sense, Foucault would acknowledge the Marxist claim that ideas tend to preserve power relations. Yet he would disagree with the proposition that such ideas constitute "false" knowledge or ideology that somehow conceals the truth. Indeed, it is the very "truth" of such ideas that makes the power they constitute more complex and insidious than the formulations of power found in either Durkheim or Marx.

One of the strengths of Foucault's approach to power is that it overcomes the tendency toward conspiracy theories and points out the many subtle ways that power infiltrates the social body. This represents a significant advance in our ability to understand how power operates and, by extension, where the most promising points of resistance are. As noted in the previous section, the frequency of both authorized and wildcat strikes has declined significantly in recent years, indicating the problematic nature of these forms of resistance within the current system. Increasingly, and in ways that Foucault would likely find amusing, unions are engaging in "work to rule" actions as forms of resistance. This approach enables compliance with the *legal* terms of the collective bargaining agreement while encouraging noncompliance with the *extralegal* terms described in *Discipline and Punish*. From a Foucaultian perspective, resistance at those points where power meets the social body is probably more effective than attempting to pursue the resolution of disputes through the grievance process.

At another level, Foucault helps us to understand collective bargaining law in the United States by shifting the focus away from a power elite model whereby elite members presumably gain disproportionate control over the legislative and judicial processes and manipulate them for their own gain. Using the Foucaultian approach I have discussed, it is possible to see the broader contours of a system of power/knowledge that cannot be reduced to specific actors. But neither is Foucault's approach wholly structural. Another strength is that it enables a focus on social bodies as objects of power without attributing social relations to the suspect motives of the ruling class.

Foucault has given us a fresh and exciting model of power that forces us to rethink our traditional approaches to the subject. The discussion above constitutes one exercise in the application of that model. While the exercise may yield interesting insights, I would argue that it achieves its maximum potential when combined with elements of neo-Marxian models that explore larger patterns of social inequality. This is important in a theoretical as well as a political sense. Foucault helps us to understand the "microphysics" of power, but without some way to make sense of the larger patterns and social consequences of this power, we are left with few strategic possibilities for promoting social change. Primarily there is the problem of organizing effective forms of resistance beyond individual actions that are taken and understood in isolation from others similarly affected.

Moreover, there is the empirical reality that the benefits of current social and cultural arrangements accrue to some segments of society far more than to others. This is particularly true in the realm of work. The "level playing field" analogy and widespread adherence to narrowly prescribed procedural rights can provide evidence in support of a Foucaultian view of the disciplinary aspects of power over individuals, but they can also lend support to a view that sees social class as a valuable explanatory device for understanding the various avenues along which power will travel.

I would argue in favor of a synthesis incorporating the detail of a Foucaultian analysis with the broader social vision of a class-based approach. I see considerable compatibility between the Foucaultian view of normalization as part of a disciplinary system and the neo-Marxian perspective on ideology as a "lived" truth that extends beyond mystification. Such a synthesis would reject the idea that all social life, "in the final analysis," can be understood in terms of social class; it would also reject the conclusion that political activity is necessarily limited to individual resistance at the points where power meets the social body. I believe this synthesis offers the most promising approach for a more comprehensive understanding of the relationship between law and power, as well as a more promising political agenda.

THE NORMALIZING POWERS OF AFFIRMATIVE ACTION

Mark Yount

Begin from the body, "the inscribed surface of events".[1] On March 11, 1985, a bus conductor in the state of Gujarat is tied up and buried alive.[2] On September 22, 1990, the live body of Sushil Kumar is set afire with kerosene.[3] As the United States Senate fails by one vote to override a presidential veto of the Civil Rights Act of 1990, among the bodies positioned in the balcony is David Duke. "I came to Washington to lobby against this bill. The President and the Congress are getting my message."[4]

---

[1] Michel Foucault, "Niezsche, Genealogy, History," in *The Foucault Reader*, ed. Paul Rabinow (New York: Pantheon, 1984), p. 83.
[2] John Wood, "Reservations in Doubt: The Backlash Against Affirmative Action in Gujarat, India," in *Public Affairs* 60 (Fall 1987): 423.
[3] *The Philadelphia Inquirer*, "Student Kills Himself Over Indian Job Plan," September 23, 1990.
[4] *The Philadelphia Inquirer*, "Veto Override Falls Short by One Vote," October 25, 1990.

Or consider parts of bodies: Across a television screen a white hand crumples a job rejection letter. A voice addresses this hand:

> You needed that job and you were the best qualified. But they had to give it to a minority because of a racial quota. Is that really fair? Harvey Gantt says it is. Gantt supports Ted Kennedy's racial quota law that makes the color of your skin more important than your qualifications.[5]

In 1978 a girl's ears are cut off. She has drawn water from a well reserved for caste Hindus. Hers is the body of an untouchable.[6]

These are bodily inscriptions of affirmative action. Sushil Kumar, a graduate student, burned himself to death to protest a government plan to reserve more federal jobs for low-caste Hindus. The bus conductor burned alive five years earlier was the target of a protest with similar ends, but different in this respect, that the burned body had to be tied up first: burned against *its* will as an expression of the will of other bodies. Here in the United States the contest of wills over affirmative action is less blatantly violent, less shocking, more familiar. The purpose of this essay is to disturb that familiarity by analyzing the issue through the Foucaultian categories of power/knowledge. We are badly in need of this disturbance: "Practicing criticism is a matter of making facile gestures difficult."[7]

I will begin by viewing affirmative action as a shift in how discrimination is problematized. This is connected (conceptually and historically) with the normalizing function of evolving regulations, bureaucracies, and (un)enforcement strategies. Liberal and conservative arguments struggle over the operations of the norm, but there is tension between what these discourses *claim* and the lines of power they reinforce. Once we have exposed those tensions, the constellation of power/knowledge will be more evident in the distribution of "attitudes" about race and affirmative action. We shall see that there is a circular dependence of discourse upon attitudes and of attitudes upon discourse, with both operating in a network well described by Foucault's analysis of power/knowledge.

---

[5]*The Philadelphia Inquirer*, "Helms Uses Race Against Foe," November 2, 1990.
[6]Thomas Sowell, *Preferential Policies: An International Perspective* (New York: William Morrow, 1990), p. 92.
[7]Michel Foucault, *Politics, Philosophy, Culture: Interviews and Other Writings, 1977–1984*, ed. Lawrence D. Kritzman, tr. Alan Sheridan et al. (New York: Routledge, 1988), p. 155.

Ultimately, that analysis will redirect us to the violence I have opened with here. Foucault's analysis may finally prove *too* disturbing, may *preclude* solution, may itself be troubled by the difficulties of the world.

PROBLEMATIZING AND NORMALIZING

Affirmative action is an issue of power in at least two senses and from at least two perspectives. An oft-cited objection to it, both in principle and in its particulars, is that it represents an unwarranted intrusion of government power at the expense of individual rights: those of employers *and* employees, of colleges *and* students. But advocates of affirmative action will do more than defend this exercise of power by the state. They will testify to the more important power function of affirmative action as both a promissory note and a measure of progress: the empowerment of peoples who have historically been denied their political and economic share. It is in that history (*in medias res*) that the discourse of affirmative action begins.

Instead of seeking an absolute origin for this discourse, let us follow Foucault in searching for "always the relative beginnings . . . , more the institutionalizations or the transformations than the foundings or foundations."[8] Summary histories of affirmative action policy in the United States trace the phrase "affirmative action" to one of two executive orders. John F. Kennedy's Executive Order No. 10925 of 1961 required all employers who are government contractors to "take affirmative action to ensure that the applicants are employed, and that employees are treated during employment without regard to race, creed, color or national origin."[9] More often cited is Lyndon Johnson's Executive Order No. 11246 of 1964, which added this rationale:

> Imagine a hundred yard dash in which one of the two runners has his legs shackled. He has progressed 10 yards while the unshackled runner has gone 50 yards. At this point the judges decide that the race is unfair. How do they rectify the situation? Do they

---

[8]*Foucault Live: Interviews, 1966–1984*, tr. John Johnston, ed. Sylvere Lotringer (New York: Semiotext(e), 1989), p. 46.
[9]Quoted in Sowell, *Preferential Policies*, p. 126.

merely remove the shackles and allow the race to proceed? Then they could say that "equal opportunity" now prevailed. But one of the runners would still be 40 yards ahead of the other. Would it not be the better part of justice to allow the previously shackled runner to make up the forty yard gap; or to start the race all over again? That would be affirmative action towards equality.[10]

Earlier legislative and judicial acts had attempted to remove the most obvious of these shackles so that procedures would be fair and be fairly followed. Johnson's executive order offered a different discourse and a different rationale, and it is that shift that is still at issue in the controversy over affirmative action.

Should our social policy be colorblind and genderblind from this point forward? This had already been a hotly contested question (at least concerning race), but now the terms of that contest would shift; partisans would answer differently a question that would no longer be the *same* question. Before, the question was not whether colorblindness was *sufficient* but whether it was *necessary*. Before, the ideal of colorblind policy had been opposed by a color consciousness whose principal intent was the continued subjugation of the American Negro. Its attitude was what is now called "traditional racism," and its constitutional policies opposed the claims of civil rights with the confederate banner of "states' rights." "The racial question" offered its two sides these competing rights claims, each cast in terms of procedural, rather than substantive, entitlements.

The discourse of "affirmative action" grafted considerations of substantive justice directly onto policies that had been formulated in procedural terms. It would not be long before the argument for "colorblindness" would come from the other side: no longer the *same* argument, especially in its implications for groups long victimized by discrimination. "Discrimination," "civil rights," and especially "equal opportunity" would now be drawn into a shifted problem, into a new *problematization*. Foucault explains:

> Problematization doesn't mean the representation of a pre-existent object, nor the creation through discourse of an object that doesn't exist. It's the set of discursive or non-discursive practices that

[10]Quoted in S. Sambasivam, "Affirmative Action and Reverse Discrimination," *Indian Philosophical Quarterly* 16:2 (April 1989): 197–198.

makes something enter into the play of the true and false, and constitutes it as an object for thought (whether under the form of moral reflection, scientific knowledge, political analysis, etc.).[11]

Now "equal opportunity" would *mean* in ways not possible before, and new measures of truth and falsehood would be generated to measure claims of fairness, of innocence, of progress. This problematization not only would act as an event but would enter structurally into the field it generated, pervading and directing the subsequent discourses and strategies it required. This problematization would subject contractors, employers, and institutions to a new range of regulation—to the production of new measures, new data, and new documentation—and it would demand attention (however cynical) to the *substance* of discrimination.

For the proponent of the civil rights movement, including women's rights, this would seem an incontestable gain, for two (related) reasons. First, affirmative action requirements would offer means of enforcing the procedural rights previously secured only de jure and not de facto. Nondiscrimination (as a procedural value) might now be realized, since discriminatory hiring practices could be identified and punished. Second, the discourse of affirmative action promises attention to the substance of the problem. Absent that attention, even a best-case scenario—one barring *all* present and future discrimination—still leaves the burden of all past discrimination on those already most victimized. Their resultant "equal opportunity" would be as ironic as the equality of law that forbids rich and poor alike from sleeping under bridges. By any reasonable measure, the shift of attention from de jure to de facto equality of opportunity was absolutely crucial to the pursuit of justice, and most objections to affirmative action on grounds of procedural justice seem mean in comparison.

But as justified as its ideals are, other questions arise with the *practice* of affirmative action. Let us first focus on the connection between the problematizing function of affirmative action and its normalizing function. Like its complement, this normalizing belongs more to the order of structure than to that of events. It invests an increasing range of offices, of studies, of employment strategies, as the objectives of the policy proliferate in finer and finer detail. To some extent these effects are intended by individuals, but such objectives operate without need of

---

[11]"The Concern for Truth," in *Foucault Live*, p. 296.

individual intention.[12] To shift the terms in which a problem is construed is not only to announce an ideal or to release a play of statements; it belongs to the new arrangements of discourse that the apparatus of inspection and enforcement shifts as well, that bodies are redirected along with memoranda.

Executive Order No. 11246 was amended by Executive Order No. 11375 and implemented by Revised Order No. 4, which first stipulated the *form* that affirmative action would take: to set "goals" and "timetables" for employment of minorities and women into job categories in which they are "underutilized."[13] In mid-1969 the Secretary of Labor introduced what came to be called "the Philadelphia Plan," which set forth specific goals and timetables for minority employment in six skilled crafts and required contractors in the Philadelphia area to conform to these standards in order to be awarded bids for federally assisted contracts.[14] As the Supreme Court later ruled in *Teamsters* (1977), "absent explanation, it is ordinarily to be expected that nondiscriminatory hiring practices will in time result in a work force more or less representative of the racial and ethnic composition of the population in the community from which employees are hired. . . ."[15] The rationale is persuasive, and consistent with a program attentive to the substance of employment opportunity.

In Foucaultian terms, however, it is through such discourse that the *problematizing* function of affirmative action enjoins a *normalizing* function. To have any appearance of validity, an employer's goals and timetables

---

[12] As Foucault puts it: "Power relations are both intentional and nonsubjective. . . . [T]hey are imbued, through and through, with calculation: there is no power that is exercised without a series of aims and objectives. But this does not mean that it results from the choice or decision of an individual subject. . . ." *The History of Sexuality, Volume I: An Introduction*, tr. Robert Hurley (New York: Pantheon, 1978), pp. 94–95.

[13] Alan Goldman, *Justice and Reverse Discrimination* (Princeton: Princeton University Press, 1979), pp. 204–205.

[14] James Jones, "'Reverse Discrimination' in Employment," in Joseph DesJardins and John McCall, eds., *Contemporary Issues in Business Ethics* (Belmont: Wadsworth, 1985), p. 431. Jones notes (p. 439n) that this program was legally challenged, but upheld by both the federal district court and the Court of Appeals of the Third Circuit. *Contractors' Association of Eastern Pennsylvania v. Secretary of Labor*, 442 F.2d 159 (3d Cir. 1971), cert. denied, 404 U.S. 854 (1971).

[15] 431 U.S. 324 (1977), quoted in Carl Hoffmann, Patty Reed, and Nancy Keeshan, "Defining Minority and Female Utilization by Employment Practices: Is It Consistent with OFCCP Regulations?" in *Selected Affirmative Action Topics in Employment and Business Set-Asides: A Consultation/Hearing of the United States Commission on Civil Rights, March 6–7, 1985* (Washington, D.C.: Government Printing Office, 1985), p. 34.

would have to be based on statistical calculations: how many workers of which protected group would be needed in which job categories by when and as compared to what? This determination would require not only statistical assessments of the employer's own workforce but comparative measures within the industry, within the job classification, in terms of the general population and in terms of any of several measures of availability for the labor pool. This would require official and unofficial demographic measurements, regional and local statistics, broad standards of comparison and statistics tailored to the individual case. All of these statistics and relationships of statistics would have to be generated and maintained in multiple orders of detail: details suited to scrutiny by the Equal Employment Opportunity Commission (EEOC), the Office of Federal Contract Compliance Programs (OFCCP), and, if necessary, the courts. One estimate using data from the early 1980s suggested the costs of the process might be "perhaps more than $1 billion a year in administrative costs alone."[16]

The language around which those great statistics mass is simple enough. Section 60–2.11(b) of Title VII of the Civil Rights Act of 1964 defines "underutilization" as "having fewer minorities or women in a particular job classification than would reasonably be expected by their availability."[17] Both job categories and membership in protected groups could be defined well enough to avoid serious contention. But how was "availability" to be determined, and which expectations would count as "reasonable" ones? It is around this point that the legal-juridical and the social-scientific domains fuse in networks of administration, litigation, and employment. Having turned from a discourse of pure procedural integrity, the laws are now only understandable and enforceable through demographic comparisons. Both utilization and availability have to be quantified and measured against standards whose appropriateness can only be established statistically. The distance between utilization and availability constitutes an "inequality gap," which (once measured) will in turn require timetables that can only be set by statistical formulae, which themselves will be determined by the demographics of *actual* hiring tendencies (either local, regional, or national). So the law has had to be interpreted through

---

[16] Jonathan Leonard, "What Promises Are Worth: The Impact of Affirmative Action Goals," *The Journal of Human Resources* 20 (Winter 1985): 18.

[17] Quoted in Charles R. Mann, "Underutilization and Discrimination: Do They Have a Meaningful Relationship?" in *Selected Affirmative Action Topics*, p. 3.

social-scientific expertise, entailing a hermeneutics of the workforce as well as of the law.

The expertise applied to this scrutiny of populations is demanded in advance by the objectives of affirmative action policy. But according to a logic Foucault calls "power/knowledge," the demand runs in both directions: it is equally true that this expertise demanded redefinition of "equal opportunity." Let us substitute this for what Foucault writes of sexuality:

> If [equal opportunity] was constituted as an area of investigation, this was only because relations of power had established it as a possible object; and conversely, if power was able to take it as its target, this was because techniques of knowledge and procedures of discourse were capable of investing it. Between techniques of knowledge and strategies of power, there is no exteriority. . . .[18]

The strategies of power/knowledge operative in the case of affirmative action show especially well how the confluence of law and social-scientific expertise results in normalization. From the apparently simple legal injunction against employment discrimination, the presence or absence of discrimination is legally determined on a case-by-case basis through analysis of hiring and promotion patterns. The procedural ideal is thus measured against a substantive standard of its fulfillment. That is exactly what affirmative action *needed* to be—and is even the basis of its moral claim, since justice unfulfilled is not justice at all. But the most objective and reliable measures we know are statistical ones, and the ruling standard for these statistics is the norm. This proliferation of statistical measures in a legal-administrative network thus offers the most direct evidence there could be of normalization. Particular measures abound, and each can only function in this legal-administrative-demographic-economic network by the sustaining claim that it is the *best* norm, that it best defines which expectations are "reasonable" ones. Opportunities will be found equal or not in accordance with whichever norm is designated most normal, as judged by the norms of social-scientific expertise.

---

[18]*The History of Sexuality* p. 98.

DISCIPLINE AND LAW

These are "two absolutely heterogeneous forms of discourse":[19]

> The discourse of discipline has nothing in common with that of law. . . . [T]his is not the juridical rule deriving from sovereignty, but a natural rule, a norm. The code they come to define is not that of law but of normalization.[20]

This difference of the disciplinary and the legal pervades enforcement as well:

> What is specific to the disciplinary penalty is nonobservance, that which does not measure up to the rule, that departs from it. The whole indefinite domain of the nonconforming is punishable. . . . It differentiates individuals from one another, in terms of the following overall rule: that the rule be made to function as a minimum threshold, as an average to be respected, or as an optimum to which one must move. . . . It is opposed, therefore, term by term, to a judicial penalty whose essential function is to refer, not to a set of observable phenomena, but to a corpus of laws and texts that must be remembered, that operates . . . quite simply by bringing into play the binary opposition of the permitted and the forbidden. . . .[21]

The enforcement of affirmative action policy depends on this disciplinary scrutiny, which measures degrees of conformity and nonconformity, and even degrees to which nonconformity might be excused. The more variability there is among measures of "utilization," the more variation there will be in judicial assessments of corporate defenses, especially as those defenses turn on differing interpretations of "reasonable expectations." A striking case of such variation is reported by Hoffmann Research Associates, who compare two Charlotte, North Carolina, food wholesalers that were sued for race discrimination in the mid-1970s.[22]

---

[19] Michel Foucault, *Power/Knowledge: Selected Interviews and Other Writings, 1972–1977*, ed. Colin Gordon, tr. Colin Gordan et al.: (New York: Pantheon, 1980), p. 107.

[20] Ibid., p. 106.

[21] Michel Foucault, *Discipline and Punish: The Birth of the Prison*, tr. Alan Sheridan (New York: Pantheon, 1977), pp. 178–179 and 182–183.

[22] Hoffmann et al., "Defining Minority and Female Utilization," pp. 36–39.

The firms were the same size, shared the same markets over the same geographical region, and neither had any extensive training program for its employees. The district court found both companies in violation of fair hiring practices, both times on grounds of "underutilization" of black workers as measured against their "availability." But *how* that availability was calculated differed greatly:

> The analysis shows that in the same city, the same industry, and for companies of the same size that deal in the same markets, black availability for wholesale food sales positions ranged from under 10 percent to well over 32 percent. That range translates to a total of 32 jobs that might have gone to blacks in just these two companies.[23]

Recall again the "power of the norm" to introduce, within a system of formal equality "as a useful imperative and as a result of measurement, all the shading of individual differences."[24]

The courts have also applied a case-by-case approach where voluntary affirmative action programs have been *challenged* (as in *DeFunis* and *Bakke*). Eric Schnapper describes the catch-22 that such defense involves:

> Undeniably the very best defense for any such program would be an allegation and proof that the defendant had in the past engaged in invidious discrimination against the beneficiaries of the program. But such a claim and evidence would amount to a confession of judgment in any future lawsuits by the victims of that earlier discrimination, and would present an irresistible invitation for such litigation. But few sensible defendants would attempt to justify a challenged program in that manner. The evolution of the case-by-case approach of affirmative action plans, as the Supreme Court is doubtless well aware, has thus led to a situation in which the defendants simply cannot be relied on to present the relevant defenses, *the real parties in interest are not before the courts*, and the case or controversy requirements of Article III may not be met.[25]

---

[23]Ibid., p.39.
[24]Foucault, *Discipline and Punish*, p. 184.
[25]"An Exercise in Judicial Restraint," *New Perspectives* (Winter 1985): 15 (italics added).

If the courts have applied variable (and even conflicting) standards, enforcement of equal employment law by EEOC and OFCCP has been even less uniform. The EEOC received 80,000 complaints a year by 1976, but only half of the complaints *recommended* for action were investigated, and of those only 6 percent were "successfully resolved," though one EEOC chairperson estimated 80 percent of the complaints to be valid.[26] Where there has been prosecution, it has not always (and perhaps not often) been effective, even in closely watched cases. After the EEOC accused Bell Telephone of discrimination against blacks and women, Bell entered a consent decree and promised to undertake affirmative action. Bell was able to satisfy the EEOC by reducing its "segregation index" from 91 percent in 1970 to 78 percent in 1983, even though the company could have reduced segregation to 43 percent by 1981 just by filling vacancies without regard to gender over that period, and even though the total number of women in crafts positions rose by only six in thirteen years.[27] Through the 1980s EEO enforcement has been further diluted, and not only as a consequence of conservative administration. The hearings structure itself inclines in favor of the employer charged with discrimination, partly because findings of discrimination require more levels of review than findings of nondiscrimination. Thus, over a five-year period, agencies rejected an average of 45.6 percent of findings of discrimination recommended by EEOC hearing examiners, while rejecting only 7.7 percent of the recommended findings of *no* discrimination.[28]

While the EEOC has underenforced nondiscrimination in private and federal sectors, the OFCCP has underenforced nondiscrimination in companies with federal contracts. One measure of this underenforcement is how tiny even its successful settlements have been:

[26]Carter Wilson, "Affirmative Action Defended: Exploding the Myths of a Slandered Policy," *The Black Scholar* 17 (May/June 1986): 22.
[27]Barbara Bergmann, "The Common Sense of Affirmative Action," in *Selected Affirmative Action Topics*, pp. 29–32. Improvement in Michigan Bell's segregation index was partly a function of increasing male representation in clerical jobs, but even more affected by *removal* of women from clerical jobs, as women lost approximately twice as many jobs as men in these categories during the period at issue.
[28]Florence Perman, "The Players and the Problems in the EEO Enforcement Process: A Status Report," *Public Administration Review* 48 (July/August 1988): 828. Perman references Joseph Sellers, President of the Washington Council of Lawyers, and footnotes: Committee on Government Operations, *Overhauling the Federal EEO Complaint Processing System: A New Look at a Persistent Problem* (November 23, 1987), p. 33.

> In 1973 and 1974, $54 million was awarded in 91 settlements, averaging $63 per beneficiary. . . . In 1980, in an even more skewed distribution, $9.2 million was awarded to 4336 employees in 743 conciliation agreements. . . . These beneficiaries represented less than two-tenths of 1 percent of all protected-group employees at just the reviewed establishments.[29]

More recently, the OFCCP between 1981 and 1987 was characterized as an agency "in substantial disarray" in a report by the majority staff of the Committee on Education and Labor of the U.S. House of Representatives.[30] Florence Perman, former Director of the Federal Women's Program of the U.S. Department of Health and Human Services, summarizes part of those findings in her status report on EEO enforcement as of 1988:

> According to the report, among the factors contributing to the disarray during 1981–1987 was OFCCP's decision to cease collecting relevant statistics, issuing written policies, and developing training programs for the field staff. Other negative changes involved decreasing the time for compliance reviews to increase productivity; lowering the journeyman-level grade of the compliance staff from GS-12 to GS-11; the use of informal policy making; and prohibiting the OFCCP staff from "requiring federal contractors, to establish ultimate goals and multi-year timetables, goals above availability and make-up goals" in their affirmative action plans, although contractors are required under EO 11246 [Sec. 202(1)] to develop such plans.[31]

Such unenforcement is not, as some might think, a way of resisting the normalizing effects of affirmative action. The shift of bureaucracy, of staffing, and of (un)enforcement strategies does not break with normal-

---

[29] Leonard, "What Promises Are Worth," pp. 5–6.

[30] Majority Staff, Committee on Education and Labor, U.S. House of Representatives, *A Report on the Investigation of the Civil Rights Enforcement Activities of the Office of Federal Contract Compliance Programs, U.S. Department of Labor* (October 1987). This report is cited in Perman, "The Players and the Problems." Perman points out that the reason this report was submitted as that of the majority staff was that "the Committee's minority staff could make only two of the on-site visits" (p. 831).

[31] Perman, ibid., p. 831.

izing, but marks another shift in the operations of the norm. If power were simply a commodity exercised from above, we might think that a change of administrations or philosophies might sweep fairly clean; but even clichés of the immovable bureaucracy ought to raise doubts that such a model could be applied here. On Foucault's view, the power belongs to the system rather than the sovereign, and its struggles are fought out in the farthest capillaries of the power/knowledge network. So to oppose state interference in civil society, or to champion the individual against the state's totalizing, will only substitute one term of this complicitous system for another.[32] As Foucault observes:

> But I believe that we find ourselves here in a kind of blind alley: it is not through recourse to sovereignty against discipline that the effects of disciplinary power can be limited, because sovereignty and disciplinary mechanisms are two absolutely integral constituents of the general machanism of power in our society.[33]

> Just to look at nascent state rationality, just to see what its first policing project was, makes it clear that, right from the start, the state is both individualizing and totalitarian. Opposing the individual and his interests to it is just as hazardous as opposing it with the community and its requirements.[34]

What is at stake in the shifting operations of "equal opportunity" is not freedom from a norm-pervasive system, but a struggle within that system about what will *count* as the norm. This struggle has been played out at the discursive level, where both liberal and conservative arguments serve to rationalize power/knowledge positions. These arguments serve the less articulate forces of interest, offering reassurance for attitudes that are

---

[32]This, of course, is the defining characteristic of conservative and libertarian approaches. Jeremy Rabkin goes so far as to deny that equal opportunity programs (and "the so-called Civil Rights Act of 1984" in particular) even advance the cause of civil rights, since the central idea of civil rights (he holds) is to constrain governments, rather than private action. Equality was "a secondary and derivative principle." Rabkin is particularly irked that schools may not remove pregnant teachers or students "whether married or not," and that vocational counselors must give the same advice to women as to men. See "A 'Civil Rights' Snare," *New Perspectives* (Winter 1985): 3–7. *New Perspectives* is published by the U.S. Civil Rights Commission.
[33]"Two Lectures," in *Power/Knowledge*, p. 108.
[34]"Politics and Reason," in *Politics, Philosophy, Culture*, p. 84.

sometimes immovable and sometimes at the highest pitch of vacillation. Since those attitudes are themselves shaped by these competing discourses, we must examine the arguments in order to understand the forces that operate through them. But we will have to attend just as carefully to the distribution of attitudes in order to see how lines of power/knowledge constellate around the issue of affirmative action. Even if liberal and conservative arguments are not *equally* dubious, let us disturb the assurances each side finds in its discourse. Only then can we appreciate how far the problem extends.

LIBERAL ARGUMENTS

Arguments supporting affirmative action are often divided into past-regarding and future-regarding. The gist of the first type is that affirmative action is an appropriate way of compensating those who have been victimized by a history of discrimination. This was an obvious and prominent factor where lower-caste Hindus and African Americans were concerned, but the protected status of other racial and ethnic groups and of women is now as evident by the same appeal. The second type argues that one need not appeal to the past at all to justify affirmative action, since sufficient grounds can be found by comparing the inequalities that now exist to the equality we recognize as a goal. On this view, affirmative action is an important instrument of progress in social justice. The success of either type of argument would justify affirmative action, though the rationale for that policy and the details of particular programs might differ considerably, with consequences for its further implementation.

If groups victimized by past discrimination had by now attained equity to white males, both types of argument would be moot. It is the existence of inequalities in the *present* that supports both types of argument: first, as evidence that past wrongs are not yet remedied and thus require some form of recompense; second, as confirmation that we are far enough removed from the goal of equality to require "affirmative" action to realize equality in the future. Everything turns on existing inequalities by race and gender, especially in employment and education, where affirmative action programs are most at issue. If there is no problem, there is no argument for affirmative action.

But what if the problem is so extensive that affirmative action programs cannot possibly achieve their ends? What if they can neither effectively compensate victims of past discrimination nor bring about the equality we seek? The following analysis will suggest that the problem is serious enough to require *some* kind of "affirmative action," but that affirmative action in its present form cannot even approximate a solution. There are two stages to the argument: one concerning the extent of the problem and one concerning the (in)effectiveness of affirmative action as a solution. Employment and wage differentials between black and white workers may be the exemplary case for affirmative action, so let us take our focus there.

In 1988 median family income for blacks was just 57 percent of that for whites, with blacks having lower income in constant dollars than they had in 1970. Full-time black workers earned 73 percent as much as their white counterparts, with black workers paid substantially less in every job category. The percentage of blacks who worked but fell below the poverty level was 16.6 percent, barely less than the 17.2 percent for whites who did *not* work. And black families with the householder having one or more years of college were more than four times as likely to be below the poverty line as comparable white families (11.5 to 2.7 percent).[35] It is indisputable that black workers are underemployed and underpaid. In the language of equal opportunity policy, they are "underutilized." As economists measure these differentials, though, there are two components involved: underutilization and productivity differential. Even in the absence of discrimination, we would not expect two groups to be equally represented in the workforce (or in positions requiring higher skills) if one group was substantially better qualified. Since only job-related qualifications can claim to be free of discrimination, "better qualified" here must mean "having greater productive ability," counting by that whatever is demonstrably job-relevant. Economists are thus able to calculate what percentage of employment or wage differentials is due to productivity differentials, and the remaining percentage constitutes underutilization in the stricter sense. This remaining underutilization value

---

[35] Statistics taken from the Census Bureau's *Statistical Abstract of the United States, 1990*, pp. 444–461. See tables 716, 719, 733, 734, 737, 743, 747, 748, and 749. Family and personal income for Hispanics is only slightly higher than for blacks, and full-time income is actually lower than that for blacks. Differentials in median personal income are even greater by sex, where 1987 figures show women making less than half what men do.

thus reflects "current market discrimination," since it reflects the difference in treatment of comparably qualified workers.[36]

Estimates of the underutilization component of the wage-rate gap between blacks and whites have ranged from 40 to 60 percent, while estimates of the underutilization component in employment disparity generally run over 80 percent.[37] Again, these are the differences that remain *over and above* differences in education, productivity, and other job-related qualifications. I stress: there is that great a difference in the employment and payment of comparably qualified blacks and whites; there is that much "current market discrimination."

But this is *not* the extent of discrimination in general, even as it relates to employment opportunity. Differentials of "productivity" are not innocent measures, as David Swinton's closer analysis shows.[38] Assume that blacks and whites have equal "inherent" abilities:

> In fair human capital markets, blacks and whites of equal ability would acquire equal human capital as long as they had equal resources and taste. Assuming taste equal, differences in the acquired abilities of black and whites must be attributed to differences in resources and discrimination in human capital markets. However, since differences in resources must result from differences in historical paths of earnings, it follows that, under the conditions posed, all resource differences must, themselves, be due to historical discrimination. It follows, therefore, that differences in productive abilities are, themselves, just the present day legacy of historical discrimination.[39]

The argument could be carried even farther by examining the first two assumptions. Suppose the "inherent" abilities of African Americans and

---

[36]David Swinton, "Underutilization, Discrimination and Equal Employment Opportunity," in *Selected Affirmative Action Topics*, p. 58.

[37]Ibid., p. 58. Swinton suggests that the reality is worse than even these figures indicate, and he argues that the productivity component is overstated, the underutilization component is *under*stated, and the recent trend is for the worse. He also addresses specific variables often appealed to by conservatives: economic studies have shown that "attitudinal variables have little discernible impact on economic outcomes," and numerous studies "have failed to find differences in the work ethic or expectations of black and white workers" (p. 59).

[38]This argument is taken entirely from Swinton's article, ibid., pp. 59–60.

[39]Ibid., p. 60.

white Americans were *not* equal: surely the greatest part of that difference would follow from differences in prenatal care. So a disadvantaged position in "human capital markets" would affect even factors we would otherwise call "inherent." Or suppose, as we are often reminded, that black and white tastes are *not* equal: along what lines would they differ? What we find is that blacks and whites of similar social strata and social class backgrounds have similar occupational aspirations, and that black aspirations only diverge "in the very lowest income levels (the strata of the working class below the poverty level)."[40] Here, too, the difference is traceable to existing economic disadvantage. *All* of these differences stem from past or present differences in *access to resources*.

It is hard to imagine a more persuasive argument for a past-regarding affirmative action policy. African Americans have been denied fair access to resources and markets, and all measures of existing wage and price differentials are traceable to that history of discrimination. As for future-regarding affirmative action, the more extensive and entrenched discrimination is, the more crucial it is that we take affirmative action to offset this inherited injustice and move toward a society of substantive equality, especially with nearly half of black children now living below the poverty level.[41]

But can affirmative action do this?

William Feinberg has applied mathematical models to determine the time needed to reach equality with affirmative action programs under different conditions, with particular attention to the plan the Supreme Court upheld in the *Weber* decision.[42] The plan challenged by *Weber* provided training for higher-paid crafts jobs at Kaiser Aluminum's Gramercy, Louisiana, plant, and it reserved approximately 50 percent of the openings in this category for blacks and other minorities. Justice Brennan's majority opinion stated that the plan was to end "as soon as the percentage of black skilled craft workers in the Gramercy plant approximates the percentage of blacks in the local labor force," which at that

[40]Howard Sherman and James Wood, *Sociology: Traditional and Radical Approaches* (New York: Harper and Row, 1989), p. 207.

[41]45.1 percent compared to 15 percent of white children. Both numbers are higher than those for the percentage of all persons below the poverty level, but there, too, the black/white ratio is about 3:1. These 1987 figures are reported in tables 747 and 743 of the Census Bureau's *Statistical Abstract of the United States, 1990*, pp. 460 and 458.

[42]William Feinberg, "At a Snail's Pace: Time to Equality in Simple Models of Affirmative Action Programs," *American Journal of Sociology* 90:1 (July 1984): 168–181.

time was 39 percent.[43] Feinberg shows that, if we assume no attrition among those blacks recruited into this program, continued use of the 50 percent recruitment formula would achieve equality to the labor force proportion in thirty-four years.[44] That is the best-case scenario: this temporary program would have a thirty-four-year life span.

But is there any basis for assuming no black attrition? The more realistic assumption is that black attrition will parallel that of whites, in which case it would take sixty years for the percentage of black workers in the program to reach 39 percent. During those sixty years, however, the proportion of black workers in the "outside" population will *also* have grown, with the net result that even one hundred years would not be enough to achieve proportionality to the labor force. Black attrition could even be *greater* than white during a period of economic contraction if seniority were a factor in job retention, and seniority would be the *last* factor to become proportional by race. Feinberg suggests that, if his model had taken age structure and other demographic factors into account, "the times to equality probably would have been somewhat lengthened."[45] Another study of national demographics projected that, even assuming *elimination* of discrimination in employment and education, "it would take almost 50 years for the black-white earnings ratio to reach .95."[46] But any figures based on the above assumption are naive at best. We have not begun to fathom how far and how deep our racism runs. Or our sexism.

Without affirmative action matters are even worse, as even a total elimination of discrimination in hiring and promotion could not remedy today's inequalities by the bicentennial of the emancipation proclamation. As an example, if the Gramercy program recruited blacks in proportion to their availability in the labor force, the program would fail to attain 39 percent black representation even in one hundred years.[47] Worse than that, there is no reason to suppose that discrimination will be eliminated, especially in the absence of vigorously enforced affirmative action programs. Employment of blacks and white women between 1974 and

---

[43]Ibid., p. 169. Feinberg cites *United Steelworkers of America* v. *Weber* (1979), p. 2730.

[44]Ibid., p. 172. The most relevant data for this case can be found in the chart on that page.

[45]Ibid., p. 180.

[46]Thomas Daymont, "Racial Equity or Racial Equality," *Demography* 17 (November 1980), 379–393. Cited in Feinberg, ibid., pp. 169–170.

[47]Feinberg, ibid., p. 172.

1980 increased significantly faster in those contractor establishments subject to affirmative action than it did in noncontractor establishments.[48] Moreover, since many of the highest-paying jobs require graduate education, and since black enrollments are dwindling even with some affirmative action programs, educational opportunity would surely be even more restricted without affirmative action. One study concluded that black enrollment in medical and law school would drop from the then current 8.2 percent to about 2 percent; another indicated that 60 percent fewer blacks and 40 percent fewer Hispanics would be learning medicine.[49] We can conclude, then, that affirmative action has at least some salutory effect.

But there is *so* much to remedy, and we are *so* far from equality, that affirmative action seems to fail the very conditions that justify it. We will never finish compensating for the past; we will never arrive at the promised future. Feinberg's conclusion to the data analyzed earlier is moderately stated:

> Affirmative action programs are slow to correct the results of past racial discrimination. Clearly, such programs have a great structural disadvantage in attempting to overcome the arithmetic as well as the social consequences of the past, and we do a great disservice if we do not recognize that disadvantage.[50]

Swinton draws a more pointed conclusion from his analysis of underutilization and productivity differentials:

> As long as whites have disproportionate shares of economic power, guaranteeing equal opportunities for blacks implies ensuring that whites do not discriminate against blacks. . . . However, the strength with which EEO policy is implemented, at any point in time, is a political decision, and whites also dominate the

---

[48] Jonathan Leonard, "What Was Affirmative Action?" *American Economic Review* 76:2 (May 1986): 359. See also Jonathan Leonard, "What Promises Are Worth," pp. 1–20. There Leonard argues that firms that promise more minority hiring and promotion actually *do* deliver more, though the gains still fall short of what was promised.

[49] Irving Thalberg, "Themes in the Reverse Discrimination Debate," *Ethics* 91 (October 1980): 139. Thalberg cites a study itself cited in Allan Sindler, *Bakke, DeFunis, and Minority Admissions: The Quest for Equal Opportunity* (New York: Longman, 1978).

[50] Ibid., p. 181.

> political process. . . . There is no way out of this paradox for the reformist, since reform does not alter the basic distribution of resources of power. . . . Black economic well-being must either be made independent of white behavior or blacks must have the capacity to ensure favorable white behavior. . . . This implies a need for a permanent increase in the power and resources of blacks.[51]

Affirmative action as we know it cannot accomplish this kind of black power. It can and does "reform" employment procedures that would otherwise leave an even bleaker picture. But the odds are overwhelming, the arithmetic staggering, the means too modest. The casualties of the reformed system mount.

It might be argued that affirmative action only needs to be enforced to work, especially if coupled with commitment to broader equality of access to education and other resources. But there are two problems with such an argument. First, the statistics for the Gramercy plant showed that following the affirmative action plan *could* not achieve proportional representation. Second, the fate of the Civil Rights Act of 1990 reminds us again of Swinton's point: that any commitment or enforcement stems from a political process controlled by (male) whites. What this shows is that the very "working" of affirmative action is accomplished by mechanisms that effectively prevent any great redeployment of power in employment (or education). Swinton is right. Affirmative action offers a vision of empowerment, but it does not offer anything like a permanent increase in the power and resources of blacks.

Since affirmative action programs fall far short of progress toward substantive justice, the arguments supporting such programs must serve other objectives, intended or not. The net effect of discourse supporting affirmative action is twofold. Though such programs are not capable of achieving the substantive justice claimed as their rationale, they at least help promote a narrower sort of procedural justice by making it harder to arbitrarily exclude well-qualified workers on grounds of race or gender. This primarily benefits white women and better-educated people of color. But the gain of this first effect carries with it a second effect with very different "benefits." By focusing on opportunity for individual members of these protected groups, the terms of the debate both reflect and reinforce

---

[51]Swinton, "Underutilization," pp. 63–64.

the individualism of classic liberalism and, along with that, the primacy of market operations. It is precisely *as* a mechanism of reform that affirmative action reaffirms the very networks it would modify. Here is a striking statement of that point:

> At their core, the OFCCP regulations really ask a company to study its workforce and perfect its internal labor markets by eliminating any existing impediments to a free market. . . . In short, the regulations invite a company to become an active participant in developing and controlling its labor market.[52]

We will need to examine other arguments and attitudes before we can fully appreciate the lines of power that operate through such discourse, but this much is clear. Liberal arguments collaborate with conservative ones to constrain the debate to affirmative action as we know it. Given that definition, opposing arguments can only contest the mechanisms, and not the more encompassing structure they all accommodate. The discourses differ, but all are variable plottings of the market's less debatable norm.

CONSERVATIVE ARGUMENTS

Just as the promises of liberal discourse exaggerate what they are defending, righteous objections to affirmative action imply that these programs are something more than adjustments to a system unchallenged in its fundamentals. The more intense the debate is, the more fundamental the point at issue appears, until all discourse of "equal opportunity" is locked into this *specific* point. Nicholas Capaldi's "big lie" strategy offers the most extreme denial of grounds for affirmative action and also subsumes the controversy under partisan political categories. The facts do not substantiate claims about "alleged oppression," he writes, and "there is little or no evidence to support the contention that a lack of jobs or discrimination in available jobs is the serious problem."[53] Rather, the very

---

[52]Hoffmann et al., "Defining Minority and Female Utilization," p. 50.
[53]Nicholas Capaldi, *Out of Order: Affirmative Action and the Crisis of Doctrinaire Liberalism* (Buffalo: Prometheus Books, 1985), pp. 144, 146. Note the logic of the definite article in

existence of oppression is fabricate by Democrats because "affirmative action's list of 'oppressed' people is a list of potential clients for the Democratic party."[54]

Michael Levin recalls Capaldi by noting parenthetically, "I leave unchallenged the dubious claim that women . . . have been greatly wronged."[55] (And from his abstract: "I also make fun of the results of such a policy and contemptuously ignore the claims of feminists about women.") Levin takes on the "shackled runner" rationale by arguing on personal identity grounds that it makes no sense to speak of what *that* runner might have achieved without his shackles. For one thing, affirmative action asks us to count one runner's *possible* effort for as much as the other runner's actual effort, which "suggests that the Rangers should get the Stanley Cup because they would have won it if they tried."[56] But even this "possible effort" would have been that of a different person, since "ability to compete" is a cluster of "deep" abilities intimately connected with the self. Levin's understanding of the self is well illustrated by his observation that "abilities like intelligence correlate strongly with personality and moral character."[57] For Levin, the documented inequalities to which people of color are subject show them to be "victims" only of their own moral failing.

Another argument will show us who the *real* victims are, and this is the familiar labeling of affirmative action as "reverse discrimination." By this invidious violation of procedural justice, it is white males who become (in the title of Frederick Lynch's book) "invisible victims."[58] Sidney Hook characterizes affirmative action as a "form of punishment," based on the concept of collective guilt and evidenced by "manifest injustices committed against white males."[59] Nathan Perlmutter, National Director of the Anti-Defamation League of B'nai B'rith, asks whether a quota can ever be benign:

Capaldi's phrase "the big problem." If something else might be a bigger problem (itself a dubious claim), then we ought not be too bothered by economic oppression.

[54]Ibid., p. 147.

[55]Michael Levin, "Reverse Discrimination, Shackled Runners, and Personal Identity" *Philosophical Studies* 37 (February 1980): 139.

[56]Ibid., p. 140.

[57]Ibid., p. 144.

[58]*Invisible Victims: White Males and the Crisis of Affirmative Action*, noted in Frederick Lynch and William Beer, "'You Ain't the Right Color, Pal': White Resentment and Affirmative Action," *Policy Review* 51 (Winter 1990): 64–67.

[59]Sidney Hook, "Rationalizations for Reverse Discrimination," *New Perspectives* (Winter 1985): 9. Brought to you by the U.S. Civil Rights Commission.

It is certainly not benign with respect to an innocent third party who is passed over for employment or promotion, or who is dismissed because he or she is not a member of a privileged group. The fact that today white males may be the victims of preferential treatment, while 30 years ago it was black males, cannot whitewash the discriminatory procedure. Only the victims have changed.[60]

The Anti-Defamation League of B'nai B'rith argued along these lines when it supplied counsel for DeFunis, who was denied admission to the University of Washington law school. Though thirty-eight white students were admitted with scores lower than DeFunis, his attorneys noted they were not questioning the use of criteria beyond strictly observed entrance requirements, but were only objecting to preferential action on behalf of nonwhite students.[61] In the more celebrated *Bakke* case, Dean Tupper of the Davis medical school was allowed to select five admittees each year (usually rich and white) without reference to the screening process.[62] The man who urged Bakke to challenge the Task Force quota also opposed Tupper's quota, but he never suggested to Bakke that he was losing out to those candidates. Thus one rebuttal to the "white male victim" argument is that in cases like these it is hypocritical to claim that the white man's loss is attributable to gains by people of color or women. They may be losing out to some wealthy white man's nephew, and *that* seems not to trouble critics of affirmative action.

But look again at the B'nai B'rith's claim: *only the victims have changed*. This is the point most widely attacked, and it is this point that reveals the most about objections to affirmative action. DeFunis would have to go to the University of Oregon instead, and Bakke would have to go to a school of lower choice on his list. Neither of them would be shot on his way to school as James Meredith was. As Michael Davis succinctly puts it, affirmative action programs simply deprive whites "of the *greater* chance for a minimally decent life."[63] It is this greater chance, this relative privilege, that we white males are reluctant to part with.

[60]"Testimony of Anti-Defamation League of B'nai B'rith," in *Selected Affirmative Action Topics*, pp. 194–195.
[61]Celia Zitron, "Reverse Racism: The Great White Hoax," *Freedomways* 15:3 (1975): 189.
[62]The account given here is from Thalberg ("Themes," p. 150), who takes it from Swinton.
[63]"Race as Merit," *Mind* 92 (1983): 362.

What is the basis of that "greater privilege"? Recall how Swinton's analysis of underutilization showed that even productivity differentials between black and white workers were a function of a history of discrimination. The same type of argument could be extended to educational "productivity," and on numerous grounds. Predominantly black schools are usually underfunded, set in areas underpatrolled by police, and attended by children of parents who were themselves undereducated relative to their white counterparts. And since schools are more segregated today than they were in 1954, since most public schools are funded by property taxes (on these segregated neighborhoods), and since the educational attainment of a child correlates most closely with the parents' social class, the same conclusion follows for education as for employment. Differences between blacks and whites are thus a function of the fact that resources and opportunities have historically been less available to blacks than to whites, all owing to sustained and intransigent racism. Such are the "privileged groups" Perlmutter so envies.

What we require to secure our status as white male victims is an argument that our relative advantage is not a privilege but a right. That is the argument that affirmative action is a violation of "merit"-based practices in employment and education: that minorities and women are being given positions they have not earned, and that these positions should go instead to those who are "most qualified." Thus Bakke is *entitled* to a position if someone with lower scores was admitted. Dean Tupper's candidates complicate the situation, of course. "Being related to a rich person willing to promise a donation to the university" is not the sort of "qualification" most have in mind; nor is "being Henry Ford's son" the usual measure of managerial ability. There it is clearly *power* that qualifies: it is Tupper's college; it is Henry Sr.'s company.

There are still other complications in measures of white male merit, of which I will distinguish two types. Richard Wasserstrom argues that "there is no reason to think that there is any strong sense of 'desert' in which it is correct that the most qualified deserve anything."[64] If two tennis players could beat everyone else in a town with only one court, would either be "victimized" if there were time limits on court use? This underscores the opposition view's reliance on the assumption that positions *must* be

---

[64]"A Defense of Programs of Preferential Treatment," in Des Jardins and McCall, eds., *Contemporary Issues*, pp. 415–416. The example given is a variation on one given by Wasserstrom. For a more extended analysis, see Davis, ibid., pp. 346–367.

regarded as competitive rewards. But even if they were, and were based strictly on qualifications, what *counts* as qualification is less obvious than most assume. Educational attainment is relevant to many jobs but irrelevant to others; a high score on a verbal exam will not correlate with a firefighter's commitment to saving lives and property.[65] Much past and present discrimination takes the form of imposing "objective" standards that are not job-relevant, but that serve to reduce representation of those already underrepresented.[66] By forcing scrutiny of such requirements, affirmative action encourages better recognition of the range of characteristics that might carry "merit" for a particular position. (Recall the earlier characterization of affirmative action as "perfecting internal labor markets.")

It is sometimes supposed that where there is affirmative action a less qualified workforce results, and this is clearly derived from the most basic assumption that positions would otherwise be assigned on the basis of merit. Here, too, the assumption is unsupported. A study of the attitudes of male police officers reported that, "both before and after assignment of women to patrols, male officers rated female officers as 'less competent.'"[67] But another study taking a sample of 254 cities found no significant difference in the effectiveness of police forces with (comparatively) high utilization of women as compared to those with low utilization.[68]

This difference between attitudes and reality also enters into another argument against affirmative action: that it undermines the self-respect of persons included by such programs. A person might still prefer a craft job in which she is not fully respected to a clerical job in which she is not fully respected, and might thus favor affirmative action even if this cost were

---

[65] I take this example from Carter Wilson, "Affirmative Action Defended," p. 20.

[66] Let me add to the firefighter example a highbrow one drawn from Thomas Sowell, *Preferential Policies*, pp. 135–137. Sowell believes he can challenge the claim that blacks are underpaid in college faculties by factoring in differences in their qualifications, including "the professional ranking of the department from which the Ph.D was obtained" (p. 136). Will historically black colleges have had proportionate voice in those rankings?

[67] Peter Bloch, *Policewomen on Patrol*, Vol. 1 (Washington, D.C.: Police Foundation, 1973), cited in Brent Steel and Nicholas Lovrich, "Equality and Efficiency Tradeoffs in Affirmative Action—Real or Imagined? The Case of Women in Policing," *The Social Sciences Journal* 24:1 (1987): 55.

[68] Steel and Lovrich, ibid., pp. 53–70. Measurement of police effectiveness was based on three variables standard in assessments of police departments generally: crime rate, rate of clearance of reported crimes by arrest, and cost of operation. For all three measures no statistically significant difference was found, and the same is true of independent surveys of citizen confidence.

entailed. But the costs are not imposed by the *program*; it is the male officers in the study cited above who impart disrespect. The problem is attitude-induced, and we will see in the next section how extensive such attitudes are. The net effect is that extensive prejudice makes this objection to affirmative action self-fulfilling, even extending suspicion to women and people of color who attained their positions through "regular" channels. Sadly, the truth of this argument is that self-respect *can* be victimized by the persistent prejudice of others, and even by internalized norms.

The argument opposing affirmative action that is most consistent with my analysis here is that affirmative action helps those who need it least, or (more plausibly) that it least helps those who need it most. Christopher Jencks puts it this way:

> As Title VII increased both the potential cost of hiring the "wrong" blacks and the potential cost of not hiring any blacks at all, it forced employers to intensify their search for the "right" blacks. This presumably explains why the wages of black men with college degrees and of black men over 35 with high school diplomas rose faster than those of their white counterparts, while the wages of black men under 35 without college degrees lagged behind those of their white counterparts.[69]

Robert Beauregard notes that even set-asides for minority business "are more likely to benefit the black middle class than the black working class," since "such programs do not specify the number of minority workers within the firm, only the racial composition of the owners."[70]

Alan Goldman translates these empirical observations into a normative argument against affirmative action, arguing that those "who belong to a group that has generally been treated unjustly but who have themselves not been mistreated deserve no compensation."[71] Yet Carter Wilson poses an argument that, while not a direct response to Goldman, challenges Goldman's assumptions:

---

[69]"Affirmative Action for Blacks: Past, Present and Future," *American Behavioral Scientist* 28:6 (July/August 1985): 752.

[70]"Tenacious Inequalities: Politics and Race in Philadelphia," *Urban Affairs Quarterly* 25:3 (March 1990): 433n.

[71]*Justice and Reverse Discrimination*, p. 197.

> The dramatic rise in unemployment among black males, the increase in the number of families in poverty, the rise in female-headed households are all indicative of the continuing oppression of blacks. Since existent affirmative action policies do not affect economic structure, they provide opportunities only to those blacks who have indeed pulled themselves up by their bootstraps.[72]

The set of African Americans who "themselves have not been mistreated" (Goldman's phrase) is virtually a null set. As Justice Marshall remarked in his *Bakke* opinion:

> It is unnecessary in twentieth century America to have individual Negroes demonstrate that they have been victims of racial discrimination. . . . [It] has been so pervasive that none, regardless of wealth or position, has managed to escape its impact."[73]

But isn't it possible to give full credit to those who have made themselves "the right blacks" (Jencks's phrase) and still question affirmative action programs that effectively ignore those whose "wrongness" is no fault of their own? It is not hard to assent to this conclusion of Goldman's: "Even if all members of a group are relatively deprived, degrees of deprivation can still be determined, and equal opportunity or justice calls for helping those on the bottom first rather than last (as occurs if left to the market)."[74]

There is only one problem with this argument against affirmative action: it is not an argument against affirmative action; it is an argument against leaving affirmative action to the market. To argue that since affirmative action programs do not help those "on the bottom" they ought to be rejected or further limited is misanthropic. The criticism that *does* follow, which I take to be absolutely correct, is that more profound measures of affirmation and empowerment are required. The liberal, reformist programs now in place have had good effects but woefully

---

[72]"Affirmative Action Defended," p. 23

[73]Cited in Thalberg, "Themes," p. 146. For a partial indication of how even the black middle class is subject to invasive prejudice, see Joe Feagin, "The Continuing Significance of Race: Antiblack Discrimination in Public Places," *American Sociological Review* 56:1 (February 1991): pp. 101–116.

[74]*Justice and Reverse Discrimination*, p. 197.

insufficient ones. Therefore liberal defenses of affirmative action are themselves woefully insufficient. But who could sincerely believe that those who oppose affirmative action are *more* concerned for young, uneducated, unskilled black males or for unemployed mothers? No one can think that it is the concern of a U.S. Civil Rights Commission that "remains committed to affirmative action, but sees it as a remedy that should be limited in scope."[75] If the objective were to help those worst off, an opposite conclusion would follow: we would *un*limit the scope of our "remedies." This proliferation of conservative arguments can only serve as rationale to other inclinations, can only rationalize lines of power with very different objectives.

THE DISTRIBUTION OF ATTITUDES

We have seen how extensively the histories of racism and sexism are entrenched in present socioeconomic structures. Racism and sexism are not only "attitudes" or "practices": they are inflections of the systems through which bodies are established as labor, selected or excluded, and deployed or denied. There is no "root" of the problem to be found in the prejudices of individuals or in behaviors we might hope to modify (or mollify). The gross inequalities of race and sex are simply not eradicable defects of an otherwise sound social body, as the confluence of liberal and conservative discourses on affirmative action suggests. We will see people of color malnourished, sent to the worst schools, exposed to drugs and homicide: then we will give them five points on their police exam. If that is unfair—and it surely is—it is not for the reasons offered by opponents of affirmative action. But if *that* much is true, it also follows that nothing like "fairness" can be achieved through the kind of affirmative action programs now in existence. Once opportunities have been blocked as massively as they have for people of color and for women generally, *the blockages belong to the system.*

We have drawn on the categories of power/knowledge to show how this configuration of blockages defines and limits the operations of affirmative action. But Foucault reminds us that:

[75] *Selected Affirmative Action Topics*, p. iii.

those who resist or rebel a form of power cannot merely be content to denounce [its] violence or criticize an institution. . . . What has to be questioned is the form of rationality at stake. . . . The question is: how are such relations of power rationalized?[76]

The arguments against affirmative action surveyed in the previous section are only the most studied attempts to rationalize these relations of power. We saw that the arguments *for* affirmative action also rationalize relations of power by focusing the debate within a narrow range of market modifications. Close analysis of whites' attitudes about affirmative action, discrimination, and opportunity is even more revealing. We shall see how discourse, popular attitudes, politics, and economics all interconnect (without any of these simply being the basis of the others) and how they are distributed to sustain configurations of power that block the advancement of people of color.[77] There is a logic to this distribution, a "tactics" to these interlocking blockages, a structural racism that pervades us without being reducible to the good or bad intentions of any individuals—a soft machine of segregation.

A 1984 Harris poll found that 67.6 percent of whites accepted affirmative action programs when quotas were excluded.[78] It has been shown that antidiscrimination legislation has been enacted when supported by a clear public majority.[79] Bush's labeling of the Civil Rights Act of 1990 as a "quota bill" shows how rationalization can be used to *oppose* such legislation.[80] As James Kleugel has observed (in the marvelously

---

[76]"Politics and Reason," p. 84.

[77]In focusing on racial inequality I do not mean to suggest that gender inequality is less a problem. But I also want to avoid treating these inequalities as strictly parallel, which they seem not to be. Affirmative action programs often lump diverse groups together, and this is itself symptomatic of the normalizing effects of such stratagems. The relations between race and gender and class inequality are famously complicated, but at least some connections are suggested later in this section.

[78]Cited in Lynch and Beer, "'You Ain't the Right Color, Pal,'" p. 64.

[79]Paul Burstein, "Public Opinion, Demonstrations, and the Passage of Antidiscrimination Legislation," *Public Opinion Quarterly* 43:1 (Spring 1979): 157–172; also Paul Burstein, "Social Protest, Public Opinion and Public Policy: The Case of Civil Rights" (paper presented at the 1981 annual meeting of the American Sociological Association). These papers are cited in James R. Kleugel and Eliot Smith, "Affirmative Action Attitudes: Effects of Self-Interest, Racial Affect, and Stratification Beliefs on Whites' Views," *Social Forces* 61:3 (March 1983): 798.

[80]Attorney General Thornburgh used this quota-calling to oppose a crime bill provision that would allow black defendants convicted of capital crimes to introduce statistical

titled, "If There Isn't a Problem, You Don't Need a Solution"), "as long as public discussion of social policy to reduce the black-white gap in average socioeconomic status remains centered on quotas, the way seems clear for political actors to ignore taking further action to redress this injustice or even cut back on existing programs."[81] But *why* are whites—perhaps 90 percent of us—(and many blacks) so opposed to quotas?[82]

Surveys have shown a substantial decline in what experts call "traditional racism," that is, "attitudes denying the legal and social equality of blacks to whites."[83] What has superceded traditional racism has been identified as "new" or "modern" or "symbolic" racism. But as Cardell Jacobson observes, "the new racism is not all that new."[84] Jacobson's factor analysis of data from a 1978 Harris poll showed the highest correlates of the new racism scale to be the stereotype scale and the personal intimacy index, suggesting that "the new racism is a form of aversion racism." Consider the following 1990 survey results.[85] Of nonblack respondents, 78 percent said blacks are more likely than whites to "prefer to live off welfare" and less likely to "prefer to be self-supporting"; 62 percent said blacks were more likely to be lazy; 56 percent said blacks were violence-prone; 53 percent said blacks were less intelligent. Hispanics were the object of equal levels of prejudice.

Given white folks thinking black folks are lazy, violent, and dumb,

---

evidence before sentencing to show a racial imbalance among death-row inmates in their states. Thornburgh objected that to allow this would be to impose "racial quotas on our death penalty laws" (*The Philadelphia Inquirer*, "House Passes Anti-Crime Bill Expanding Death Penalty," October 6, 1990).

[81]"If There Isn't a Problem, You Don't Need a Solution: The Bases of Contemporary Affirmative Action Attitudes," *American Behavioral Scientist* 28:6 (July/August 1985): 779.

[82]Kleugel and Smith, "Affirmative Action Attitudes," p. 797. Lynch and Beer, "'You Ain't the Right Color, Pal'" cite a March 1988 poll with a figure of 80 percent of whites and 50 percent of blacks so opposed.

[83]Kleugel and Smith, ibid., p. 800.

[84]"Resistance to Affirmative Action: Self-Interest of Racism?" *Journal of Conflict Resolution* 29:2 (June 1985): 327. 'New' or not, such a category indicates the persistence of racism. I am skeptical about the decline of 'traditional' racism, since even now only 57 percent of white Americans favor a law prohibiting a homeowner from refusing to sell to a buyer because of the buyer's race. David Boldt of *The Philadelphia Inquirer* cites these figures ("Exploring the Myths of Racism: The Picture Isn't Black and White," February 24, 1991) in arguing that white attitudes toward blacks have been increasingly positive: "Still short of an overwhelming majority, but the trend, as the expression goes, seems significant."

[85]*The Philadelphia Inquirer*, "Survey Finds Whites Still Hold Biases," January 9, 1991. The survey was conducted by the National Opinion Research Center of the University of Chicago.

rumors of the demise of racism are premature. But white people *believe* that racism is a thing of the past. In the National Election Surveys of 1972 and 1976, 71.2 percent of whites agreed with this statement: "Blacks and other minorities no longer face unfair employment conditions. In fact they are favored in many job and training programs."[86] A recent poll of white Philadelphians found 18 percent admitting that blacks get less than their fair share, while 25 percent thought blacks are getting *more* than their fair share.[87] These related attitudes coalesce to a conclusion in a 1977 survey question posed to whites: "On the average blacks have worse jobs, income, and housing than white people. Do you think these differences are _____ ?" "Because most blacks don't have the motivation or will power to pull themselves up out of poverty" was the leading response, given by 65.8 percent.[88]

James Kleugel explains how these beliefs of whites are theory-driven, shaped as much by assumptions about how opportunity works in America as by negative racial affect.[89] Whites want to believe that a problem no longer exists because unjustified inequality (for blacks, women, or anyone else) would disrupt an unspoken syllogism. This syllogism "begins with the premise that the opportunity to achieve is plentiful and equally available to all persons, deduces that individuals are therefore responsible for their own economic fate, and concludes that consequent economic inequality is generally just."[90] Kleugel contrasts this "dominant ideology thesis" with the "modern racism" thesis in that the latter explains contemporary racism as rooted in affect; the former "stresses the emotionally neutral or cognitive sources of this belief."[91]

That the underlying assumption here *is* ideology is not hard to establish: Michael Reich has shown that "racial inequality has a disequalizing effect on the white income distribution," thus benefiting capitalists and hurting white workers by weakening workers' solidarity and bargaining strength.[92] But the attitudes operative here cannot be reduced to

---

[86] Kleugel, "If There Isn't a Problem," p. 765.

[87] The survey, conducted by Michael Hooper of Temple University, was reported in David Boldt's column "Exploring the Myths of Racism."

[88] Kleugel, "If There Isn't a Problem," p. 767. The data are from the 1977 General Social Survey.

[89] Ibid., pp. 773–779.

[90] Ibid., p. 774.

[91] Ibid., p. 773.

[92] "Who Benefits From Racism? The Distribution Among Whites of Gains and Losses

superstructural effects, founded in relations of production, and imposed in a hierarchy of economic power. A Foucaultian analysis has to admit the function of ideology, while insisting that it is not *only* that. The assumptions that pervade and direct our bodies do not dominate us from above or mystify from without, as if masking an underlying truth or blocking the one true path of liberation. Racism was not invented by capitalists; and though capital may have been invented by racists, relations of race and of economics are dependent variables in the constantly shifting equations of a network of powers.

It is incorrect, then, to separate the operations of a "dominant ideology" from those of racial affect. Such ideology is not solely, or even primarily, "cognitive" and is surely not "emotionally neutral" (as Kleugel suggests). If the function of Kleugel's syllogism were emotionally neutral, it could only persuade on rational grounds. Thus we would expect it to be rejected by those who themselves are materially and emotionally burdened by lack of opportunity. Blacks, for instance, do not share the attitudes or assumptions about their own opportunities that whites have of them, and they thus consistently support even those affirmative action programs opposed by whites.[93] But how can it be that whites' beliefs about blacks' opportunities show little variance by socioeconomic status level, as we in fact find?[94] If Kleugel is right, why can't white victims of structural inequality see through this syllogism as most blacks do? Our whiteness must somehow distribute our beliefs toward conclusions that cognition alone could never support. To effectively resist awareness of reality—the massive inequalities of opportunity—requires affective strategies unsuper-

---

From Racial Inequality," *The Journal of Human Resources* 13:4 (Fall 1978): 541 and 525. See also Sherman and Wood, *Sociology*, p. 222.

[93]Cardell Jacobson found that black respondents strongly endorsed all eight affirmative action items on which they were surveyed, with the positive response averaging 78.7 percent. He also found "strikingly little" variance in the attitudes of blacks by socioeconomic variables: "Neither the middle-aged nor the young were more supportive of affirmative action than older blacks. Salaried blacks were no more supportive than hourly wage workers, and middle-income and middle-class blacks were no more supportive than high-income or low-income blacks. And neither social class, income, nor sex was statistically significant." Professionals and those with higher levels of education did show more support, but only by a margin of 2 percent. "Black Support for Affirmative Action Programs," *Phylon* 44 (December 1983): 307.

[94]Kleugel, "If There Isn't a Problem," p. 781n. Kleugel cites James R. Kleugel and Eliot R. Smith, "Whites' Beliefs About Blacks' Opportunity," *American Sociological Review* 47:4 (August 1982): 518–532.

vised by conscious calculations.[95] We must locate the white man's logic of opportunity within a more extended rationale that is impacted in emotions, attitudes, and politics as well as economics.

Drawing on this mass of data and interpretation, we can now construct the rationale of the "new" racism. If blacks no longer face discrimination, nothing now holds them back, in which case they ought to have attained "their fair share." But if blacks have already attained their fair share, the fact that there are still affirmative action programs *proves* that they are deriving an unfair advantage over white males (who are thus Lynch's "invisible victims"). On the other hand, if blacks have not attained equal status even in the absence of racism, there must be something wrong with them, in which case they don't deserve affirmative action (since they are just lazy, violent, etc.). By this logic affirmative action is either unnecessary or undeserved, so the very existence of such programs *rationalizes* white resentment of blacks (the backlash effect). A few affirmative action programs are able to offset massive inequalities that can thus be reinterpreted, if not altogether ignored. And it is racial aversion that structures perception and sustains this ignorance or denial of existing inequality: we do not *want* to know. This circle of attitudes, assumptions, and (mis)perceptions thus serves to *justify* resentment toward blacks. And that means that this resentment/aversion must not be "racist," *because* it is justified. And since racial prejudice is now justified by this affective rationale, what might once have counted as racism will no longer be so—certainly not among people like ourselves.

Perhaps the only thing "new" about this racism is its refusal to be recognized as racism. But we have also seen that the institution of affirmative action serves as a premise for this refusal of racism. "New" racism is not just a backlash against affirmative action, as if the two were opposites (the way liberal discourse makes it seem). "New" racism is structurally inseparable from these liberal modifications and from a discourse that exaggerates the effects these programs have. The tactics by which affirmative action opposed "old" racism allow it to rationalize racism in a new form. Regardless of intentions, affirmative action has been instrumental in the rearrangement of racism from its "traditional" form as

---

[95]One index of ambivalence turned up in a survey studied by Kleugel and Smith ("Affirmative Action Attitudes," p. 804). Whites *supported* affirmative action programs (76.2 percent), university quotas (59.5 percent), and employment quotas (51.4 percent), while they "personally" felt that such programs would be *unfair* (64.5 percent)!

overt segregationism to the form outlined above: a new rationale for old attitudes. We have traced in affirmative action the connections between problematizing and normalizing, between the disciplinary and the legal, between discourse and affect; we now find that mechanisms for resisting one form of racism are instrumental in producing and rationalizing another. Such are the normalizing powers of affirmative action.

RESISTANCES

Would it be better, then, if affirmative action programs were discontinued? No. We have seen that what is needed is not less, but *more* affirmative action. To remove affirmative action would not remove the rationale for racism in our society, much less remove racism itself. To remove affirmative action in order to secure the "rights" of white males would likely have an opposite effect. The message received would be that the mission is accomplished, the shackles removed, the race a fair one from this point forward. We can predict that such racism would just operate differently, that racism would be redeployed yet again, cutting new channels of aversion and constructing new blockages to opportunity.

So what are we to do?

Unfortunately, Foucault's analysis of power upsets this *question* as much as it upsets the prevailing liberal and conservative alternatives. Who is this "we" that could act on such a scale? Foucault's genealogy takes all relations to be relations of power, relations of power to be relations of force, and relations of force to be relations of war. War metaphors dominate the *Power/Knowledge* period, as power pits "all against all." "We all fight each other," spoke Foucault, with the first and last components being individuals "or even sub-individuals."[96] The view that "we" as a society can address the problems of racism or sexism would, by Foucault's genealogy, be another normalizing gesture. But if Foucault's analysis makes us wary of programmatic solutions, it isn't evident that anything like a "solution" is even *possible* on his terms. What hope is there for those who lose the most in this war of all against all? Shivaji Singh, an upper-caste landlord in the Bihar state of India, is stockpiling weapons for war with the lower castes

---

[96]"The Confession of the Flesh," in *Power/Knowledge*, p. 208. For power-as-war, see esp. pp. 114, 123, 132, and 208.

over affirmative action: "We're just waiting for the other side to come on the battlefield."[97] But by Foucault's account we are all already on the battlefield, of which these weapons are but one deployment.

Where Foucault cannot suggest solutions he does offer strategies. The genealogist begins from the victim's knowledge: "a particular, local, regional knowledge, a differential knowledge incapable of unanimity and which owes its force only to the harshness with which it is opposed by everything surrounding it. . . ."[98] Genealogy can even be *defined* as "the union of erudite knowledge and local memories which allows us to establish a historical knowledge of struggles and to make use of this knowledge tactically today."[99] Rather than one "locus of great Refusal," "there is a plurality of resistances, each of them a special case. . . ."[100]

Here are two gradients of resistance within the field of "equal opportunity," one in education and one in employment. Bakke's arguments suppose that the quantitative measures of grades and test scores operate as measures of *entitlement* to admission. Affirmative action arguments dispute that entitlement claim, but it is also possible to develop other measures of qualification. "Multi-intelligence" is thus one area in which specific intellectuals might articulate, and even legitimate, the "disqualified knowledges" of groups underrepresented in higher education.[101] This would follow the rationale of Justice Stevens in *Johnson v. Transportation Agency*, where the Court supported use of gender classifications, but suggested that "in many cases the employer will find it more appropriate to consider other legitimate reasons to give preferences to members of underrepresented groups."[102]

Janette Webb and Sonia Liff argue that job requirements are social constructions that need to be rethought.[103] The "liberal model" of equal opportunity assumes that all applicants shall be assessed on their merits and matched to an employer's fixed demand characteristics. A

---

[97]*The Philadelphia Inquirer*, "Caste Divisions Run Deep in India," October 21, 1990.
[98]Ibid., p. 82.
[99]"Two Lectures," p. 83.
[100]*The History of Sexuality*, p. 96.
[101]See, e.g., Samuel Henry, "Toward a Theory of the Desegregation of the Workplace," *The Black Scholar* 16 (September/October 1985): 23–30.
[102]Cited in John Nalbandian, "The U.S. Supreme Court's 'Consensus' on Affirmative Action," *Public Administration Review* 49 (January/February 1989).
[103]"Play the White Man: The Social Construction of Fairness and Competition in Equal Opportunity Policies," *Sociological Review* 36 (August 1988): 532–551.

"radical" approach would be to appoint persons of underrepresented groups even though they are less well qualified. But this is a false dichotomy:

> Women fail not because they are less able to carry out the tasks; they are excluded because of the way that necessary qualifications are defined. The competition is structured against women because the job is perceived as requiring skills, experiences and working patterns far more likely to be found amongst men, or indeed seen as inherently male. What should be asked of employers is not that they accept less qualified, less able women in preference to men, but that they rethink what the job requires in ways that do not rule out competent women.[104]

Both admission measures and job requirements might be rethought in ways that could significantly advance women and people of color. But notice that these modifications are still subject to the markets of labor and education and to the discretion of those on the favored side of power differentials. Won't the "new racism" that pervades these markets and these persons make such changes unlikely, make even the need for change seem dubious, even make it seem that change should restore "balance" by advancing white males?

The more genealogy lets us see the shape of the structural racism and sexism of our society, the less likely effective resistance seems within that theoretical perspective. Foucault's work after the first *Sexuality* volume offers an alternative, however, by opening up possibilities not reducible to power. Foucault reminded interviewers that his interest had always been more in truth than in power, and if truth is *of* power, his last works suggest that truth is of "ethics" as well. An interview on the topic of "Social Security" published in 1983 (between the first and second volumes of *Sexuality*) is especially suggestive, since what Foucault says of social security could well apply to equal opportunity and to affirmative action as we know it.[105]

Foucault calls for decentralization (predictably), but at the same time his language seems either to propose or to presuppose the kind of community genealogy seemed to rule out. The "empiricism" he calls for is now implicated in social planning:

---

[104]Ibid., p. 549.
[105]"Social Security," in *Politics, Philosophy, Culture*, pp. 159–177.

> We have to transform the field of social institutions into a vast experimental field, in such a way as to decide which taps need turning, which bolts need to be loosened here or there, to get the desired change; . . . bearing in mind that a whole institutional complex, at present very fragile, will probably have to undergo a restructuring from top to bottom.[106]

Such an experimental field cannot be operated from points of resistance, each a local affair. It would seem instead that "we" as a society must effect change. Even so, Foucault still insists that "every human relation is in some degree a power relation," and he cautions that we should not "believe society capable, by mere internal regulation, of solving the problems that it is presented with. . . ."[107] The changes demanded for (and by) such an experimental field cannot even be conceived in the conceptual categories that now dominate our approaches to such problems. "For the moment, then, we completely lack the intellectual tools necessary to envisage in new terms the form in which we might attain what we are looking for."[108]

The tone is cautionary, but not forbidding. There *might* be such tools; the moment might *yet* come. But what we seek will not be found in a war of all against all.[109] Instead,

> I believe the decisions made ought to be the effect of a kind of ethical consensus so that the individual may recognize himself in the decisions made and in the values that inspired them. Only then would such decisions be acceptable, even if there might be protests here and there.[110]

The terms of power are thus only part of the truth. Genealogy exposes lines of conflict that traverse all relationships; it disrupts both liberal and conservative optimisms and makes us wary of facile solutions and facile surrenders. But genealogy cannot, I think, reveal or construct an "ethical consensus"—even one admitting the dissent Foucault would welcome. To

---

[106]Ibid., pp. 165–166.
[107]Ibid., p. 168.
[108]Ibid., p. 166.
[109]Not as war, and not as rape or as child abuse. Foucault's remarks on rape and on child abuse on pp. 200–204 of the same collection of interviews are unfortunate, to put it mildly.
[110]Ibid., p. 174.

even aspire to that requires another "truth." If we follow Foucault, we should seek that truth in the disqualified and oppressed; we should articulate the knowledge that has been made dumb by subjugation and recover the "rude memory" of struggle, still seeking a consensus in which we might recognize ourselves. *That* will be our affirmation.

I will close by suggesting a liaison of perspectives that have been antithetical, but seem required here. Add to Foucault's genealogy (with its Nietzschean heritage so misogynist and so opposed to mere compassion) the "care perspective" finding its articulation through the work of Carol Gilligan and other theorists of "women's ways of knowing."[111] Gilligan's work exemplifies the most important features of genealogy, beginning with her critique of the power relations that produce knowledge of moral development and her recovery of the "different voice" disqualified by Kohlberg's norm. Gilligan and others have made tactical use of this popular knowledge, finding new ways to link it with the cutting edges of theory. These researches rigorously advance Foucault's anti-science, whose aim is "to entertain the claims to attention of local, discontinuous, disqualified, illegitimate knowledge against the claims of a unitary body of theory which would filter, hierarchise and order them in the name of some true knowledge and some arbitrary idea of what constitutes a science and its objects."[112]

There are many of these different voices, too many of them disqualified, only partially audible. One tone among them that Gilligan and other feminist ethicists would give voice to is that of care. The more we rely on the example of Foucault's genealogy, the more we need to hear that voice. Absent that care we can watch the lower castes ambushed on Shivaji Singh's battlefield. Only if we care about the child born in the ghetto, about all the relationships born and broken in that milieu (to mention only the exemplary), only then is there any hope that "we" can begin to dissolve the blockages of a racist, sexist system. Insist that unrelieved

---

[111] Gilligan's most influential work is *In A Different Voice* (Cambridge: Harvard University Press, 1982). Eva Feder Kittay and Diane Meyers have compiled a variety of responses to Gilligan in *Women and Moral Theory* (Totowa: Rowman & Littlefield, 1987). *Women's Ways of Knowing* is by Mary Field Belenky, Blythe Vicker Clinchy, Nancy Rule Goldberger, and Jill Mattuck Tarule (New York: Basic Books, 1986). Foucault, as much as anyone, would lead us to suspect any claim to *a* voice, especially one unifying as much as half the world. I recommend Irene Diamond's and Lee Quinby's fine anthology *Feminism and Foucault: Reflections on Resistance* (Boston: Northeastern University Press, 1988) as an indication of the range of uses and rapprochements of Foucault and feminist thinking.

[112] "Two Lectures," p. 83.

"underutilization" means unrelieved human pain, and a more genuinely affirmative action becomes possible. But, correlatively, anyone who can care and still leave the lines of power unchallenged only feeds that system with her good intentions. The point of criticism, the point that enables our greater affirmations, is simply this: what is does not need to be the way it is. The refusals, resistances, and creations that issue from that point may yet form a "we," where new inflection will transform what will no longer be the same question: what can we do?

Part VI

HEALING INSTITUTIONS

ON NOT KNOWING WHO WE ARE
Madness, Hermeneutics, and the Night of Truth in Foucault

John Caputo

In this essay I argue that Foucault's thought is best construed as a hermeneutics of who we are. This is a hermeneutics that turns not on uncovering the truth but on living with the untruth or with what Foucault calls very early on the "night of truth," the truth that there is no capitalized "Truth," no "truth of truth." It is thus a hermeneutics that confesses from the start that we do not know who we are, and it is a hermeneutics of who we are not. Contrary to the received view of Dreyfus and Rabinow,[1] I argue that Foucault's thought thus does not move "beyond hermeneutics," but rather beyond a certain "tragic" hermeneutics toward what I will call a "hermeneutics of refusal"—beyond a hermeneutics of "identity" toward a hermeneutics of "difference." I will take my point of departure from

---

[1] Hubert Dreyfus and Paul Rabinow, *Michel Foucault: Beyond Structuralism and Hermeneutics*, with an Afterword by Michel Foucault, 2d edn. (Chicago: University of Chicago Press, 1983), hereafter cited as *BSH*.

Foucault's early writings on madness, although I am also interested in what he says later on about Christian "confessional techniques." At the end I will attempt to push out beyond Foucault by addressing the question of what I will call certain "healing gestures." I move there in a direction that, while it was not taken by Foucault, is perhaps suggested by him and that constitutes a hermeneutics, not of refusal, but of response and redress.[2]

TRAGIC HERMENEUTICS: MADNESS AND THE NIGHT OF TRUTH

In his earliest writings on "mental illness" (*maladie*) Foucault drew a fascinating portrait of *déraison*—"unreason," the failing or giving way of reason—"before" it was interned and reduced to silence. By the nineteenth century, unreason had been constituted as "mental illness," an object for the "psychology of madness" (*folie*), which overwhelmed madness simultaneously with the external force of internment and the internal force of moralizing. The effect of psychology was to foreshorten "the experience of Unreason," an experience in which, Foucault says, "Western man encountered the night of his truth and its absolute challenge," which once was and still is "the mode of access to the natural truth of man."[3]

What Foucault had in mind at that time could readily be described as a "destruction of the history of psychology" that parallels Heidegger's project of a "destruction of the history of ontology" in *Being and Time*.[4] Were psychology to reflect on itself, it would effect a kind of *Destruktion* that would be at the same time the *retrieval* of a more essential truth. It would suffer a kind of auto-deconstruction, coming undone under its own

---

[2] For the background of the present study, see the argument that I develop for a "cold" or "radical hermeneutics" in my *Radical Hermeneutics: Repetition, Deconstruction and Hermeneutics* (Bloomington: Indiana University Press, 1987), hereafter cited as *RH*.

[3] Michel Foucault, *Mental Illness and Psychology* (hereafter cited as *MIP*), tr. Alan Sheridan, with a Foreword by Hubert Dreyfus (Berkeley and Los Angeles: University of California Press, 1987), p. 74. This is a translation of the 1962 French edition, *Maladie mentale et psychologie*, which is an extensive revision of the 1954 edition, *Maladie mentale et personalité*. The important difference between these editions is examined carefully by James Bernauer, *Michel Foucault's Force of Flight: Toward an Ethics For Thought* (Atlantic Highlands: Humanities Press International, 1990), pp. 24–36 and Appendix 1.

[4] Dreyfus discusses Foucault's interest in Heidegger in his instructive Foreword to *MIP*, pp. ix, xviii-xix, xxviiiff.

eye. That is because psychology is the alienated truth of madness, the truth in a "derisory" or alienated form that precisely on that account harbors within itself and maintains contacts with something "essential." While deriding madness under the hypocritical veil of moralizing internment, psychology "cannot fail to move toward the essential," toward that originary point from which it itself arises as a science, namely, "those regions in which man has a relation with himself."[5]

> If carried back to its roots, the psychology of madness would appear to be . . . the destruction of psychology itself and the discovery of that essential, nonpsychological because nonmoralizable relation that is the relation between Reason and Unreason.[6]

Beneath its moralization by the humanist reformers—viewing madness as somehow a moral failing, an effect of ill will—lies its more essential truth. Psychology cannot master the truth of madness because the truth of madness is the soil from which psychology springs, the prior, anterior sphere of unconcealment of which it is itself the alienating, scientific derivative. Madness is the founding experience from which psychology derives, from the distortion of which it itself arises. Occasionally, Foucault points out, the founding, originary experiences of madness do find a voice—in artists like Hölderlin, Nerval, Roussel, and Artaud—and "that holds out the promise to man that one day, perhaps, he will be able to be free of all psychology and be ready for the great tragic confrontation with madness."[7] The poetic experience of the truth of madness, being prior to the scientific truth of psychology, is a more radical unconcealment of madness.

"Mental illness" is "alienated madness," madness in an alienated form. The aim of Foucault's work at this point is to bring us "face to face" with madness in its unalienated truth, to let it speak in its own voice, which is not the voice of reason or science, to regain "madness freed and disalienated, restored in some sense to its original language."[8] But what can this original experience be? What would unreason say were its voice restored? What is the truth of madness, the truth that madness knows but

[5] *MIP*, p. 74.
[6] Ibid.
[7] *MIP*, p. 75.
[8] *MIP*, p. 76.

we have silenced? Madness is "difference," extreme, disturbing difference, inhabiting a "void." The Renaissance took the "risk" of exposing itself to this void. It let itself be put into question by madness, without shutting it away. It allowed itself to be invaded by the "Other," the "insane." It allowed the familiar, the *heimlich*, to be invaded by the strange and *unheimlich*. It allowed reason to be tested by unreason: "it thought itself wise and it was mad; it thought it knew and it knew nothing."[9] But in the seventeenth century there began what Foucault describes as "the negative appraisal of what had been originally apprehended as the Different, the Insane, Unreason."[10]

So we have in the last two hundred years constituted *homo psychologicus*, the object of psychological science. Psychological man is a substitute that puts in the place of man's "relation to the truth"[11] the assumption that psychological man is himself "the truth of the truth." By this Foucault means that the "real"—let us say "cold"—truth of our divided condition is explained away and forgotten by the "truth" of psychological science and its purportedly scientific explanations of an inner mental pathology. But the truth of truth, the truth of psychology arrives too late, only after madness in its truth has been closed off. Indeed, psychology itself is constituted as a science only on the basis of having closed off madness and turned it into a phantom of itself. Psychological truth is a way of forgetting the truth and reducing it to silence. Foucault refers to this truth that psychology allows us to forget, and that can be recognized in the modern world only in "lightning flashes" with names like "Nietzsche," as a "tragic split" and "freedom."[12]

Foucault thus pursues in these early writings a very original approach to madness. He is not interested in its "physiological" basis, which he does not deny, or in its "cure," which he does not oppose,[13] but in the "truth of madness," in what the mad—shall we say—"know" or "experience." He is not addressing its physiology or its therapeutics but its "hermeneutics" and the way in which psychological science conceals, represses, forgets, and silences the truth of madness (rather the way that Gadamer thinks that "method" objectifies and alienates "truth"). In these early writings the mad "know" something that we want first to diagnose and then to treat (and in

[9]*MIP*, p. 77.
[10]*MIP*, p. 78.
[11]*MIP*, p. 87.
[12]*MIP*, p. 88.
[13]*MIP*, p. 86.

recent years simply to anaesthetize with powerful psychotherapeutic drugs) whereas Foucault wants to linger with it for a while, to listen and to learn from it, to hear what it has to say.

What do the mad know? What truth would they speak if we lend them an ear? A "tragic" truth, the truth of a "split," let us say, a tragic knowledge. This is the sort of truth that would kill you—or drive you mad—of which Nietzsche spoke. Was Nietzsche's madness a function of what he knew? Was his knowledge a function of his madness? Foucault suspends both alternatives because they are both causal, etiological; he subjects both questions to a kind of *epoché* that puts both physiological and therapeutic questions out of action. His interest is hermeneutic: he wants to hear what one says who has been driven *in extremis*. While Foucault does not cite it here, one is reminded of the passage in *Beyond Good and Evil* in which Nietzsche repudiates the need to have the truth "attenuated, veiled, sweetened, blunted and falsified"—which is pretty much what Foucault thinks happens to madness in psychology. Foucault seems to have in mind what Nietzsche calls the "elect of knowledge" who are almost destroyed by their knowledge, which carries them off into "distant, terrible worlds."[14]

The mad, in these early writings, have experienced a terrible truth; they sail on dangerous seas, have been released from ordinary constraints; they are extreme points of sensitivity to the human condition. They are not truly "other" than "us." That is only the alienating gesture in which "we" constitute ourselves as sane and normal and constitute "them" as "other." The mad speak of a truth to us for which we have neither the nerve nor the ear, which is the truth of who we are. They instruct us about our hostility, meanness, aggressiveness, combativeness.[15] "Man has become for man the face of his own truth as well as the possibility of his death."[16]

---

[14]Friedrich Nietzsche, *Beyond Good and Evil*, tr. R. J. Hollingdale (Baltimore: Penguin, 1972), no. 39 (p. 50), no. 270 (pp. 189–90). See my discussion of these texts of Nietzsche in *RH*, p. 189.

[15]Madness is a mirror of ourselves. It tells us who we are. If the mad exhibit "infantile regressions," it is only because childhood itself is infantilized to begin with, unrealistically insulated from real conflict. If madness takes on the form of "schizophrenia," it is because the mad reflect the contradictions of a world in which man can no longer recognize himself, because the social world itself is marked by struggle, hostility, and foreignness. It is the world that is mad, alienated, unfree, divided, and contradictory, and it is such madness that the mad take as their model and in which the world refuses to see itself. See *MIP*, pp. 80–81.

[16]*MIP*, p. 82.

Foucault is not saying that the mad are the true philosophers but rather that they are precisely not philosophers at all, that they are the most forceful testimony to the breakdown of philosophy. They speak not with philosophical knowledge but with tragic knowledge. They have broken through the veil that philosophy lays over reality and that, in the form of psychology, philosophy tries to lay over them. The mad speak *de profundis*, from the depths of an experience in which both the reassuring structures of ordinary life and the comforting reassurances of scientific or philosophical knowledge have collapsed. They experience the radical groundlessness of the world, the contingency of its constructs, both social and epistemic; they speak of and from a kind of ineradicable terror. They speak to us from the abyss by which we are all inhabited; they are voices from an abyss.

This discussion, which Foucault inserted as the new "Part II" of the 1962 revised edition of *Mental Illness and Psychology*, is an incisive summary of *Madness and Civilization*[17] published a year before, whose "Preface" and "Conclusion" it closely parallels. *Madness and Civilization* opens with a reference to the madness of not being mad, the dangerous and unhealthy (*in-sanum*) condition of failing to recognize that "we," too, are a little mad, invaded also by unreason, and that it is mad to want to make reason a wholly insulated and pure region. He speaks of the madness of sovereign reason, the madness of a reason that thinks it has purified itself of the madness that inhabits us all, whose exclusion constitutes us as "us," the madness that speaks in a "merciless" language of madlessness. The goal of *Madness and Civilization* is to arrive at a zero point, a point *before* madness is divided off from reason, before the lines of communication between the two are cut, before reason looks sovereignly—that is, without risk or threat—upon madness as its pure Other. This is a region where "truth" and "science" do not obtain, which is prior to and older than science, which is older than the merciless "difference" between reason and madness, a region of an originary undifferentiatedness in which reason mingles with and is disturbed from within by its other. Such a return to the original scene of madness will isolate "the action that divides madness," the "originative . . . caesura" by means of which reason and science are made to stand on the side, or better to look on from above, while

---

[17]*Madness and Civilization: A History of Insanity in the Age of Reason*, tr. Richard Howard (New York: Pantheon, 1965), hereafter cited as MC. This is an abridgment of *Histoire de la folie à l'âge classique* (Paris: Gallimard, 1972).

unreason spreads out beneath its gaze as its object.¹⁸ Then unreason is constituted as madness, crime, or mental disease. That deprives madness of its voice—reduces it, in Lyotard's words, to a *différend* in which it is impossible for madness to state its case¹⁹—and establishes the monologue of reason with itself that we call psychology and psychiatry.

The Greeks, by way of contrast, thought of *sophrosyne* and *hybris* as alternate possibilities—of moderation and excess—within *logos*, but they did not constitute some sphere of exile, of *a-logos*, outside logos.²⁰ The discourse on madness conducted by Europe since the beginning of the Middle Ages gives a "depth" to Western reason that irrupts in some of its greatest artists and poets (Bosch, Nietzsche, Artaud).²¹ Reason without unreason is a smooth surface, a superficial transparency; reason with unreason speaks from the depths, *de profundis*. Unreason reduced to its scientific "truth," constituted as a scientific object, is a surface event, a thin, transparent, placid object. If that depth is still apparent in the "dispute" conducted between reason and madness in the Middle Ages and Renaissance, the depth is gone and the dispute is hushed in the silent corridors of the mental institution. The task of *Madness and Civilization* thus is one of archeological restoration, a vertical plumbing of the dark sedimented depths from which *homo psychologicus* emerges, of which it still bears a faint trace, reminding us of these hidden depths even as it tries to make us forget them.

What is the "great motionless structure"²² lying beneath the surface that is reducible neither to the drama of a dispute nor to an object of knowledge? Foucault's answer is again the tragic ("the tragic category"). By the tragic he means a radical breach or split within human being, a profound rupture that makes it impossible for reason to constitute itself as an identity, to close round about itself, to make itself reason and light through and through. Reason is always already unreason; the truth of man is this untruth.²³ The attempt to find the "truth of truth" is the attempt to

---

¹⁸*MC*, p. ix.
¹⁹Jean-François Lyotard, *The Differend: Phrases in Dispute*, tr. G. Van Den Abbeele (Minneapolis: University of Minnesota Press, 1988), p. xi.
²⁰*MC*, p. ix.
²¹*MC*, p. xi.
²²*MC*, p. xii.
²³"Untruth" is an expression used by Heidegger to say that there is always a radical core of untruth within truth; truth is not truth "all the way through"; concealment is the hidden ground of unconcealment, a wresting of unconcealment from a prior concealment. See "On the Essence of Truth," tr. John Sallis, in *Martin Heidegger: Basic Writings*, ed. David

expunge this untruth, to take leave of a more disturbing and disturbed region, to simplify and reduce human beings to pure reason by constituting the twin transparencies of reason on the one side and madness as the object of knowledge on the other.

In the "Conclusion" to *Madness and Civilization*, after tracing the story from the great confinement to the birth of the asylum, Foucault returns again to the theme of the tragic. At the end of the story, by way of a conclusion to his discussion of the asylum, he mentions the advent of Freud. Freud, he says, reproduces in the person of the psychiatrist the confining structure of the institution of the asylum. For that reason, "psychoanalysis has not been able, will not be able, to hear the voices of unreason, nor to decipher in themselves the signs of the madman." Psychoanalysis can unravel some of the forms of madness (it even has let it speak[24]), but it remains a stranger to "the sovereign enterprise of unreason."[25]

Were they freed from the fetters of moralizing internment, the voices of unreason would speak of "human truth" and "dark freedom," Foucault says. That is the role of the artists who lend unreason an ear, who give it a voice, or lend it a canvass. Of Goya's *The Madhouse*, Foucault remarks: ". . . within this madman in a hat rises—by the inarticulate power of his muscular body, of his savage and marvelously unconstricted youth—a human presence already liberated and somehow free since the beginning of time, by his birthright."[26] In *Sleep of Reason* "man communicates with what is deepest in himself."[27] In Goya we experience madness as "the birth of the first man and his first movement toward liberty,"[28] the freedom to dissolve the world and even to dissolve man himself. The madman, Foucault suggests, lives *in extremis*, at the limits of the constitution of the world, where the world threatens to come undone, to deconstitute itself in a kind of pathological parallel to Husserl's famous hypothesis of the thought-experiment of the destruction of the world. But where, in Husserl, such a deconstitution would leave sovereign consciousness still

---

Krell (New York: Harper & Row, 1977), pp. 132–135. Foucault seems to think of unreason as a prior untruth and concealment embedded in the core of reason.

[24] *MIP*, p. 69.
[25] *MC*, p. 278.
[26] *MC*, p. 279.
[27] *MC*, p. 280.
[28] *MC*, p. 281.

standing, Foucault suggests that, in Goya's work, the reduction of the world leads us back to naked unreason.

In Nietzsche unreason acquires a voice of "total contestation" of the world, contestations that restore "primitive savagery."

In Sade we discover the truth of nature, the savage truth that nature cannot act contrary to nature, that every desire arises from nature. As an "ironic Rousseau," Sade teaches the ethic of a more savage "fidelity to nature," "natural liberty." But Sade pushes on beyond the truth of natural freedom to the "total liberty" of pure subjectivity that dashes even nature itself by its violence. Sade traverses the terrible path from "man's violent nature" to the "infinity of nonnature,"[29] thus to a point where nature itself breaks up and reveals its own nature, its dissension and abolition. Sade dwells at that limit point where the world comes undone, where it is unmade, at "the limits of the world that wounds" the mad heart.[30]

In Goya and Sade unreason finds a way to transcend reason in the path of violence and thus finds a way of "recovering tragic experience beyond the promises of dialectic."[31] The tragic always means the split, the rupture of human being—without the dream of dialectical rejoining and reconciliation—and here it means the unmaking and destruction of the world that reason builds around itself.

The final pages of *Madness and Civilization* are devoted to Nietzsche, who represents the tragic voice par excellence, the dominant voice from the abyss. Foucault's early writings are very much keyed to *The Birth of Tragedy* (and not, like the later writings, to *The Genealogy of Morals*), to which, Foucault says, all of Nietzsche's texts belong.[32] Nietzsche is the philosopher of the tragic category, that is, of unreason and of the undoing of philosophy. What interests Foucault about Nietzsche is that his writing fell silent under the blow of madness, that his final word to us after a lifetime of writing was the howl of madness followed by silence.

Foucault is not leading up to the conclusion that madness is, in Heidegger's language, the "origin of the work of art," but to an opposite conclusion, that it spells its death. "Pure" madness is not the origin of the work of art but its abolition; there is no work where there is pure madness. Madness is but the parting gesture of the artwork, its final word or

[29]*MC*, p. 284.
[30]*MC*, p. 285.
[31]Ibid.
[32]*MC*, p. 288.

nonword just as it subsides into chaos. The work of art springs not from pure madness but from the invasion of reason by madness, from the tension or confrontation between reason and unreason, Apollo and Dionysus. But it is rendered impossible if this tension is broken from the side either of pure reason or of pure unreason.

The work of art carries out a kind of *epoché* of the world, suspending its hold on us, which it does just to the extent that it is "interrupted" by madness, or exposed to it and held in communication with it. The work of art puts the rationality of the world in question, making the world, and not the madman, guilty, arraigning the world before the work of art. What is the world's fault? What has it done wrong? For what is it to be held responsible? For what does it owe reparation? The guilt of the world is that it has suppressed the world of unreason, and it is precisely the restoration of unreason that the work of art demands, or better, the "restoration of reason *from* that unreason and *to* that unreason."[33] So it is not precisely unreason that is restored to itself so much as it is reason that is restored to itself, to its originative belonging-together with unreason. Reason is itself only insofar as it also unreason; otherwise—and this is how *Madness and Civilization* began—it is quite mad. Foucault has turned the tables—or the couch—on the doctor. Now, instead of the madman as patient silently observed by the figure of science, the world itself is put into question by the madman as artist, by a very Dionysiac artist.

These early works of Foucault are not only or even primarily histories of psychology and madness. As archeologies of the silence to which unreason is reduced in the asylum, they offer a positive view of being human, a view best expressed by the "tragic category." Human beings are inwardly divided, inhabited by an abyss, by both reason and unreason. We dwell in both the truth and the untruth. In such a view, neither "science" (the human sciences) nor "morals" can be what they are (or want to be) all the way through. They are at best limited, incomplete, or distortive, and hence in need of correction—the view that Foucault held in the 1954 edition of *Mental Illness and Personality*. At worst, they are useless illusions and even hypocritical attempts to suppress the unreason by which they are inhabited and hence they are beyond correction—the view both of the 1962 edition and of *Madness and Civilization*. The human sciences promote the illusion that unreason is a disturbance to be quelled, an abnormality to be normalized, a cry to be silenced. Ethics promotes the

[33] Ibid.

illusion that virtue is a unity, that the law is universalizable, that conscience is God's voice, suppressing the violence and confusion by which we are inhabited.

Against the illusions of science and morals Foucault advocates a more originary tragic experience, an experience of reason's undoing and auto-deconstruction by unreason, which is the "truth" of the human condition. This truth is destroyed if it is allowed to evaporate into the "truth of truth." The truth is the night of truth, the midnight hour when reason allows itself to be interrupted and invaded by unreason. That happens in certain works of art that flash like lightning in the night of truth, illuminating for a moment a more originary and cragged human landscape.

BEYOND TRAGIC HERMENEUTICS

Foucault's early writings came under fire both by his critics and by Foucault himself. In the first place, these texts are marked by a kind of phenomenological naiveté. The goal of the early writings, which is to find an "undifferentiated" experience of unreason, before it is differentiated into reason and madness, before the lines of reason are drawn in its virginal sands, perfectly parallels the phenomenological goal of finding a realm of pure "prepredicative" experience, prior to its being carved out by the categories of logical grammar. To be sure, where Husserl thought to find pure *Sinn* lying beneath the categories of logical *Bedeutung* (in *Ideas Towards a Pure Phenomenology*,§§124–127), Foucault suggests that we will find a pure *Unsinn*, a kind of perfect, pure, free, natural, undistorted, prepredicative madness, beneath the categories of the prison or the asylum. It was with this in mind that Derrida said it is an impossible dream to think that one could write the history of madness from the standpont of madness itself. Writing and history already represent the standpoint of reason and are already violent; they have already incised this virginal terrain with their cuts and divides.[34]

---

[34]"The attempt to write the history of the decision, division, difference runs the risk of construing the division as an event or a structure subsequent to the unity of an original presence, thereby confirming metaphysics in its fundamental operation." Jacques Derrida, *Writing and Difference*, tr. Alan Bass (Chicago: University of Chicago Press, 1978), p. 140; see Foucault's hostile response, "My Body, This Paper, This Fire," tr. Geoffrey Bennington,

This point is well made and Foucault has clearly not avoided this objection. Still, we should recall that in the concluding pages of *Madness and Civilization* Foucault makes it plain that pure madness gives rise only to silence, that it leads to the end of the work of art. Now that surely implies that no work of history or of archeology could ever enter the domain of pure madness. The voices of unreason issue in works or art, or works of any sort, only inasmuch as they interrupt, invade, intermingle with and confront reason. So Foucualt is aware that there is no access to a "pure" madness or unreason, to a pure, ante-historical essence of madness, but only to the confrontation of reason and unreason in this or that concrete historical context.

Secondly, in a not unrelated way, Foucault himself criticized *Madness and Civilization* (he never spoke of the first book, in either edition, on mental illness and opposed its republication) on the grounds that it labored under the "repressive" hypothesis, that is, the notion that power works by excluding and repressing:

> I think that I was positing [in *Madness and Civilization*] the existence of a sort of living, voluble and anxious madness which the mechanisms of power and psychiatry were supposed to have come to repress and reduce to silence. . . . In defining the effects of power as repression, one adopts a purely juridical conception of such power, one identifies power with a law which says no, power is taken above all as carrying the force of a prohibition.[35]

It is certainly true that in *Madness and Civilization* Foucault thought that unreason is repressed, suppressed, excluded, silenced, denied, obstructed, and occulted by reason. On that point I think he was quite right and, furthermore, that virtually the whole power of his book rests precisely on his being right about that. Furthermore, I do not think he means to retract this point. In an interview also given in 1977 he says that the repressive mechanisms of *Madness and Civilization* were "adequate" to his purposes in

---

Oxford Literary Review 4:1 (1979): 5–28. For a good account of the acrimonious character of this exchange between Foucault and Derrida and for a very sensible appraisal of the convergence of their thought around the themes of power and ethics, see Roy Boyne, *Foucault and Derrida: The Other Side of Reason* (London: Unwin Hyman, 1990).

[35] *Power/Knowledge: Selected Interviews and Other Writings, 1972–1977* (hereafter cited as P/K) ed. Colin Gordon, tr. Colin Gordon et al. (New York: Pantheon, 1980), pp. 118–119.

that book, that "madness is a special case—during the Classical age power over madness was, in its most important manifestations at least, exercised in the form of exclusion; thus one sees madness caught up in a great movement of rejection."[36] However, Foucault was subsequently led by way of his investigations into the history of sexuality to see another mechanism of power, the productive one, which proceeds not by repressing and saying no but which "traverses and produces things . . . induces pleasure, forms knowledge, produces discourse."[37] But this other form of power reflects not so much a change in Foucault's thinking as a discovery about a change that takes place in the later history of power and madness:

> However, in the nineteenth century, an absolutely fundamental phenomenon made its appearance: the interweaving, the intrication of two great technologies of power: one which fabricated sexuality and the other which segregated madness. The technology of madness changed from negative to positive, from being binary to being complex and multiform. There came into being a vast technology of the psyche, which became a characteristic feature of the nineteenth and twentieth centuries."[38]

One important result of this interweaving is that "sexuality" assumed the place—as the truth of madness—that Foucault would have earlier said belonged to the "tragic category." That is an important point to which I shall return below. The essential thing to see at the moment, however, is that at a certain point, instead of being repressed, unreason is forced to talk. At a certain point, one that evolves from the confessional practices of the Church in the seventeenth and eighteenth centuries, instead of being doused with water, berated with moral criticism, and subjected to a rigorous regimen, the mad are encouraged to say what they have on their mind, to associate freely, to dredge up their dreams, to tell us all about themselves and their parents (especially their parents) and childhood, to reveal their innermost secrets, to bring them out in the public view of the world—in short, to talk, talk, talk, for in the talking is the cure.

Now it would be a mistake to think that the repressive hypothesis is

[36] P/K, pp. 183–184.
[37] P/K, p. 119.
[38] P/K, p. 185.

somehow inconsistent with productive power. In fact, the two are quite compatible and, indeed, produce a similar effect. I would even say that the hypothesis of a productive power is a continuation of the repressive hypothesis by another means. The unreason by which reason is inhabited is again silenced, this time not by real, physical, institutionalized silence but still more effectively, and rather more pleasurably, by talk. The notion that more and more talking is an effective way to silence what requires a voice was noticed early on in the nineteenth century by Kierkegaard, who found that the idle chatter of the press addressed to the "millions," and the numerous compendia of Hegelianized Christian doctrine that were being turned out by the dozens, were proving to be an exceptionally effective way to silence the quiet terror of authentic faith.[39] One of the most famous Kierkegaardian pseudonyms bore the name Johannes de Silentia because he was charged with the task of describing the indescribable "fear and trembling" of Abraham, who was quite unable to explain himself to others and whom everyone else took to be quite—well—mad. Kierkegaard played such silence against the foil of the sane and sensible "stockbrokers of the finite" with whom he draws a consistent contrast throughout *Fear and Trembling*.[40] In an age of top-down monarchical power, outright repression will do just fine; but in the democratic age of the "millions," productive power does an even better job of silencing.

The fact of the matter is that unless power has a univocal essence, unless power means just one thing, it is impossible to sustain the idea that power is only or essentially or primarily "productive" and not also repressive. Power is only a descriptive category for Foucault and it means many things, in keeping with the plurality of historical situations in which it is deployed. There is no power as such; we can only describe the "how" of power relations.[41] Power is now repressive, now productive, and now something else that Foucault had not noticed, and later on something else that perhaps has not yet come about. So there is nothing about Foucault's later adoption of the hypothesis of productive power to invalidate his notion that the work of reason is to silence and reject the voices of unreason by which it is inhabited, and hence to invalidate the early notion

---

[39]See Søren Kierkegaard, *Two Ages: The Age of Revolution and the Present Age*, tr. Howard Hong and Edna Hong (Princeton: Princeton University Press, 1978), pp. 68ff., esp. pp. 92–102.

[40]*Fear and Trembling and Repetition*, tr. Howard Hong and Edna Hong (Princeton: Princeton University Press, 1983), p. 36.

[41]*BSH*, pp. 217 and 219.

of the "tragic category." On the contrary, the two exist in a continual "interweaving" and "intrication."

The strongest challenge to the continued viability of "tragic hermeneutics" in Foucault's work is voiced by Dreyfus and Rabinow, who claim that after *Madness and Civilization* Foucault simply disavows any form of "hermeneutics," and specifically, using Ricoeur's term, the "hermeneutics of suspicion." By "hermeneutics" Dreyfus and Rabinow mean the unmasking and ferreting out of a repressed truth that tells the truth of man. In his "Foreword to the California Edition" of *Mental Illness and Psychology* (1987) Dreyfus says that even the 1962 revised edition remains under the spell of a Heideggerian conception of "'anxiety' in the face of madness" that is silenced by morality and science. Foucault is convinced that there has been a "repression of a deep, nonobjectifiable truth."[42] So there is still a "conspiracy theory" at work in this book, a notion that something is being suppressed that, if we could just face up to it, would result in liberation (in the way that Heidegger talks about being ready for anxiety). In the first edition of the book, Foucault thought it was a matter of facing up to the alienation produced by social contradiction; in the second edition, he has succeeded only in replacing a Marxist conception of social alienation with a Heideggerian-existential conception of "strangeness" (*Unheimlichkeit*), but the overall (hermeneutic) scheme of disalienating madness into its unalienated, liberating truth remains intact.

In the following years, Dreyfus argues, Foucault came to reject any such "hermeneutics" and with it the claim that there is some deep truth begging to be deciphered, some latent content that awaits "commentary,"[43] some meaning at once more hidden and more fundamental that demands a "hermeneutics,"[44] some interrogation of "the being of madness itself, its secret content, its silent, self-enclosed truth"[45] that would traverse what is said about madness at any particular historical time. There is no message from the depths. Madness is simply constituted in different ways at different times and nothing is being left out. There is no inexhaustible

---

[42]*MIP*, p. xxxii.
[43]Michel Foucault, *The Birth of the Clinic: An Archaeology of Medical Perception*, tr. A. M. Sheridan Smith (New York: Pantheon, 1973), pp. xvi–xvii.
[44]Michel Foucault, *The Order of Things: An Archaeology of the Human Sciences*, tr. Alan Sheridan (New York: Pantheon, 1970), p. 373. Dreyfus and Rabinow use this text to set the terms of their own understanding of hermeneutics.
[45]Michel Foucault, *The Archaeology of Knowledge and the Discourse on Language*, tr. A. M. Sheridan Smith (New York: Pantheon, 1972), p. 32

residue, no cover-up story, no buried saving truth.[46] There is no ahistorical essential structure of madness (analogous to the ahistorical structure of *Dasein* yielded by the existential analytic), but only the changing, historical constitution of human beings. For Dreyfus and Rabinow, the critique made in Volume I of *The History of Sexuality* of the search for a secret self—sexuality—as a "construction of modern thought," and hence as an important kind of modern power, is to be applied to *Madness and Civilization*. The latter sought to locate that secret, not in sexuality to be sure, but in "the sovereign enterprise of unreason" that is delivered over to us in flashes of lightning with names like Nietzsche and Hölderlin.[47] But Foucault was led to give up this hermeneutic ontology that locates the transcendental being of unreason behind the play of the historical appearances of madness and *homo psychologicus*. He turns his attention instead to the patient description of the multiple historical forms in which modern man is constituted.

But if that is so, then what difference do the different historical constitutions of madness make? If madness is just produced in various ways, if nothing is repressed, lost, or silenced, why worry about what historical form the historical constitution of madness takes? If nothing is repressed, then nothing is to be liberated. If nothing is repressed, then there is nothing to offer resistance and no historical formation is better or worse than another. As Dreyfus and Rabinow themselves query at the end of their book, "What is wrong with carceral society? Genealogy undermines a stance which opposes it on the grounds of natural law or human dignity. . . . What are the resources which enable us to sustain a critical stance?"[48]

A good deal of what Foucault wrote in the years that followed *Madness and Civilization* raises just those objections. In the remaining sections of this essay I shall argue that an adequate answer to them turns on understanding what becomes of the hermeneutic impulse that is so clearly evident in the early writings, that it turns, in short, on seeing that Foucault has moved beyond a certain hermeneutics, but not another hermeneutics more radically conceived.

---

[46]*MIP*, p. xxxiii.
[47]*MC*, p. 11.
[48]*BSH*, p. 206.

THE HERMENEUTICS OF REFUSAL

In "The Subject and Power," the Afterword to the Dreyfus-Rabinow book, Foucault speaks of the two "pathological forms" of power, two "diseases of power"—fascism and Stalinism—that the twentieth century has known.[49] Are we to think that these are "alienated power," power gone wrong, power that divests human beings of something unalienated or even inalienable? Foucault says they are marked by an "internal madness," but that such madness is merely the extension of contemporary "political rationality," of a kind of unlimited rationalization. Are we to think that this, then, is something like a political equivalent of the "other form of madness" that consists in not being mad, a political analogue of the "merciless language of nonmadness"?[50] Are we to think that something is lost, repressed, or occulted by fascism and Stalinism?

Foucault puts these expressions in scare quotes. They are normative expressions that seem to edge out beyond a felicitous positivism. He is perhaps concerned that he is drifting in the direction of the earlier writings that speak of a more originative sphere. He is worried that he is making himself look like the "doctor." In the next paragraph the metaphor switches to Kant, to what Lyotard calls Kant's "critical watchman,"[51] and Foucault speaks of a need for a Kantian-like critique of the limits of political reason that keeps watch for "excesses."[52] Still, although it is helpful—this is what the Frankfurt school has already done—it is not enough, he says, to study the Enlightenment and the excesses to which it has led "if we want to understand how we have been *trapped in our own history.*"[53]

We are trapped in our history. We, who? Trapped? Then what is the opposite of being trapped? Does being trapped mean that something has been prohibited, occulted, blocked off, or repressed,[54] that is, trapped? What would it be like to be untrapped? *What* would be untrapped? What is the "we" who would be untrapped?

Instead of pursuing the strategy of the Frankfurt school, of analyzing

---

[49]*BSH*, p. 209.
[50]*MC*, p. ix.
[51]See "Judiciousness in Dispute, or Kant after Marx" in *The Lyotard Reader*, ed. Andrew Benjamin (Oxford: Basil Blackwell, 1990), pp. 328 et passim.
[52]*BSH*, p. 210.
[53]Ibid (italics added).
[54]Cf. *P/K*, p. 183.

the "internal rationality" of such excesses, Foucault says that he thinks it would be more instructive to approach such processes of subjection by way of a consideration of the "resistance" that is offered to them, of the "antagonisms" that they engender.[55] Insanity and illegality, for example, are (negative) indicators of what a society calls sanity and legality. Consider the "struggles" we witness nowadays against the power of men over women, of psychiatry over the mentally ill, of bureaucracy over people at large. Such struggles "assert the right to be different and they underline everything which makes individuals truly individual" and they fight against everything that "ties [the individual] to his own identity in a constraining way," which reduces the individual to the identity of "madman," "mentally retarded," "alcoholic," "handicapped," etc.

These struggles, he says, "are not for or against the 'individual,' but rather they are struggles against the 'government of individualization.'"[56] It is not as though Foucault has a normative idea of what an individual should be in the name of which he thinks these struggles should be waged. What the individual should be is none of Foucault's business. More importantly, the very business of coming up with normative ideas of what the individual should be, and of developing administrative practices and professional competences to see to it that such individuals are in fact produced, is precisely the problem, not the solution; it is precisely what these struggles are against.

In sum, he says, all such struggles "revolve around the question: 'Who are we?'"[57] But Foucault's idea is not only *not* to answer this question but to see to it that no one else is allowed to answer it either. He wants to keep this question open, and above all to block the administrators and professionals and managers of all sorts from answering this question, thereby closing us in on some constituted identity or another that represents a strictly historical, that is, contingent constraint. That is what it means to be "trapped by our history." There are too many theories out there of what Foucault earlier called "the truth of truth," of the scientific or therapeutic truth of who we are, too many ready responses to the question "Who are we?" Foucault's program is to block off or delimit the truth of truth—and to leave us to what the earlier writings called our (simple) truth, to the truth that there is no truth of truth, or to what

[55] *BSH*, p. 211.
[56] *BSH*, p. 212.
[57] Ibid.

Heidegger would have called the untruth of being human. Foucault wants to defend the impossibility of reducing us to truth, to shelter the irreducibility and uncontractability of being-human, its refusal of identity and identification, its refusal of an identifying truth. Such refusal issues from the irrepressibility of being human, from its irrepressible capacity for being-different.

Foucault thus has an entirely negative idea of the individual. He struggles against any "positive" theory of the individual that takes itself seriously, that thinks it has the truth of truth, that thinks it can affirmatively say or positively identify who we are. He opposes all "cataphatic" discourse about the individual, discourse that tries to say what the individual is or should be, and he does so in the name of a kind of "apophatic" discourse, of preserving a purely apophatic freedom. The gesture is actually quite classical, reminding us, as James Bernauer argues, of negative theology.[58] What you say God is is not true, Meister Eckhart wrote; but what you do not say God is, that is true. Foucault wants to keep open the negative space of what the individual is *not*, of what we *cannot* say the individual is, to preserve the space of a certain negativity that refuses all positivity, all identification, that is always in the end a historical trap. To paraphrase the Meister, whenever the social sciences tell us who we are, that is not true; but what they do not say about who we are, that is true. Whatever lays claim to being the truth of truth, that is not true; but whatever concedes that we do not know the truth of truth, that is true. Whatever way the individual is historically constituted is not true; but whatever alternatives there are to the way we are constituted, that is true.

The modern exercise of power on Foucault's account represents a peculiar "double bind"[59] that produces individuals (productive power) just precisely in order to block off individuality (repressive power). Modern power combines the production of individuals ("individualization techniques") along with the repression of individuality and difference ("total-

---

[58] I have found James Bernauer's work (see note 3) to be singularly insightful in its approach to Foucault and quite consonant with my own notion of "radical hermeneutics," a notion I developed in connection with Derrida, not Foucault. For more on Bernauer's notion of Foucault's negative theology, see his "The Prisons of Man: An Introduction to Foucault's Negative Theology," *International Philosophical Quarterly* 27:4 (December 1987): 365–381, and the excellent conclusion of *Michel Foucault's Force of Flight*, pp. 175–184, on "ecstatic thinking." For more on the long-range consonance between Foucault and Derrida, which focuses on the question of reason and unreason, see Boyne, *Foucault and Derrida*.

[59] *BSH*, p. 216.

ization procedures").⁶⁰ Far from having abandoned the repressive hypothesis, the double bind depends upon the combined and simultaneous effect of both productive and repressive power, upon their "interweaving" and "intrication."⁶¹

Productive power takes its rise from the spread of "pastoral power" over the social body.⁶² In pastoral power the pastor gives himself over to the production of an individual soul (the "individual" is an invention of the Christian confessional). The pastor needs to know what is going on in individuals' hearts, to get inside their minds, to have them "confess" their innermost secrets, in order to give spiritual direction. Pastoral power depends upon producing the truth, the truth of truth, in order thereby to produce good Christians. In the modern world pastoral techniques are multiplied everwhere: among the police, state investigative functions, criminal justice and social work professionals; among medical and health care professionals; among clinical and counselling psychologists and psychiatrists; educationists; demographers; etc. Wherever a "file" is kept, wherever an individual "case history" is to be written, the "individual" is the target of knowledge and power, of power/knowledge.

Against this totalizing, normalizing production of individuals, Foucault holds out for the "individual." This is the double bind. Not the individual in the sense of the individual case history, of the "subject" whose secret code we—psychiatrists, moralists, or educationists—know, but rather the individual who resists all secret codes, who has no identity, who is not reducible to one or another of the hermeneutic techniques of pastoral power, who is marked by the "right to be different."⁶³ Against the positive production of individuals in keeping with some normative standard, Foucault holds out for the negative freedom of the individual to be different. Whatever the social engineers want the individual to be, that is what the individual wants not to be, what the individual refuses to be.

So what philosophers must do is ask not, like Descartes, "what am I?"—as if there were a general answer—but, like Kant ("what is the Enlightenment?"), who are we *now*, at this particular moment of our historical constitution. Who are we high-tech, late capitalist, mobile, post-Enlightenment—shall we say—postmodernists? And how can we be

⁶⁰*BSH*, p. 213.
⁶¹*P/K*, p. 185.
⁶²*BSH*, p. 215.
⁶³*BSH*, p. 211.

otherwise? Or better still: "Maybe the target nowadays is not to discover what we are but to refuse what we are. We have to imagine and to build up what we could be to get rid of this kind of 'double bind' which is the simultaneous individualization and totalization of modern power structures."[64] The idea is to liberate us not only from the state but from the sort of individualization that the state produces. The idea is "to promote new forms of subjectivity through the refusal of this kind of individuality which has been imposed on us for several centuries."[65]

Foucault's position is comparable to Lyotard's call for continual experimentalism, not only in art but in the artwork that we ourselves are, for the formation of new forms of subjectivity, for finding what Lyotard calls new idioms that provide a space for the right to be different.

We are now in a position to address the question of just what difference the different historical constitutions of madness make. If madness is just produced in various ways, if nothing is repressed, lost, or silenced, why worry about what historical form the historical constitution of madness takes? If nothing is repressed, then nothing is to be liberated, there is nothing to offer resistance, and no historical formation—including fascism and Stalisnism—is better or worse than another. It is, I think, clear that Foucault does believe that something is repressed, and the very cogency of speaking of a "double bind" depends on it. The claim that every historical constitution is a contingency that threatens to become a historical "trap" means that something is being trapped. The idea that no particular historical constitution is exhaustive or totalizing means that there is always a residue, an irreducibility, a fragment that cannot be incorporated.[66] I do not mean a transcendental residuum like Husserl's pure consciousness, or a historical essence or nature of being human, but rather a purely negative, always historical capacity for being-otherwise, which is what Foucault means by freedom.

That is the answer to the objection that Foucault's writings provoke after *Madness and Civilization*, that he treats human beings as a kind of pure *hyle* capable of taking on indefinitely many forms, of being historically

[64]*BSH*, p. 216.
[65]Ibid.
[66]The motif of the irreducible residue, the unassimilable fragment, the remains, the leftover that cannot be *relevé*, is central likewise to Derrida's *Glas*, tr. John Leavey and Richard Rand (Lincoln: University of Nebraska Press, 1986), which like so much of recent French philosophy is on the lookout for something that cannot be consumed and incorporated into the Hegelian "dialectic." Cf. *MC*, p. 285.

constituted in an indefinite multiplicity of forms, no one of which is any better or worse than another. Foucault clearly distinguishes the power that is exerted over material objects, for example, by means of instruments, from the power that individuals exert over other individuals, which is not power over things but power over freedom. Power is not a mere violence exerted on an object, like cutting wood or bending a piece of steel. Violence or force are effected on a "mere passivity."[67] But the power in which Foucault is interested is exerted over "the other," over another person who acts and reacts. Power is a set of actions upon other actions. Nor is power *consensus*, a free renunciation of one's own freedom for the sake of a general arrangement. "Power relations" occur in the space between pure force and free consent, and they may or may not obtain in the presence of either. Power is a matter neither of pushing boulders about with great bulldozers nor of a pure dialogue between Platonic souls.

Power is a way inducing, seducing, conducing (*conduire*, conduct [v.], conduct [n.]); power is conductive. It is stronger (more coercive) than what Husserl calls "motivation," which is pure intentional freedom, because it is a way we have of being led (*ducere*) around (*con*), but like motivation it belongs in a quasi-intentional sphere of human behavior and is not to be reduced to physical causality. Power is a way of "governing," shaping, forming—the seventeenth-century religious orders that Foucault discussed in *Discipline and Punish* called the time of apprenticeship in the order years of "formation." Power sets up (*stellen, auf-stellen*) or frames out (*Ge-stell*)[68] a certain preset range of possibilities within which action can take place, broad "ducts" through which actions are led; power "structures the field" of actions.[69] Thus "power is exercised only over free subjects, and only insofar as they are free."[70] Slavery is not power but constraint because in slavery the range of possibilities has been "saturated," that is, determined to a specific outcome (*determinatio ad unum*). Power is exerted only over beings capable of being recalcitrant and intransigent. Power implies freedom since without freedom power is just constraint or force. Power and freedom belong together agonistically, in an ongoing "ago-

---

[67]BSH, p. 220.

[68]There are late Heideggerian tones in late Foucault: where Heidegger has analyzed the *Gestell* that is the "essence of technology," in its application to nature, Foucault discusses the *Gestell* that is applied to us in the various "technologies of the self," or technologies of behavior.

[69]BSH, p. 222.

[70]BSH, p. 221.

nism," a stuggle, in which there are winning and losing strategies, a victorious consolidation of power on the one hand or successful strategies against power on the other hand. If power is cunning and pervasive enough, it will coopt freedom; if freedom is resistant and persistent enough, it will cause power to tremble.

Power is not something that could be removed, the result being a perfectly free society. A society without power would not be a society but a physical aggregate; as soon as human beings come together (and when have they not?), in virtue of their coming together, power relations spring into being. A society is essentially a network of power relations that are more minute than its larger institutional structures. The idea for Foucault is not to abolish power relations—that would make no sense—but to alter them by means of winning strategies, to open up new possibilities, to restructure the field such that something else (being otherwise) is possible.[71] Such an alteration is driven on by the ongoing agonism between power and freedom that sees to it that any field of power is an unsteady state, an unstable and hence ultimately open, alterable system. The idea is to keep open "the free play of antagonistic" relations, to refuse to let the social system harden into place with stable mechanisms that are overeffective in regulating conduct.[72]

So far from excluding or reducing freedom, power over freedom implies resistance. Freedom for Foucault is a kind of irrepressibility, a refusal to contract into an identity, a continually twisting loose from the historical forms of life by which it is always already shaped. Freedom is not a nature or essence but a lack of nature or essence, a capacity for novelty and innovation. Bernauer calls it "transcendence,"[73] the capacity to move beyond a particular historical constitution. That is in keeping with Bernauer's guiding motif of Foucault's "negative theology" (God transcends whatever we say about God), which I would say is rather a "high" theology for Foucault. I think Foucault has in mind a more modest freedom from below, a refusal, a resistance, a certain stepping back, not so much a *trans*cendence, let us say, as a *res*cendence.

We are now in a position to evaluate the claim of Dreyfus and Rabinow that, by turning himself over to detailed genealogies of the various ways

---

[71]*BSH*, p. 223.
[72]*BSH*, p. 225.
[73]"This . . . force of resistance, this Foucaultian spirituality, bears witness to the capacity for an ecstatic transcendence of any history that asserts its necessity." *Michel Foucault's Force of Flight*, pp. 180–181.

in which bodies and minds are historically constituted, Foucault moved beyond all hermeneutics. This claim is tied up with the claim that he simply dropped the idea of the repression of something deep and replaced it with the notion of describing the surface of productive relations of power.

I would say that this position is partly right. In the early writings Foucault clearly believed in the "secret" and in finding the hermeneutic key to the secret. The hermeneutics of suspicion he practiced at that point (suspecting psychology of repressing the tragic truth) turned on a positive idea of who we are, a particular—indeed, I would say a Dionysiac—idea of a "tragic unreason." The authoritative account of who we are was to be found in *The Birth of Tragedy*, an account the human sciences would like to dismiss or forget. It is clear that by the time of the last works he had given up the idea that there is some *positive* idea of "who we are" to be recovered, some *particular* identity that is being repressed that needs to be shaken loose ("destruction") and retrieved.

But if he has dropped the idea that there is some particular identity that is being repressed, he has not given up the idea that *something* is being repressed, something much looser, more unspecifiable and indefinite, something negative and unidentifiable. It is no longer an *identity* we need to recover (a secret tragic identity) but a *difference*. It is no longer a positive ideal that needs to be restored but simply a certain capacity to resist the identities that are imposed upon us just in order to set free our capacity to invent such new identities for ourselves as circumstances allow.[74] In short, the movement has not been beyond hermeneutics-and-repression but beyond a hermeneutics of identity (a positive tragic hermeneutics) to a hermeneutics of difference (a negative hermeneutics of refusal).

The later writings turn on the idea that there is always something other than or different from the various historical constitutions of human beings, some "freedom" or resistance that is irreducible to the several enframing historical forms of life, some power-to-be-otherwise, some being-otherwise-than-the-present that radically, irreducibly, irrepressibly belongs to us, to what we are (not). We never are what we are; something

---

[74]Foucault does not have a theory of pure or radical freedom, of the sort suggested by his early work on Binswanger, but of a circumscribed or circumstantial freedom, a capacity for contextual alteration, for modification of the circumstances one finds oneself by way of refusal. It is also a theory of local revolt as opposed to total revolution. See John Rajchman, *Michel Foucault: The Freedom of Philosophy* (New York: Columbia University Press, 1985), Ch. 2, "The Politics of Revolt."

different is always possible. That is why I say that Foucault has not dropped the hermeneutic project. He has not abandoned a certain hermeneutics, a negative hermeneutics, a hermeneutics of refusal, of what we are not, a kind of "radical hermeneutics."[75] In such a hermeneutics there is no question of deciphering a "master name," of reapprehending through the "manifest meaning . . . another meaning at once . . . more hidden but more fundamental."[76] On the contrary, such a hermeneutics turns on the loss of fixed or determinate meaning, and on an understanding of being human as an abyss that refuses identification, contraction, or reduction to a fixed meaning. If Foucault has abandoned the hermeneutics of suspicion, it is in favor of a hermeneutics of refusal.

Foucault's more radical hermeneutics rejects the idea of the truth of truth, of some nameable, masterable truth of being human. It rejects a whole series of humanisms of truth—*homo psychologicus*, *homo economicus*, *homo religiosus*, including his own earlier contribution to this scheme, *homo tragicus*. But he has done so, not in order to skim along the surface of positivistic descriptions, but in order to open a hermeneutic depth, a depth of negativity: that we do not know who we are. He has abandoned the truth of truth, the mastery of knowledge, in favor of the "cold truth," of the truth that there is no truth of truth, of the truth that our being is always already disturbed by untruth, which means an irreducibility to truth. The essence of such Foucaultian freedom, were there such a thing, is its untruth,[77] its irreducibility to the truth of truth. *Beneath* the layers of *homo psychologicus* and of all the "idols" of the human sciences, of all the "graven images" of modernity that we might collectively call *homo cyberneticus*, Foucault hears the murmerings of a capacity to be otherwise. The later writings respond to a plea that quietly calls for something different. Conductive, productive power is de-ductive: by leading us along (*con*) certain paths, it leads us away from (*de*) others, cutting off, closing off, the capacity to differ. Productive power is interwoven with repressive power. It wants to produce human beings of a certain sort because it is at the same time "anxious" about the human capacity for being-otherwise; it

---

[75]The notion of a hermeneutics that gives up on the idea of a hermeneutic secret, of uncovering the master name, and that finds itself in an abyss is developed in my *RH* in dialogue with Derrida. See *RH*, Chs. 6–7. For a more systematic account of what a "radical hermeneutics" as a whole would look like, see *RH*, Chs. 8–10.

[76]*The Order of Things*, p. 373.

[77]I am playing with Heidegger's famous assertion in *Basic Writings*, p. 130: "The essence of truth reveals itself as freedom."

is not a little anxious about difference. Far from giving up on the idea of hermeneutic anxiety, *pace* Dreyfus, I think the power of Foucault's analyses, early or late, depends on that anxiety.

We do not know who we are, not if we are honest about it. That is a hermeneutic point, albeit a negative one. It is the issue of a certain kind of radical facing up to the facts that neither ethics nor the human sciences can tell us who we are or what to do. It is, I would say, the issue of a certain "responsiveness" to the abyss that we are, to the capacity to be different. Dreyfus is mistaken to think that Foucault gave up on the hermeneutic idea of "facing up to the truth,"[78] by which I mean the "cold truth," the truth that there is no truth of truth, the truth that is invaded by untruth. Whatever is called "Truth" and adorned with capital letters masks its own contingency and untruth, even as it masks the capacity for being-otherwise that lets our being human spin off into an indefinite future about which we know little or nothing, which fills us with a little hope and not a little anxiety.

BEYOND FOUCAULT: HEALING GESTURES

I wish to close with a word about madmen and confessors, a word that Foucault does not himself utter but that belongs to the space he opens up. Foucault's analysis of the normalization of the mad in psychology and psychiatry, and of the normalization of the faithful in the confessional, addresses the anxiety of modernity about difference and abnormality, and it does so in a most incisive way. But it does not address another issue and another concern, the issue of what healing means in such an analysis.

Let us return to the question of madness. Madness is a "disturbance" but in a twofold sense both of what is "disturbing" and of what is "disturbed." Foucault does a masterful job of showing what is "disturbing" about madness. To put it in the terms of *Being and Time*, Foucault treats madness as a certain way the world is "understood," not in a theoretical sense, of course, but in the sense of *Weltverstehen*, of a practical understanding that is heavily "mooded" or "tuned" (*bestimmt*). The disturbing thing about the mad is the nagging fear that they are "at-tuned" to something, to some deep set dis-sonance, from which the rest of "us" seek to be protected. We

---

[78]*MIP*, pp. xxviii–xxx.

are apprehensive that, living at the margins of normal life, *in extremis*, the mad have been exposed to something the rest of us prefer to ignore. "We" are beset by an apprehensiveness that our sane, healed, whole lives mask a deeper rupture, that the tranquility of the sane is acquired only by repressing the "up-set" of the mad. We are disturbed that "the disturbed" are responding to a certain *turbatio* that is "there." "We" find the disturbed disturbing. That is what gives Foucault's analyses their bite.

But madness is also a being-disturbed, *patheia*, a way of suffering that causes pain. The mad suffer from their attunement, from what they experience/feel/undergo. Their ruptured lives are the site of a wound. They live with terror; they wrestle with demons; their works are impaired, ruined, brought to halt. Their lives are disrupted and destroyed, "disturbed." They have fallen prey to madness. They need healing. Their cry of pain is also a call for help. They lay claim to us, we who are whole (enough) to help, we who are perhaps not so much whole and sane as just a little less mad. There are, after all, only a few Nietzsches, Hölderlins, and Van Goghs among the mad. It was in the long run better to let Van Gogh and Nietzsche alone, to let mad genius run its course into the dark night of truth. But for the majority madness does not mean genius but pain, and they cry out for help, not for the immortality of the work of art.

I take it that there is nothing in what Foucault says that opposes "a strategy of cure"[79]; it is simply not his subject. Indeed, I see in his work the makings of a certain therapeutic "direction," let us say of a therapeutic of not-knowing. Such a therapeutic does not come from on high (so this is a somewhat Levinasian direction), does not proceed from the heights of science or *episteme*, and so does not suffer from the illusion that it knows what madness is (when madness is not clearly physiological). Such a therapy of not-knowing would take madness "seriously," that is, as an Other from which we ourselves have something to learn. Indeed, it undergoes a change of direction by letting the mad come to us from "on high," in their extreme Otherness. It does not look on the mad as "patients" in the sense of "objects" of medical knowledge, but as *patiens*, as ones who suffer greatly, who suffer, as Nietzsche says, from their knowledge. Such a patient would not be an object of knowledge but an author or subject of knowledge, one from whom we have something to learn. Such patients are not stretched out before the medical gaze as objects but come to us from on high, lifted up by their suffering. We are

---

[79] *MIP*, p. 76.

not panoptical observers of madness, but we are ourselves put into question by the mad, seen and interrogated by them, above all, solicited by them. We have something to learn from the mad. We are instructed by them; they have set foot where the sane fear to tread. They tell us, unhappily, who we are; they tell us of our own unhappiness. The mad are not the subject of a medical observation but the source of a call that calls upon us and demands our response.

The mad do not ask for analysis and objectification by us but friendship, support, companionship, solace, joy. The healing gesture, the gesture meant to heal their suffering, is not intended to explain anything away or fill in the abyss but simply to affirm that they are not alone, that our common madness is a matter of degree, that we are all siblings in the same "night of truth." The healing gesture is not to explain madness, if that means to explain it away, but to recognize it as a common fate, to affirm our community and solidarity.

A comparable point can be made about the "confessional practices" of the seventeenth and eighteenth centuries that Foucault has so adroitly analyzed. The meticulous ruminations of an Alphonse Liquori into the most secret recesses of the soul are lurid exercises in a kind of confessional voyeurism, which are useful only as candidates for an inverted, perverted *ars erotica*. But they are also, and more importantly, from what I would like to call a more authentically religious point of view, profoundly insufficient and, I would say, quite irreligious. The institutionalization, regularization, and methodologization of "confession" is a religious perversity. The confessor (in the sense of *confiteor*, I confess) is a "sinner." "Sin" is like "madness": it is a larger-than-life term for life *in extremis*, at the limits, for life that has strayed beyond the safe and reassuring boundaries of everyday life, beyond the wide swaths of normalcy cut by our everyday practices. Sin is not reducible to wrongdoing—no more than madness is reducible to error. It is an expression, perhaps a mythic expression—that is arguably the status of "madness," too—that provides an idiom for a deeper breach, a profound rupture in the human heart. We are divided against ourselves. Like the madness by which we are all beset and upset, and from which we have something to learn, sin bears testimony to a deep divide. But, unlike madness, sin is not a disturbance in the sphere of reason and "truth," but in the sphere of justice and the "good." "Sin" seeks to give words to profound self-diremption, a rupture, a radical unhappiness in our condition.

I believe that sin requires a healing gesture very analogous to madness, a gesture of compassion and commonality. The sinner tells us who we are, tells us of our own unhappiness. Sin is not the object of a Liquorian gaze, not a secret to be ferreted out by confessional techniques, not an object of interrogation. Sin is not an object at all, but the Being of the being we ourselves are.[80] The language of sin provides an idiom for what Levinas calls the "murderousness" of freedom, the murderousness of *our power*. We who are free and well fed, we who are whole and hearty, fit and on the move, we who move easily about within the relations of power, are murderous and we cause others to suffer. "Sin" likewise provides an idiom for our weakness, our infidelities to those who depend on us. Sin is not the Other but who we are. Sin is the Other within. Sin comes to us from on high and gives us something to understand by telling us who we are, by telling us of the abyss within.

Again, the healing gesture handed down to us by the best religious traditions is not analytic objectification, not minute, ruminating subjectification; the great healing gesture that sweeps down over us in Buddhism is called the "great compassion" and in the New Testament "forgiveness." Jesus was the discoverer of forgiveness, Hannah Arendt says.[81] Forgiveness loosens the knots of the social network, in the relations of power, even as revenge draws them tighter and makes them more intractable and oppressive. Forgiveness opens the space of the social network; it makes the future possible and denies to the past its role as fate. Forgiveness makes new forms of subjectivity possible, even as revenge condemns us to repeat the past in endless cycles. Forgiveness releases and opens; revenge traps, incarcerates, and closes. Forgiveness is not given to minute interior rehearsing of the past and intensive subjectification, but is rather dismissive and forgetting. Go and sin no more! Forget it! Forgiving is active forgetting. Forgiveness does not ask questions, but understands that it has itself been put in question by sin. Forgiveness lets itself be interrogated; it does not interrogate. Forgiveness readily makes itself guilty for the sake of the other. Forgiveness asks who among us can cast

---

[80]That is fundamentally the argument of Kierkegaard's *The Concept of Anxiety*, tr. Reidar Thomte (Princeton: Princeton University Press, 1980), which is the reason that Heidegger had a fairly easily time of rewriting this concept in a detheologized form in *Being and Time*.
[81]*The Human Condition* (Chicago: University of Chicago Press, 1958), pp. 236–243. "Trespassing is an everyday occurrence which is in the very nature of action's constant establishment of new relationships within a web of relations, and it needs forgiving, dismissing, in order to make it possible for life to go on by constantly releasing men from what they have done unknowingly" (p. 240). Forgiving is releasing, forgetting, moving on.

the first stone; it looks lovingly on sinners, with whom it consistently consorts to the scandal of the good and the just. Forgiveness heals not by analyzing but by holding out a hand of compassion, by offering a forgiving word that affirms and confesses for its own part that we are all sinners, all siblings of the same dark night.

That is the "truth" of confession, the truth that there is no "truth of truth," no confessional techniques, no metholodogical examinations of conscience, no objectification by way of subjectification. That is also why Julia Kristeva thinks that Christian confessional practices have a notable, albeit mystified, healing power. (But then what is more mystifying than the creatures that psychoanalysis invents?) That is particularly true, she thinks, when confession centers on words of forgiveness and not on the rites of "penance," which is the view of Duns Scotus, whom Kristeva regards as the great theologian of confession.[82] Scotus of course lived before the age of subjectification/objectification, the age of the "world as a picture" (*Weltbild*), as Heidegger says, and offered an antidote to the Tridentine confessional practices that Foucault has so ruthlessly exposed.

The truth is that we cannot gain the high ground of a capitalized Truth, insulated from violence and unreason, destruction and self-destructiveness, "madness" and "sin." The truth is what Foucault called—in a wonderfully unguarded moment—the "night of truth." I do not think that Foucault's thought moved beyond hermeneutics but only beyond a certain naive hermeneutics. I think that it represents a hermeneutics of that night of truth, a cold and more merciless hermeneutics of the human condition that is, at the same time, bent subtly in a direction not at all at odds with mercy.

---

[82]"Qui tollis peccata mundi," in *Powers of Horror: An Essay on Abjection*, tr. Leon S. Roudiez (New York: Columbia University Press, 1982), pp. 131–132. Scotus located the essence of the sacrament in the word of the confessor, not in penance. Arendt says that *metanoein* (Luke 17: 3–4), understood properly as change of heart, trace your steps and sin no more, has nothing to do with "repent" (the usual translation) and penance. Cf. *The Human Condition*, p. 240, n. 78.

NOTES ON CONTRIBUTORS

JUDITH BUTLER is Professor of Humanities at The Johns Hopkins University. She is the author of *Subjects of Desire: Hegelian Reflections in Twentieth-Century France* (Columbia, University Press, 1987) and *Gender Trouble: Feminism and the Subversion of Identity* (Routledge, 1990).

JOHN CAPUTO is David R. Cook Professor of Philosophy at Villanova University. He is the author of *Radical Hermeneutics* (Indiana University Press, 1987), *Heidegger and Aquinas: An Essay in Overcoming Metaphysics* (Fordham University Press, 1982), *The Mystical Element in Heidegger's Thought* (Ohio University Press, 1978; reissued Fordham University Press, 1986), and coauthor with James Marsh and Merold Westphal of *Modernity and Its Discontents* (Fordham University Press, 1992). *Demythologizing Heidegger* and *Against Ethics* are both being published by Indiana University Press in 1993.

CHUCK DYKE is tenuously, but tenuredly entrenched in the Philosophy Department at Temple University. He desperately tries to understand the social systems in which he is enmeshed. His last two lengthy efforts in this regard are *The Evolutionary Dynamics of Complex Systems: A Study in Biosocial Complexity* (Oxford University Press, 1988) and *Patterns of Complexity: Some New Tools for the Social Sciences* (MIT Press, 1992).

JOSEPH MARGOLIS is Laura H. Carnell Professor of Philosophy at Temple University. His most recent publications include *The Truth about Relativism* (Basil Blackwell, 1991), *The New Puzzle of Interpretation* (forthcoming), *The Flux of History and the Flux of Science* (forthcoming), and a collection of commissioned essays, coedited with Tom Rockmore, entitled *The Heidegger Case* (Temple University Press, 1991).

JITENDRA MOHANTY is Professor of Philosophy at Temple University; Visiting Fellow at All Souls College, Oxford; Member of the Institut

International de Philosophie, Paris; former President of the Indian Philosophical Congress; Coeditor of *Husserl Studies*; and member of the Editorial Board of *Phaenomenologica*. He holds a D. Litt h.s. degree from the University of Burdwan. His latest book is *Reason and Tradition in Indian Thought* (Oxford University Press, 1992).

ROBERT MOORE, Jr., is currently Assistant Professor of Sociology at St. Joseph's University in Philadelphia, where he teaches courses related to the sociology of work and law. He holds a Ph.D. in sociology (1988) and J. D. (1988) with a focus on labor law from the State University of New York at Buffalo. He currently serves as Director of the Comey Institute for Industrial Relations at St. Joseph's, which offers a Certificate Program in Labor Issues for labor leaders and management officials.

MARK POSTER is Professor of History at the University of California, Irvine. His recent books include *The Mode of Information* (University of Chicago Press, 1990), *Critical Theory and Poststructuralism* (Cornell University Press, 1989), and *Postsuburban California: The Transformation of Orange County Since World War II* (University of California Press, 1991).

JOSEPH ROUSE is Professor of Philosophy and Science in Society at Wesleyan University. His principal research interests are in the philosophy of science and interdisciplinary studies of scientific knowledge. He is the author of *Knowledge and Power: Toward a Political Philosophy of Science* (Cornell University Press, 1987) and is currently working on a book to be called *The Dynamics of Scientific Knowledge: Beyond Realism, Rationality, and Social Constructivism*.

MARY SCHMELZER has been Visiting Professor of English at St. Joseph's University in Philadelphia for the past two years. She specializes in critical theory in Renaissance literature and is at present considering the relationship between the Erasmian notion of copius discourse and the shape of Renaissance prose.

MARK YOUNT has been Assistant Professor of Philosophy at St. Joseph's University in Philadelphia. His work focuses on the status of philosophy since poststructuralism, especially in terms of the implications for meaning and for subjectivity. In addition to Foucault, he has written on Derrida and Merleau-Ponty and on the problems and possibilities of what Caputo calls "radical hermeneutics."

INDEX OF NAMES

Abraham, 246
Adorno, Theodor, 46, 47, 72
Althusser, Louis, 72
Arendt, Hannah, 261, 262n
Aristotle, 6
Artaud, Antonin, 235, 239
Atleson, James, 174, 180, 181
Avery, Oswald, 152

Bachelard, Gaston, 39, 138
Bacon, Francis, 6, 139, 140n
Bales, Kurt, 43n
Bakhtin, Mikhail, 67
Bakke, Alan, 213, 214, 217, 225
Barbin, Herculine, 91n
Baudrillard, Jean, 13
Beauregard, Robert, 216
Benjamin, Andrew, 249n

Bentham, Jeremy, 127
Berg, Paul, 152
Bergmann, Barbara, 201n
Berkeley, George, 14, 114, 115
Bernauer, James, 19, 19n, 234n, 251, 255
Bernstein, Leonard, 95
Binswanger, Ludwig, 64, 256
Bloch, Peter, 215n
Boldt, David, 220n, 221n
Bosch, Hieronymous, 239
Bouchard, Donald, 69n
Boyle, Robert, 140n
Boyne, Roy, 244n, 251n
Brennan, Justice William, 207
Brunschvicg, Leon, 63
Bürger, Peter, 43
Burstein, Paul, 219n

Bush, George, 219
Butler, Judith, 13, 14, 123, 263

Canguilhem, Georges, 138
Capaldi, Nicholas, 211, 212
Caputo, John, 12, 18–19, 263
Cartwright, Nancy, 141
Clawson, Dan, 175n
Clinchy, Clythe Vicker, 228n
Copernicus, Nicolas, 139
Crick, Francis, 152
Croce, Bernadetto, 33
Cousins, Mark, 35n, 65n

Dahl, Robert, 169
Darwin, Charles, 8, 112, 113, 160
Davis, Michael, 213
Daymont, Thomas, 208n
de Beauvoir, Simone, 67
Defunis, 213, 214, 217, 225
Derrida, Jacques, 16, 53, 57, 58, 64, 72, 91, 113, 134, 243, 244n, 251n, 253n, 257
Descartes, René, 14, 63, 64, 103, 108, 111, 112, 115, 252
de Vries, Hugo, 152
Dewey, John, 106n
Diamond, John, 228n
Douglas, Justice William O., 177, 178, 179
Dreyfus, Hubert, 5n, 65n, 70n, 75n, 138n, 233n, 234n, 247, 248, 249, 255, 258
Duke, David, 191
Durkheim, Emile, 187, 188
Dyke, Chuck, 14–15, 21, 263

Edwards, Richard, 175n
Eisendrath, Craig, 23
Elkouri, Edna Asper, 173n
Elkouri, Frank, 173n

Feinberg, William, 207, 208
Findlay, J. N., 33
Fine, Arthur, 158n
Finley, Moses, 103n
Fish, Stanley, 135, 136
Fleck, Ludwik, 142
Ford, Henry, 214
Frege, F.L.G., 107n
Freud, Sigmund, 7, 20, 46, 54, 80, 240
Fuller, Steve, 156n, 159n

Gadamer, Hans-Georg, 236
Galahad, 102
Gantt, Harvey, 192
Genetech, 152
Giese, Richard, 141
Gillan, Garth, 36
Gilligan, Carol, 18, 228
Goldberger, Nancy Rule, 228n
Goldman, Alan, 196n, 216, 217
Goya, Francisco de, 240, 241
Greenblatt, Stephen, 128
Gutting, Gary, 138

Habermas, Jürgen, 11, 12, 46, 47, 48, 50, 51, 52, 54, 55, 56, 57, 58, 71, 72, 73, 74, 106n, 157n
Hacking, Ian, 140n
Harding, Jeremy, 66n
Hegel, G.W.F., 5, 11, 30, 31, 32, 33, 34, 37, 39, 44, 49, 50, 51, 52, 56, 57, 68, 72, 106n, 246, 253n
Heidegger, Martin, 5, 9, 30, 45, 49, 234, 239n, 241, 247, 251, 254n, 257, 261n, 262
Henahan, Donal, 95n
Henry, Samuel, 225n
Hill, Stephen, 175, 176
Hoffman, Carl, 196n, 199n, 211n
Hölderlin, Friedrich, 235, 248, 259
Hook, Sidney, 212
Horkheimer, Max, 46, 47, 72
Horwich, Paul, 158n
Hoy, David, 33n
Hume, David, 14, 114, 115, 123
Hussain, Athar, 35n, 65n
Husserl, Edmund, 30, 35, 37, 38, 39, 42, 45, 240, 243, 253, 254
Hyppolite, Jean, 33

Irigaray, Luce, 13, 54, 84n, 90, 91

Jacobson, Cardell, 220, 222n
James I, 130
Jencks, Christopher, 216, 217
Johnson, Lyndon, 193, 194
Jones, James, 196n

Kant, Immanuel, 14, 32, 35, 37, 40, 42, 45, 50, 58, 63, 106n, 14, 114, 116, 123, 249, 252
Kennedy, John F., 193
Kennedy, Ted, 192
Kerr, Clark, 170n
Kierkegaard, Søren, 246, 261n
Kilborn, Peter, 186n

Kittay, Eva Feder, 228n
Klare, Karl, 167n, 169n, 170n,
Klein, Calvin, 80
Kleugel, James, 219, 220n 221, 222, 223n,
Kohlberg, 72, 228
Koretz, Robert F., 168n
Krausz, Michael, 23
Krell, David, 239n
Kristeva, Julia, 262
Kuhn, Thomas, 141, 148
Kumar, Sushil, 191, 192

Lacan, Jacques, 54, 64
Lajolo, Davids, 104
Lakatos, Imré, 148n
Latour, Bruno, 142, 154n
Laudan, Larry, 148n
Lemert, Charles C., 36n, 65n
Leonard, Jonathan, 197n, 202n, 209n
Levinas, Emmanuel, 19, 57, 58n, 259, 261
Levin, Michael, 212
Lévi-Strauss, Claude, 63, 106n
Lichtenstein, Nelson, 171n
Liff, Sonia, 225
Liquori, Alphonse, 260
Locke, John, 14, 114, 115
Lovrich, Nicholas, 215n
Lynch, 223
Lyotard, Jean-François, 13, 47n, 51, 52, 53, 72, 239, 253

Mann, Charles R., 197n
Mao Zedong, 135
Mapplethorpe, Robert, 83
Marcuse, Herbert, 170
Margolis, Joseph, 10, 11–12, 23, 263
Marshall, 217
Martin, Lynn, 186, 187
Marx, Karl, 5, 10, 20, 43, 44, 45, 46, 49, 52, 55, 56, 65, 71, 72, 80, 106n, 108, 135, 148, 166, 167, 170, 188, 189, 247, 249n
McClintock, Barbara, 152
McIntyre, Alasdair, 124
Meister, Eckhart, 251
Mendel, Gregor, 152
Mensch, Elizabeth, 169n
Meredith, James, 213
Merleau-Ponty, Maurice, 30, 37
Meyers, Diane, 228n
Mill, John Stuart, 123
Mohanty, Jitendra, 5, 11, 39n, 263–264

Moore, G. E., 14, 110, 111
Moore, Robert, 17, 264
Morgan, Thomas Hunt, 152
Müller, Gustav, 33
Murphy, Allene, 23
Myshkin, Prince, 110

Nagel, Thomas, 104n
Nalbandian, John, 225n
Nerval, 235
Newton, Isaac, 139
Nielsen, Kai, 124n
Nietzsche, Friedrich, 21, 41, 42, 46, 48, 49, 65, 66, 75, 106n, 113, 228, 236, 237, 239, 241, 248, 259
Nunokawa, Jeff, 95

Olby, Robert, 152n
Oppenheimer, Robert, 8

Pasteur, Louis, 142
Peirce, Charles S., 49, 51, 57
Perlmutter, Nathan, 212, 214
Perman, Florence, 201n, 202
Piaget, Jean, 72
Pickering, Andrew, 154n
Plato, 65, 102, 115, 123, 254
Poetzl, Pamela Major, 65n
Poincaré, Henri, 15, 105
Poster, Mark, 12–13, 65n, 264
Putnam, Hilary, 157n
Pynchon, Thomas, 70

Quinby, Lee, 228n
Quine, W.V.O., 108

Rabinow, Paul, 5n, 9n, 65n, 68n, 70n, 75n, 127n, 138n, 191n, 233n, 234n, 247, 248, 249, 255
Rabkin, Jeremy, 203n
Racevskis, Korlis, 65n
Rajchman, John, 65n, 256
Raulet, Gerard, 66
Rawls, John, 123
Reagan, Ronald, 186
Reich, Michael, 221
Ricoeur, Paul, 247
Ritzer, George, 166n
Robinson, T. M., 103n
Roosevelt, Franklin, 168
Rorty, Richard, 14, 53, 47n, 106n
Rouse, Joseph, 16–17, 22, 264

Rousseau, Jean-Jacques, 241
Roussel, 235
Russell, Bertrand, 107n

Sade, Marquis de, 241
Sambasivan, S., 194n
Sartre, Jean-Paul, 12, 30, 37, 39, 63, 65, 66, 67, 68, 71, 74, 75, 76, 77
Schmelzer, Mary, 15–16, 20, 23, 264
Schnapper, Eric, 200
Scotus, Duns, 262
Shaffer, Simon, 140n
Shapere, Dudley, 148n
Shapin, Steven, 140n
Sheridan, Alan, 234n
Sherman, Howard, 207n, 222n
Singer, Linda, 81
Singh, Shivaji, 224, 228
Smart, Barry, 65n
Smith, Eliot, 219n, 220n
Socrates, 102, 103
Sowell, Thomas, 192n, 193n, 215n
Stalin, Josef, 249, 253
Steel, Brent, 215n
Stevens, Justice John Paul, 225

Stone, Katherine, 169, 184
Swinton, David, 206, 210, 213n, 214

Tarule, Jill Mattuck, 228n
Taylor, Charles, 157n
Thalberg, Irving, 209n, 213n, 217n
Thornburgh, Richard, 219n
Tomlins, Christopher L., 168n
Traweek, Sharon, 156n

Van Gogh, Vincent, 259

Wartenburg, Thomas, 159n, 161n
Wasserman, August Paul von, 142
Wasserstrom, Richard, 214
Watson, James, 152
Webb, Janette, 225
Weber, Max, 80
Whitehead, Alfred North, 107n
Wilson, Carter, 201n, 215n, 216
Wood, James, 207n, 222n
Wood, John, 191n

Yount, Mark, 17, 18, 264

Zitron, Celia, 213n

INDEX OF SUBJECTS

affirmative action, 18, 191–229
AIDS, 12–13, 83, 94–98
arbitration, 166, 171–181, 187
art, 242–243
asylum, the, 39, 141

body, the, 39, 128, 151, 165, 174, 191–192, 196

care perspective in ethics, 28–229. *See also* healing
Cartesianism, 63–64, 108–109, 111, 115
confessional, the, 19, 39, 78, 79, 140, 234, 245, 252; and healing, 260–262
consensus, 49, 50
constitution, 30, 32, 34–40; of self, 63ff.
creationism, 158–161
credentialization, 116, 117
curriculum, 116–117, 130, 133

Darwinism, 112–113, 160
death, 84–88, 94–98, 146, 237
deconstruction, 91n10, 102, 104, 234
desire, 32, 37, 132
différend, 52, 239
discipline, 165, 74–177, 181–187, 189, 199, 203. *See also* disciplines
disciplines, the, 27, 135, 137, 140, 142–143, 148. *See also* curriculum; discipline; philosophy
discontinuity, 30, 32–33, 39–40, 228
double bind, 251–252, 253

Enlightenment, the, 46, 67, 68, 70ff., 106–107, 249
epidemics, 82–88, 91–92
episteme, 30
epistemology, 32, 138, 139, 141, 142, 144, 147–150, 153–155, 156, 157–162

Index

ethics, 64, 77, 78, 118, 120, 122–123, 226, 242–243
ethos, 68, 69, 71, 75, 106, 116
Existentialism, 30

family, the, 156n33, 205
feminism, 53–54, 78, 135, 160–161, 212, 228
forgiveness, 261–262
formalism (legal), 167, 178
freedom, 38, 39, 68, 74, 169, 254–255, 256
functionalism (social/legal), 166–167, 171

Geist, 32–34
gender, 161, 194, 210, 219n77. *See also* feminism; women
genealogy, 4, 7, 11, 33, 36, 46–48, 51, 54–59, 64, 137, 138, 139, 224–228, 255–256
God, 34, 251, 255

healing, 258–262
hermeneutics, 12, 18–19, 30, 65, 77, 198, 233ff.; beyond hermeneutics, 247–248, 262; radical, 257; of refusal, 249–258; tragic hermeneutics, 234–238
history, 28, 29, 30, 32–33, 34–36, 39–40, 132, 138, 161, 167, 171, 177, 193, 225
hospital, the, 141, 165
human sciences, 137–139, 165, 166. *See also* social sciences

ideology, 148, 156n33, 170, 176, 179, 188, 221–222
individualization, 31, 250, 253
industrial pluralism, 169–170, 184, 185
institutions, 4–5, 9–10, 14, 20, 130, 157, 227, 255
intellectual, the, 8, 74; intellectual, specific, 28, 133

language, electronic, 79–80
legitimacy, 115
legitimation, 157–158, 176
liberalism, 71–72, 118, 122–125
liberation, 13, 91–92

madness, 35, 38, 39, 170, 234–243; and healing 258–260
Marxism, 135, 148, 166–167, 170, 188, 189
medicine, 28, 139
military, the, 143, 155, 156
modernism, 49–50

modernity, 46, 73, 85, 87
moral codes, 77

natural sciences, 28, 29, 36n20, 137–162
neoconservatism, 47
normalization, 45, 48, 70, 101–102, 131, 142, 171, 181, 187, 189, 192, 193, 196, 198, 199, 202, 224
normativity, 165, 174, 175–176, 179, 181, 182

ontology, 115, 116
Other, the, 37, 57–60, 236, 259

Panopticon, the, 127–136, 143, 177
pedagogy, 15–16, 127–136, 140
phase space, 105, 122
phenomenology, 30, 32, 35, 109, 243
philosophy: analytic, 14–15, 106 ff.; departments, 119–122; Foucault's thought as, 11, 27–40; and madness, 238
Poincaré sections, 105
police, 203, 215
positivism, 34, 171
postmodernism, 72–73, 127, 133, 135, 136, 252; vs. poststructuralism, 51–54
poststructuralism, 72, 76; vs. postmodernism, 51–54
power, 4–7, 27, 30–34, 35–36, 37, 70, 84–88, 94, 96, 127–128, 129, 133, 135–136, 138, 143, 144–151, 155, 157, 158, 159, 161n39, 162, 165–166, 168, 174, 179, 187–188, 189, 196n12, 198, 203, 209–210, 219, 224, 226, 227, 244–245, 254–258
power/knowledge, 6–7, 18, 137–139, 142–144, 147, 159n38, 165, 187, 188, 192, 192, 203, 204, 218, 252
power relations, 5, 246
power, repressive vs. productive, 86, 244–246, 248, 251–252, 256–258
prison, the, 28, 39, 127, 137, 141, 142, 143, 157, 165, 181
problematization, 138, 192, 193–195, 224
psychiatry, 28, 140, 165, 166, 170, 187
psychoanalysis, 37, 40
psychology, 234–238, 242
punishment, 199

race, 192, 193, 194, 196, 199–200, 204, 205–210, 213, 214, 215n66, 216–224
realism, 141n10
relativism, 16, 148, 157

religion, 159–160
resistance, 136, 162, 188, 225, 227, 229, 250, 256
rights, 148, 157, 168, 171, 172, 175, 177, 181, 182, 183–186, 189, 193, 194, 195, 203n32, 214, 224

self: the decentered, 64–65; as work of art, 66. *See also* subject
sexuality, 12–14, 38, 39, 75, 78, 81ff., 137, 151, 152, 156, 198, 245; and sex, 88–91
sin, 260–262
social contract, 177
social sciences, 28–29, 170, 187, 198. *See also* human sciences
sovereignty, 34, 130–131, 133, 139, 144–151, 153–154, 156n33, 157, 158, 203
strikes, 171, 172, 174–175, 178, 180, 182–187, 188
structuralism, 35, 69
subject, the, 6, 30, 32, 34–39, 59, 63ff., 131, 139, 167
suffering, 259

temporality, 30, 34, 40
terrorism, 53
theology, 105, 107, 108, 262
totalization, 67–68, 73–74, 91, 252
transcendental, 30, 34–36, 40
truth, 19, 28, 30, 31, 32, 73, 127, 131, 133, 135, 158, 161–162, 166, 170, 187, 188, 189, 227, 250–251, 257–258, 262; paradox of, 41–48

unconscious, 32
unions (labor), 168–169, 173, 174, 175, 176, 180, 182–185, 188
unreason, 234–243, 246

violence, 158, 192–193

war, 224, 227
women, 195, 201, 204, 205n35, 226, 228. *See also* feminism; gender
World War II, 171 ff.

www.ingramcontent.com/pod-product-compliance
Lightning Source LLC
Chambersburg PA
CBHW031547300426
44111CB00006BA/205